Ted Brewer
Explains
Sailboat Design

Ted Brewer Explains Sailboat Design

Ted Brewer

Distributed by:
Airlife Publishing Ltd.
101 Longden Road, Shrewsbury SY3 9EB, England

© 1985 by International Marine Publishing Company

Typeset by The Key Word, Inc., Belchertown, Massachusetts
Printed and bound by The Maple Press Company, York, Pennsylvania

Published by International Marine Publishing Company
Route 1, P.O. Box 220, Camden, Maine 04843
(207) 236-4837

10   9   8   7   6   5   4   3   2

Library of Congress Cataloging in Publication Data

Brewer, Ted.
    Ted Brewer explains sailboat design.

    Bibliography: p. 220
    Includes index.
    1. Yachts and yachting—Design and construction.
I. Title.
VM331.B845   1985   623.8'223   84-48686
ISBN 0-87742-193-5

CONTENTS

Preface

Yacht design in all its aspects — technical, practical, and aesthetic — has been a source of great wonder and interest to amateurs and professional enthusiasts alike for well over 100 years. I hope that this book will be of help to the amateur, and perhaps of interest to the professional, in their search for knowledge. I do not consider myself to be an expert in the field either practically or technically. I have never sailed my own boat around the world, and I am not a graduate of the Massachusetts Institute of Technology or any other prestigious school of advanced technology. All I can offer the reader is close to 30 years' experience in the field of small-boat design. I learned my craft under fine men — George Cuthbertson, Dick Telford, and Bill Luders — and I've been fortunate to meet many great sailors in my time and to sail on some wonderful yachts. I hope I can pass along a bit of the knowledge that I've gained.

My own boat's name is *U'I Papela*. It is my wife's name in Hawaiian. Without her encouragement this book would probably never have been written. If you find the book useful, you can thank her; it you find it otherwise, blame me.

May you have fair breezes and slack tides wherever you sail.

INTRODUCTION

Yacht design is partially an art and partially a science, and the proportion of each put into the vessel is related to the accent placed on performance versus that placed on comfort, aesthetics, and the client's whims. The racing yacht designer is using more science than art today; the cruising boat designer may be using art and science in 50-50 proportion or may well be putting more art than science into the design. Much depends on the type of boat that is being created; almost as much depends on the philosophy of the designer and perhaps his client, if it is a custom yacht.

Of course, sailing yachts come in a wide variety of types as well as sizes. The variety is due largely to the different philosophies of the owners. There are those who prefer to take their sailing in comfort and do not mind sailing at moderate speeds as long as the boat contains all the amenities of a small home. Others are not content unless they are sailing as swiftly as the wind allows and will live in camping comfort if it adds an extra knot to the speed.

I'm one of those in the middle. I like some comforts (a cold beer and a warm bunk), but I also like to sail fast when the breeze is up. On the other hand, I'm too impatient to sit still or buck an adverse tide when the breeze is light. I'd rather turn on the engine and go fishing or head for a nice little cove and drop the hook. I gave up racing some years ago after a very light air race when I almost died of boredom and heat stroke. That is simply not my cup of tea. Others love the challenge of competition and will drift around all day pulling on strings to get another eighth of a knot out of her as long as there is someone else out there to beat. These people may be so engrossed in racing that they won't even go out for a pleasant day's sail unless they can use the time to practice for the next race. More power to them, as the intensity of competition has added much to our knowledge of yacht design.

Perhaps the best description I ever read of the difference between racing and cruising came from a British author who wrote words to this effect: The racing skipper will press on at night even with the wind rising, carrying full sail, rail down, and trusting to a bit of luck in the hope of gaining the silver. On the other hand, in the same conditions the cruising man will tuck in a reef, make sure everything is snug, relax in the cockpit with a drink and a smoke and think about his next landfall. Two very different philosophies—but thank God there is room for them both in this best of all sports.

Still, the boat buyer is often getting a pig in a poke since he (the word "he" hereafter means he or she) may be buying the yacht for one particular feature. Perhaps it's the performance, perhaps the accommodations or even the appearance, but it's possible that other features of that particular craft are completely unsuitable for his needs. It may be a modestly canvassed ocean-going cruiser that would be out of its element on the sheltered, light air waters of Puget Sound, Chesapeake Bay, or wherever; or it may be a sleek, skinned-out racer when the buyer really should have a comfortable family cruiser for the type of sailing that he will be doing. In either case, the owner could have avoided a potentially costly mistake by investing a little time and effort in studying the art and science of yacht design. I hope this book will be a first step for yachtsmen (and yachtswomen) who are interested in learning more about their sport, their hobby, their avocation.

After almost 30 years in this business, I am still learning, and I read, avidly, every new book or technical article about yacht design that I can get my hands on. There is so much to learn, and new concepts are continually advanced. Then too, it would take years of study just to digest all the works of the past. The best advice I can give the novice is to read everything, weigh it carefully, and then come to your own conclusions based on your experience.

Go to any boat show or dealer, and the first-time sailboat buyer will find a confusing assortment of rigs, underwater shapes, and general types. The present market offers sloops, cutters, ketches, a few yawls, catboats, cat ketches, and schooners, subdivided into marconi (or Bermudan), gaff, gunter, and junk rigs, with single-spreader, double-spreader, or unstayed masts. That's above water. Below we have the choice of full keel boats, keel-centerboarders, drop keels, cutaway full keels, fin keels (both deep and narrow, and shoal and long), plus spade rudders, skeg hung rudders, or rudders hung on the keel. The novice is not the only one who can become confused. Even the experienced yachtsman can have moments of doubt when contemplating the purchase of a larger, more expensive yacht, particularly if it is of a slightly different type than the vessels he has previously owned. It's true that a little knowledge can be a dangerous thing, but when you are buying a boat, which may well represent as large an investment as your house, then what you need is a lot of knowledge. Indeed, the more, the merrier.

I hope this book will help you understand the thinking that goes into the design and construction of your next boat, whether it's a daysailer, a production yacht, or a custom design.

☐ *2*

THE TRADEOFFS

Every boat is a compromise of four basic components: speed, seaworthiness, comfort, and economy. You cannot hope to obtain more of any one of these factors without sacrificing some of one of the others. You can get more speed, seaworthiness, and comfort, but you will lose economy (you would probably have to buy a larger boat to gain in all three of those areas). The following breakdown is only general as there are many boats that will fit in between the categories listed, but it does give the reader an idea of the compromises involved.

BOAT TYPE	SEAWORTHINESS	COMFORT	SPEED	ECONOMY
Meter-type racer	10%	0%	89%	1%
IOR ocean racer	25%	10%	60%	5%
One-design racer	25%	10%	50%	15%
Club cruiser-racer	25%	20%	35%	20%
Coastal cruiser	25%	25%	25%	25%
Ocean cruiser	30%	30%	20%	20%
Trailer sailer	15%	20%	20%	45%
Motorsailer	30%	35%	15%	20%

In effect there is no free lunch. Whatever you insist on having in any one category is going to cost you in another. It is up to the owner to decide what is needed (don't let the yacht salesman decide for you) and to weigh those needs against his bank account. The important point is to decide what is needed, and in order to do that you must be realistic about your requirements. Far too often a boat buyer dreams of long voyages to foreign shores, spends his money on a heavy, sea-going cruiser, but never gets out of sight of land on his annual two- or three-week vacation. You will see these boats growing grass in every marina in the world or motoring in soft breezes because they are too slow to offer pleasurable sailing in our coastal waters. The owner of such a boat would be better off with a lighter, faster inshore cruiser or even a club racer.

Similarly, the skipper whose interests lie in relaxed sailing, exploring interesting gunkholes, and family cruising will not be happy with a deep draft, bare bones racer. The only one who can decide the type of yacht that is best for your needs is you, and the investment in money is so large that it is worth a considerable investment in time to analyze your specific requirements. If your experience is limited, then it is a wise idea to take a course in the type of sailing that appeals to you. Courses are available today for novices, for cruising, and for racing skippers. A good course is a must for the true novice to the sport. Then read all you can, talk to experienced skippers and sailors, and attend some of the lectures that are becoming more popular in our major sailing ports. There are many ways to learn, but learn you must if you are to avoid costly mistakes.

The purpose of this book is to provide you with the basics of yacht design, both to help with the selection of your next boat and give you a better understanding of the boat you now have. I hope it will prove both informative and enjoyable.

1

□
□
□
□
□
□
□
□

LANGUAGE, RESISTANCE, AND LINES

THE LANGUAGE OF THE YACHT DESIGNER

The reader must have an understanding of the terms used in yacht design before we can go into the details of various hull types. These terms are used by all designers, and if you are buying a set of plans or having a custom design created, the architect should be able to supply you with this data. Some of the ratios, such as the displacement/length ratio, may need to be worked out, but the formulas are simple and can be handled on an inexpensive calculator.

LENGTH

This one can be confusing as different builders and designers have various ways of expressing it. Length Over All (LOA) may be the length from the rail overhang at the bow to the rail overhang aft; it may be the length from the tip of the bowsprit to the end of the boomkin; or it may be the actual length on deck, omitting the small overhangs of the rails. Length On Deck (LOD) is the most honest way to express the true length. It is the length from bow to stern with rail overhangs omitted.

LENGTH WATERLINE (LWL)

LWL is the length of the yacht as measured in a straight line from the bow ending of the waterline to the stern ending. It normally excludes any rudder tip that may stick out past the end of the hull proper. Knowing the true LWL is important since it figures in many other calculations.

DESIGNED WATERLINE (DWL)

DWL is the waterline length as the boat was drawn on paper. It may be the same as the LWL but usually is not. Over the years, the boat gets heavier due to soakage, added equipment, etc., and as she settles lower in the water her waterline length increases.

BEAM

This is considered to be the greatest width of the boat but is better expressed as beam(max.) to differentiate between the beam and the waterline beam, or beam(LWL).

DRAFT

The depth of water that the yacht draws. Like the LWL, it will vary with equipment and the weight of stores, fuel, etc.

DISPLACEMENT

The displacement is the actual weight of the boat and may be expressed in pounds, long tons, or cubic feet (one long ton = 2,240 pounds = 35 cubic feet of sea water at 64 pounds per cubic foot). The displacement is also the weight of water that the hull will displace when the yacht is at rest. Since fresh water weighs only 62.4 pounds per cubic foot, it is obvious that a yacht will sink deeper into the water and so increase her draft when she is moved from sea water to fresh water.

CENTER OF BUOYANCY (CB)

The CB is the center of the displacement of the yacht. If the vessel is to float on her DWL, the center of gravity of the boat must be in line vertically with the CB. If it is not, the vessel will be out of trim, and she will change trim until her new CB is in line with the center of gravity (CG).

For example, if your boat is perfectly in trim and you decide to fit davits aft to hold a 150-pound dinghy, you have changed the center of gravity of the boat , moving it aft. The hull will trim down by the stern and up by the bow until the change in underwater shape moves the CB to the new location of the CG. The same applies athwartship. Normally the CB and the CG are on the centerline of the boat, but if you move to the rail you move the CG outboard, and the boat will heel until the new CB lines up with the CG.

The location of the center of buoyancy is usually expressed in feet abaft the bow or abaft amidships, or as a percentage of the waterline abaft the bow.

CENTER OF FLOTATION (CF)

The center of flotation is the center of the area of the waterline. When a boat changes trim due to a shift in the center of gravity, she pivots about the CF. Indeed, it is similar to the pivot in the middle of a seesaw. On normal hulls its location is somewhat abaft the CB and, like the CB, is expressed as a distance abaft the bow or as a percentage of the LWL abaft the bow.

POUNDS PER ONE-INCH IMMERSION (PPI)

The weight required to sink the boat evenly in the water one inch. The PPI is readily calculated by multiplying the waterline area by 5.333 for sea and 5.2 for fresh water. It should be noted that the PPI increases as the hull sinks into the water since the waterline area is also increasing due to hull shape.

MOMENT TO TRIM ONE INCH (MTI)

The MTI is the moment that will change the trim of the boat one inch and is expressed in foot-pounds. If the boat has a MTI of 1,500 foot-pounds and that 150-pound dinghy is hung 20 feet aft (150 × 20 =3,000 foot-pounds), then the trim will change 2 inches by the stern. That is, in theory, the stern will go down an inch and the bow will rise an inch. However, the boat trims about its CF, and as that is usually somewhat abaft amidships, the stern will move less than the bow, perhaps sinking 7/8 inch while the bow rises 1⅛ inches to make a 2-inch change in trim. For a displacement hull the MTI is approximately one-twelfth of the displacement.

WETTED SURFACE (WS)

The wetted surface is the area in square feet of the underbody including the fin or skeg and rudder. A boat with a large wetted area will have more surface friction than a boat with a smaller wetted surface and thus be slightly slower given the same driving power. This is particularly significant at slower speeds (i.e., a sailboat moving in a very

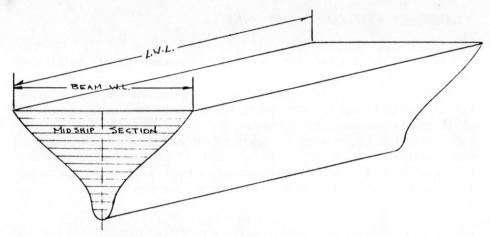

THE PRISMATIC COEFFICIENT IS THE AMOUNT OF THIS 'PRISM'
THAT REMAINS AFTER THE HULL IS CARVED OUT.

PRISMATIC COEFFICIENT

light breeze) as surface friction is then the primary cause of resistance. As the boat picks up speed, she creates waves, and these rather than the surface friction become the major part of the drag at higher speeds.

PRISMATIC COEFFICIENT (CP)

The prismatic coeffient is a nondimensional figure that relates the fullness of the ends of the hull to the area of the midship or largest station. For example, you are carving a boat model and you started with a block of wood equal to the LWL and shaped to the midship station. Now you carve away the shape at the ends. The relationship that the finished hull bears to the original chunk of wood is the Cp. The fuller the ends, the higher the Cp.

Cp can range widely, from .45–.46 for a racing sailboat intended for light air use up to .70–.75 for a planing motorboat. Actually, the proper Cp depends on the intended speed and is related to another figure called the speed/length ratio, or $V/\sqrt{L}$. The $V/\sqrt{L}$ is the speed in knots divided by the square root of the LWL. The figures below show the correct Cp for various speed/length ratios.

$V/\sqrt{L}$	Cp
1.0 and below	.525
1.1	.54
1.2	.58
1.3	.62
1.4	.64
1.5	.66
1.6	.68
1.7	.69
1.8 and above	.70

Selecting the correct Cp for a motor yacht is fairly simple since the designer can estimate the speed reasonably accurately and use the appropriate Cp in the design. It is more difficult for a sailing yacht as speed varies with wind strength. Generally, .54–.55 is the range for average conditions while a higher Cp, say .56–.58, may be used on a boat intended primarily for heavy weather.

It is better if the Cp is a bit on the high side, though, as the added resistance from having too high a Cp at low speeds is less serious than that from having too low a Cp at high speeds. Also, a high Cp should be obtained from a full stern and not from a full bow as the latter would have an adverse effect on windward performance by causing excess pitching.

DEADRISE ANGLE

This is the angle that the general line of the bottom in section view makes with the LWL. A flat bottom boat has zero deadrise while a deeply vee'd hull is said to have steep deadrise.

CENTER OF LATERAL PLANE (CLP) OR
CENTER OF LATERAL RESISTANCE (CLR)

Two terms that mean the same thing: the center of the hull's underwater area as viewed in profile. The fore and aft location is often marked on the sail plan. If not, it is easily found by tracing the hull profile on paper, cutting it out, and balancing it. Many designers omit the rudder area when working out the CLP.

CENTER OF EFFORT (CE)

The center of the area of the sails. It is usually given using 100 percent of the foretriangle area, but on boats that do not carry genoa jibs the CE may be given as the center of the working sails. More about CE and CLP under Helm Balance.

DISPLACEMENT/LENGTH RATIO

This is the displacement in tons divided by .01 LWL cubed or $Dt/(.01 \text{ LWL})^3$. The d/l ratio is a nondimensional figure that allows us to compare the displacement of hulls without regard to their LWL. The lower the d/l ratio, the smaller the waves generated by the hull as it passes through the water and the smaller the hull's wave-making resistance. A few examples of displacement/length ratios—generalities only as there can be wide diversity within each type—follow:

BOAT TYPE	D/L RATIO
Light racing multihull	40-50
Ultra-light ocean racing sail	60-100
Very light ocean racing sail	100-150
Light ocean racing sail	150-200
Light cruising auxiliary	200-250
Average cruising auxiliary	250-300
Moderately heavy cruising auxiliary	300-350
Heavy cruising auxiliary	350-400

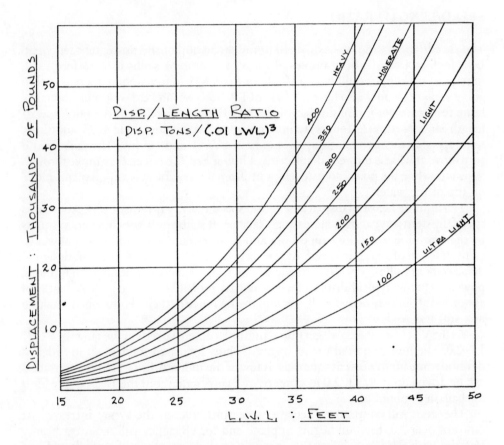

The modern trend is to lower ratios. *Finisterre*, a champion cruiser-racer of 25 years ago, had a d/l ratio of 407 and would be considered ultra-heavy by today's standards. However, she also had long bow and stern overhangs compared to modern hulls and so would pick up length as she heeled, thus reducing her d/l ratio to a much more reasonable figure when driving to windward.

SAIL AREA/DISPLACEMENT RATIO (SA/D)

Another nondimensional figure. It is derived from the sail area in square feet divided by the displacement in cubic feet to the two-thirds power, or SA/D cubic feet$^{2/3}$. The higher the SA/D ratio, the faster the boat will be in light airs. A figure below 13 or 14 is low and would be suited to a motorsailer type. Any auxiliary cruiser with a SA/D ratio of much under 15 would likely be very slow in light weather and would need large genoa jibs to give reasonable performance. The average range would be 15 to 16 for offshore cruisers, 16 to 17 for coastal cruisers, 17 to 19 on racing yachts. Ratios over 20 are usually seen only on ultra-light racers, class racers, and daysailers.

SPEED/LENGTH RATIO

The speed/length ratio was explained in the discussion of the prismatic coefficient. Let's look at a couple of examples of the $V/\sqrt{L}$ ratio: A sailboat of 36-foot LWL moving at six knots would have a $V/\sqrt{L}$ of 1.0; a 625-foot-waterline merchant ship going 25 knots would also have a $V/\sqrt{L}$ of 1.0. Both would be developing about the same resistance per ton of displacement since they are traveling at the same speed/length ratio. Next, a 25-foot-waterline motorboat skimming along at 25 knots, the same speed as the merchant ship, would have a $V/\sqrt{L}$ ratio of five. The sailboat and ship move at what is termed "displacement hull speed." In effect, they move through the water while the powerboat develops lift from its speed and is said to plane, move on top of the water.

The limiting factor of displacement hull speed is a $V/\sqrt{L}$ ratio of 1.34. Above this speed the stern wave moves increasingly farther aft so the hull loses buoyancy, squats by the stern due to lack of support aft, and requires enormous additional power to gain a fraction of a knot in speed. At speeds below a $V/\sqrt{L}$ of 1.34, the well-designed displacement hull is very efficient and can be propelled economically with minimal power. Actually, typical displacement sailboats probably average a $V/\sqrt{L}$ ratio of about .9–1.0 but may occasionally get into the 1.4 range or thereabouts when reaching in a stiff breeze.

As the $V/\sqrt{L}$ increases, we get into semidisplacement speeds in the range of $V/\sqrt{L}$ 1.5–2.0. The hulls required for such speeds show increased fullness aft in order to develop some lift to prevent squatting. A few of the modern, ultra-light cruiser-racers can be driven up to $V/\sqrt{L}$ 2.0 in a breeze with consistency, but this is about the limit for ballasted monohulls.

The stern will continue to become wider and fuller as the $V/\sqrt{L}$ increases. At ratios of over 2.0, the hull begins to plane and for efficiency will require a beamy transom with flat buttock lines, the typical fast, light dinghy hull, unballasted and dependent for stability on crew weight.

COMFORT RATIO

This ratio is one that your author dreamed up for an article in *Cruising World* magazine. The article was tongue-in-cheek but the comfort ratio has been accepted by many as a measure of motion comfort, and indeed, it does provide a reasonable comparison.

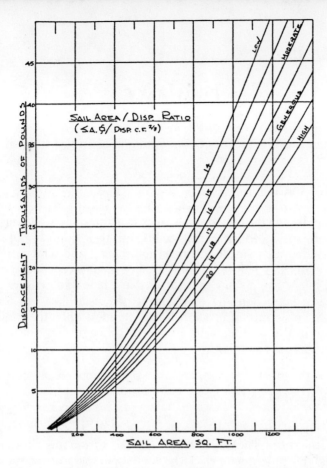

The comfort ratio is based on the fact that motion comfort depends on the rapidity of the motion; the faster the motion, the more upsetting it is to our human gyroscopes. Given a certain force, such as a wave, the speed of motion depends upon the weight of the object (the boat) and the amount of surface that is acted upon (the LWL area). Greater weight, or lesser area, means a slower motion, and thus more comfort.

Beam enters into it also as wider beam will generate a faster reaction, particularly in beam seas. In effect, the comfort ratio measures the displacement of the vessel against its waterline area, adds a factor for beam, and thus is a means to compare motion comfort for boats of various sizes and types.

The formula is as follows:

$$\text{comfort ratio} = \frac{\text{displacement, pounds}}{.65 \times (.7\,\text{LWL} + .3\,\text{LOA}) \times B^{1.333}}$$

One finds that smaller yachts, having a higher beam/length ratio, are lower on the comfort scale. Also, older designs get higher marks for comfort as they are from the era of heavy displacement and narrower beam. Comfort ratios will range from 5.4 for a Lightning class daysailing sloop to the high 60s for a heavy vessel such as a Colin Archer pilot boat. The moderate and successful ocean cruiser, such as the Whitby 42 and Bob Perry's Valiant 40, will be in the low-to-middle 30s.

RESISTANCE

The resistance of a sailing yacht to forward motion is derived from six sources:

WIND RESISTANCE

Caused by wind drag on the hull topsides, deck structures, spars, and rigging and the eddies created by these. Modern racing yachts with their slimmer aluminum spars, inside tangs and halyards, smaller diameter rod rigging, and semistreamlined deck structures have probably reduced wind resistance to an acceptable minimum. The cruising sailor might give it some thought, but on a blue water cruiser I would not trade the ease of inspection and replacement of outside halyards for the slight decrease in wind resistance of inside halyards. Besides, when the wind is aft, any added windage in the rig adds a bit to speed, although this will not always be appreciated in survival conditions.

APPENDAGE RESISTANCE

The result of eddies formed by such fittings as echo sounders, struts, exposed shafts, propellers, and apertures. The way to reduce resistance from this source is to fair the fittings as far as is possible; not much can be done about shafts or apertures. The fixed propeller is a major cause of appendage resistance, of course, and the fitting of a feathering or folding propeller can increase speed under sail surprisingly. Allowing a fixed propeller to turn freely is not the answer, though. This creates more eddies as a rule and actually slows the yacht.

SURFACE FRICTION

This forms the major part of the resistance at low speeds and is created by the area of the yacht that is in contact with the water. The amount of resistance from this source depends on the area involved, the length of the yacht, the vessel's speed, and the smoothness of the surface.

As the yacht travels through the water, it carries with it a wake called the boundary layer, and this boundary layer will vary in thickness from zero forward to as much as 4 to 6 inches aft, depending upon the size of the yacht. Next to the hull will be a thin band moving at the same speed as the hull, in effect clinging to it. This laminar film is only a few thousandths of an inch thick. As the wake gets farther from the hull, its speed decreases until at the outer edge of the boundary layer the wake is motionless.

The water in the boundary layer will normally have an eddying, turbulent motion. However, with a highly polished bottom at low speed a condition known as laminar flow may occur. This is a very smooth flow that reduces resistance substantially but is

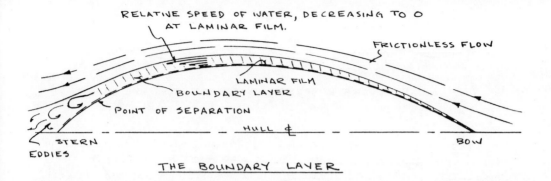

THE BOUNDARY LAYER

unlikely to occur at much above drifting speeds on the average craft. Laminar flow does occur on tank testing models due to their smooth finish and low speed, so the models have to be fitted with studs or sand strips on their leading edges in order to duplicate the normal flow on the full-sized yacht.

The normal turbulent flow is the culprit that creates the frictional resistance within the boundary layer. This resistance increases with speed and the resistance per square foot decreases with length. (The longer yacht will have proportionately less of her "rough" bottom protruding through the thin boundary layer forward.)

The modern yacht, particularly the racer, is designed with a high aspect ratio fin keel and spade rudder in order to reduce wetted surface to a minimum and so decrease frictional resistance. On an existing boat, there is only one solution to minimal resistance. Obviously, you do not want to slow the boat and you cannot increase its length or drop wetted surface in order to decrease frictional resistance, so the only answer is a carefully polished bottom. The hard racing paints are better in this regard, of course, but only if the bottom is cleaned regularly. The offshore cruiser is better off with a softer, more effective antifouling paint that will inhibit marine growth—a couple of barnacles will more than offset a week's polishing.

WAVE-MAKING RESISTANCE

As its name implies, wave-making resistance is caused by the energy used to create waves as the boat passes through the water. It is minimal at low speeds for obvious reasons but increases so rapidly with speed that at a speed/length ratio of .8 it may total 50 percent of the overall resistance. As speed increases to a $V/\sqrt{L}$ ratio of 1.4, the wave-making resistance will be close to 80 percent of the total.

The energy that creates the waves is produced by the boat, of course, and it is apparent that the deeper and longer the wave, the more power required to form a wave. The depth of the wave is controlled by the displacement and beam of the vessel; the beamy, heavy-displacement hull creates the largest wave and so has the most resistance. For this reason, beamy hulls are usually of lighter displacement (e.g., the modern ocean racer) while heavy-displacement hulls are usually narrow (e.g., the meter-class racers).

13 ☐

STERN WAVE

AT MODERATE SPEEDS WAVES ARE LOW AND SHORT

AS SPEED INCREASES, WAVES BECOME HIGHER
AND LONGER. STERN STARTS TO SQUAT.

AS BOAT APPROACHES V/√L = 1·3 WAVES LENGTHEN
TO FORM DEEP TROUGH AMIDSHIPS. STERN SQUATS
SUBSTANTIALLY.

WAVE CHANGES WITH INCREASE OF SPEED

The length of the wave is controlled by the speed of the yacht, the wave crests becoming farther apart as the speed increases until finally, at a V/ $\sqrt{L}$ of about 1.4, the wave is as long as the yacht and the vessel is supported by crests at the bow and stern with a deep hollow between. In effect, this is the limiting speed for a displacement yacht. It is evident that increasing the length of the yacht will increase the wave length and permit higher speeds. And since the wave-making resistance increases so rapidly with an increase in the V/ $\sqrt{L}$ ratio, it is apparent that one way to lower the resistance at any given speed is to spread the displacement over as long a length as possible, i.e., a long waterline hull with short overhangs.

Obviously, on a new design we can reduce wave-making resistance by decreasing the beam, decreasing the displacement, or increasing the sailing length. The tradeoffs are that reducing beam will reduce stability; reducing displacement may mean less ballast, and that also reduces stability; and a longer LWL means added wetted area and so more skin friction. Then the displacement must be properly distributed, and that's where the prismatic coefficient enters the picture. At V/ $\sqrt{L}$ = 1.1, a vessel with a Cp of .7 will have about four times the wave-making resistance of a boat of the same displacement with a Cp of .54. The shape of the ends is of great importance.

EDDY-MAKING

This is actually part of the overall wave-making resistance and is caused by a failure of the water flow to close in at the stern. If we put a flat plate crosswise to a stream, most of its total resistance would be eddy-making. This is due to the main stream of the water passing clear of the plate and leaving a low-pressure area behind the plate in which whirling eddies form and absorb energy.

Displacement hulls create eddies at the stern where the boundary layer separates from the hull, causing pressure variations and eddies abaft the point of separation. It is generally considered that the point of separation occurs where the hull surface attains an angle of about 15 degrees with the flow. The purpose of the bustles that were popular a few years ago was to move this point of separation aft, in effect making the water think the hull is longer than it really is.

On certain types of hulls, typically heavy-displacement hulls with short canoe sterns, the buttock lines may rise steeply aft, and this will create eddies and a stronger quarter wave. Modern yachts of moderate displacement well spread over a long waterline will rarely have this problem unless the stern is unduly pinched in.

INDUCED DRAG

This is the added resistance of a hull under sail caused in part by the angle of heel and the angle of leeway. As the hull heels, its lines lose their symmetry and fairness, so resistance increases. This increase will vary with each design and with heel angle but can be 10 percent or more. Generous beam, by reducing the heel angle and thus the induced drag, may more than offset the increased wave-making that the added beam created.

Induced drag due to leeway is partially a result of the keel having to produce the lift necessary to counter the sideways thrust of the sails. Then too, water is passing from the high- to the low-pressure side of the keel, creating vortices that add to resistance. And the heeled hull is not sailing in a straight line but is actually sailing at a leeway or yaw angle, which may vary from four degrees for a racing yacht up to six or seven degrees for a modern cruiser and 10 to 12 degrees for an inefficient, full-keel boat of older type. The total of all this induced drag may add from 35 to 100 percent to the straight-line resistance of the upright hull. There is not much the owner can do about this, unfortunately, so it is the responsibility of the designer to provide an effective keel design that will reduce leeway to an acceptable minimum.

It is small wonder that the sailboat is so slow compared to the displacement motorboat. Not only is the sailboat dragging along a lot of weight in its ballast keel, weight the motorboat doesn't need, but she is also moving heeled over anywhere from 10 to 20 degrees and crabbing along sideways at yaw angles of four to 10 degrees. With this enormous added resistance, we are lucky the boat will move at all.

15 ☐

THE LINES DRAWING

Somewhere in the mind of the experienced yacht designer lies a three-dimensional picture of the shape he wants for his new design. He knows what he is trying to achieve with the yacht. Whether it's a comfortable cruiser, a racing sail yacht, or a fast powerboat, he visualizes the hull form that will best perform the tasks that the client has set for the boat. His job is to lay out this three-dimensional shape on two-dimensional paper so that the builder can execute the design full size in wood, metal, or fiberglass.

The drawing that the designer produces for the builder is known as the lines drawing. Three examples are shown here of increasing complexity: a 32-foot flat bottom sharpie, a 21-foot vee bottom cat boat, and a 42-foot auxiliary cruiser.

The lines drawing shows the shape of the hull from three views: profile (or side view), plan (or view upward from the bottom), and sections (or end views). Only half the hull is drawn on the plan and section views because with skill and a bit of luck the other half of the boat will be exactly the same. The design waterline is drawn through the profile at the level the designer has calculated and hopes the boat will float.

The simple drawing of the flat bottom sharpie shows the sheer and chine lines in profile and plan view. Actually, the sheer on the plan view is, of course, the deck edge, but "sheer" is used to avoid having two different terms that mean the same line. Since the bottom of the hull is flat, the chine line in profile also represents the centerline of the hull. The stations may vary in number from eight to 16 or more and are evenly spaced along the DWL. Measurements taken from the stations provide the designer with the information he needs to calculate displacement, waterline area, CB, CF, and most of the other data discussed previously.

The slightly more complex catboat is of vee bottom form so the hull centerline and chine are at different levels in the profile view. The chine also shows in the plan view so the builder can accurately draw the stations using the points established by the centerline, chine, and sheer to obtain the shape.

The more shapely hull of the auxiliary cruiser shows waterlines laid out parallel to the LWL on the profile, and they also appear as curved lines on the plan view. Consider the hull as a layer cake with each waterline representing one layer of the cake. The auxiliary also shows diagonals. These run the full length of the hull and are developed from the straight lines on the body plan that radiate from the centerline. The diagonals are laid out on the plan view opposite the waterlines and also appear as long, gentle curves. The third set of fairing lines is the buttocks, shown in the plan view as straight lines parallel to the centerline and in the profile as long curves. Again the boat is sliced like a cake, but this time the slices run vertically.

We'll be discussing these various lines in the chapters that follow and will look at how their shapes affect performance.

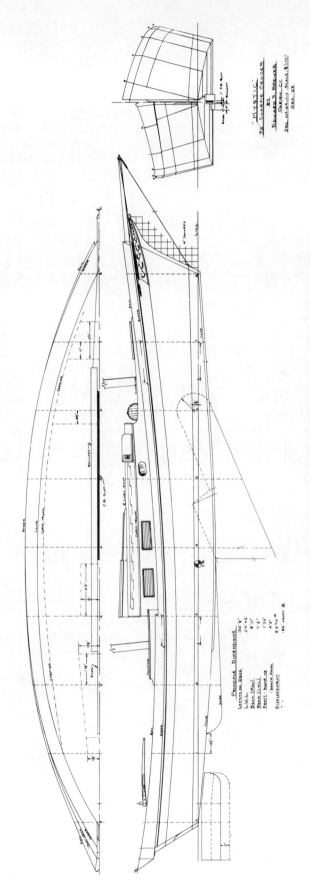

The simple lines of a double-ended sharpie. Note the drop rudder and "pink" stern.

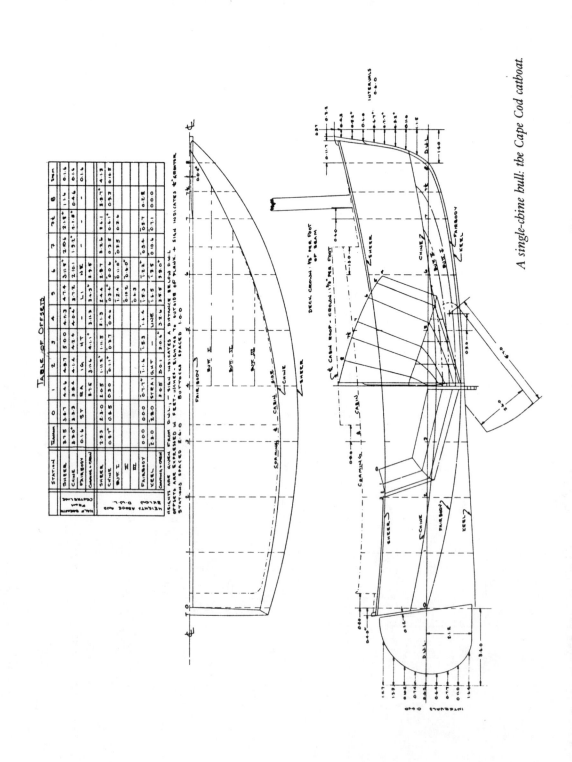

A single-chine hull: the Cape Cod catboat.

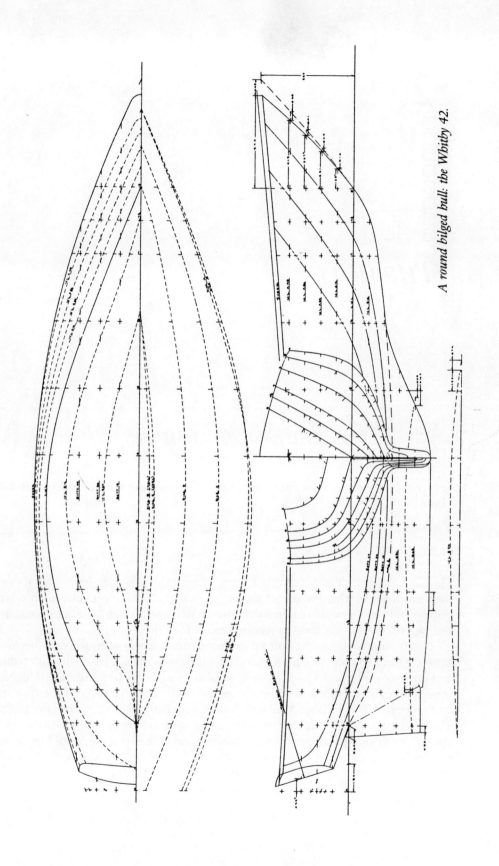

A round bilged hull: the Whitby 42.

2

□
□
□
□
□
□
□
□
□
□

THE HULL

THE BASIC HULL SHAPES

Let's consider the three basic hull forms: the flat bottom, the vee (or deadrise), and the round bilge.

FLAT BOTTOM HULLS

The flat bottom hull is the simplest form, usually the easiest to build and also the most economical. The simplest of the simple is the scow shape, in effect a box with sloping ends. It is generally limited to commercial barges, rough little duck boats, and children's toys and has little to recommend it for other uses.

Given some rocker to the bottom and some shape to the sides, the scow becomes a punt. Although today the punt hull is normally seen only in ten-to-16-foot fishing and hunting skiffs, punts have been built in sizes up to 45 feet and over. The New Jersey garvey and the Maine cargo sloops are both large examples of the type; the latter often made trips from Maine to Boston with cargoes of ice, stone, and timber. The punt can still be useful for inshore sailing, protected bays, and rivers due to its advantages of shoal draft, roominess, stability, and ease of construction. The form is not really suitable for open water, but it could be used to build a very interesting sailing houseboat that would be inexpensive and fun to own.

The sharpie is a substantial improvement over the punt where added seaworthiness is required. The type is characterized by a pointed bow, usually less rocker to the bottom, and a lower beam/length ratio than the punt. The stern may be square, rounded, or even pointed to form a double-ended hull.

Sharpies were developed in Connecticut for use in the Long Island Sound oyster fishery but spread to the Chesapeake, Florida, the Great Lakes, and even the West Coast due to their reputation for speed and seaworthiness, ease of construction, and their ability to sail on a heavy dew. They have been used in the mail service in Florida and as gunboats off the coast of Africa—a versatile type indeed.

Due to its flat bottom, the sharpie has a tendency to pound when driven hard to windward in a chop. They are fast sailers when on a reach in a good breeze, however, and one of our 32-footers has been clocked at just over 10 knots on a measured mile. They do make fine, inexpensive yachts for coastal cruising as long as they are not burdened with overly high cabins in an attempt to achieve full headroom. High freeboard and cabins can be dangerous on a relatively narrow hull such as the sharpie as the windage and raised center of gravity adversely affect stability. Due to the shoal hull and the need to keep the freeboard and cabin height moderate, it is difficult to achieve standing headroom on a good sharpie design of much under 40 feet LOA.

Another problem of the sailing sharpie is the large centerboard trunk that divides the main cabin in two. Designers have used leeboards, bilge boards, two small centerboards, shallow keels, and other devices to alleviate this. Proper planning of the interior, using the centerboard trunk as the base for the cabin table, can also be effective. In areas where draft is not a factor a good solution is to fit a fin keel. There is no rule that says the sharpie has to be a centerboard boat. Indeed, the famous Star class, developed in 1911, is essentially a modified sharpie hull with a fin keel hung under it. A well-shaped fin would add to windward ability and stability and could enable a modern sharpie design to sail along with the best of them.

Another common flat bottom hull is the dory. This form has more rocker to the bottom than the sharpie, much more flare to the topsides, and of course, the typical narrow tombstone transom. The flared topsides result in a narrower bottom than in the sharpie so the dory hull has little initial stability and heels alarmingly with a small athwartship shift in weight. This is not as bad as it sounds, though, as the hull flare quickly picks up stability as the heel angle increases. All in all, the dory has a fine reputation for seaworthiness.

My Grand Banks 22 ketch design is a modified dory shape with a somewhat broader transom than the true dory. Due to the lack of form stability, she was given a fin with outside ballast to provide more sail carrying power and has proven to be a good little cruiser. Many boats have been built to this design; one has voyaged from San Francisco to Alaska not once but several times. Even with outside ballast, the dory sails at a greater heel angle than the sharpie due to her lower initial stability. Thus, she presents her sharp chine rather than her flat bottom to the seas so pounding is less of a problem. She is somewhat slower than a sharpie due to increased bottom rocker, particularly if she is carrying the extra weight of heavy outside ballast. On the other hand, this can make the sailing dory self-righting in case of a knockdown and increases her suitability for open water use.

The 26-foot flat bottom yawl whose layout is shown is a sort of hybrid, not a

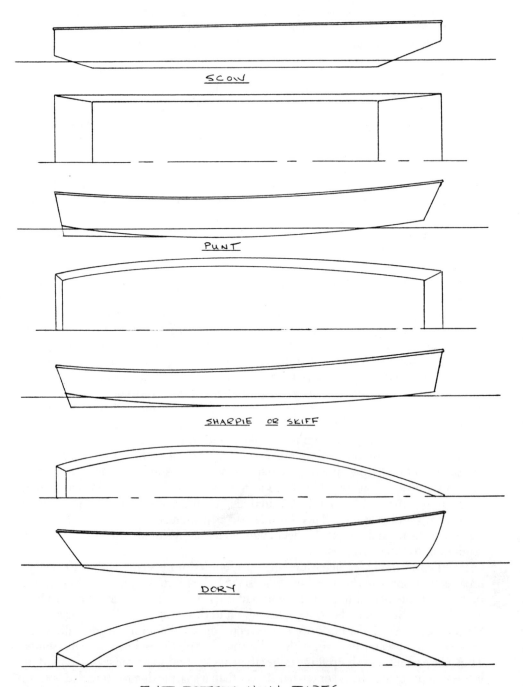

SCOW

PUNT

SHARPIE OR SKIFF

DORY

FLAT BOTTOM HULL TYPES

22

A small cruising ketch on a dory hull: the Grand Banks 22.

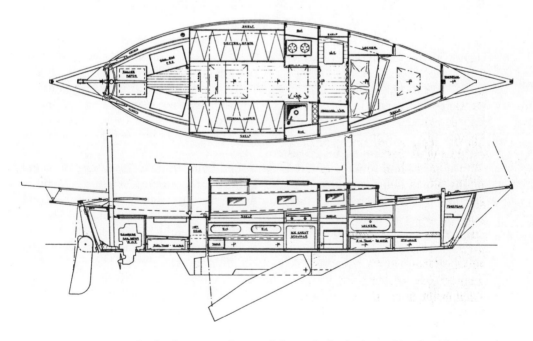

Layout of a flat bottom 26-foot yawl shows the limitations of headroom.

sharpie or a dory but simply a double-ended, skiff-like hull with some of the virtues of each type. Like all flat bottom hulls, she has the appeal of simplicity of construction and can be put together quickly and economically.

VEE BOTTOM (DEADRISE) HULLS

Vee bottom hulls afford more variety of types than their flat bottom sisters and so are harder to classify. All of the common flat bottom types have been built with deadrise modifications in an attempt to increase speed, seaworthiness, or carrying capacity. Even the lowly punt was built with deadrise in its bow and stern sections. Such craft were used with gaff sloop and schooner rigs along the Gulf Coast and built in sizes to 50 feet. They were reported to sail well. This type would also lend itself as an inexpensive, live-aboard sailing houseboat for protected coastal waters.

The vee bottom appeared rather late on the scene in America and was little used before the 1880s. Its history is obscure, but Thomas Clapham was experimenting with vee bottom sharpies in Long Island then and at the same time the flattie (a sharpie with vee sections aft) was being developed on the Chesapeake. Sketches of some of these variations are shown. Generally, the builders were widening the sterns to obtain greater reserve stability when heeled under sail and, of course, raising the chine aft so the wide stern would not be immersed and drag a ton of water behind it at normal heel angles. Clapham also raised the chine forward to provide a finer entry and so improve speed in a chop. Hulls of these various types can still make able cruisers both for sail and for low-speed power use. Readers interested in the modified sharpie, flattie, and skipjack will find a wealth of history and information on these and many other hull forms in Howard Chapelle's superb *American Small Sailing Craft*.

The descendents of these old deadrise boat hulls can be seen on our waters every day in the still active Lightning, Pelican, and other small, hard-chine, daysailing classes. As the vessels become larger, the shallow deadrise angle hulls generally give way to the deeper deadrise "yacht" type (for want of a better name). Such vessels also show more rocker to the keel, allowing them to carry greater displacement and the weight of heavy outside ballast. This in turn can make them self-righting in case of a knockdown and quite seaworthy enough for extensive voyaging. Indeed, vee bottom sailboats have circumnavigated the globe and if properly designed and built are every bit as able as their round bilged sisters.

The chine hull is rarely as fast as the round bilge, though. Tank tests of round versus chine hulls conducted at the Turkish Shipbuilding Research Institute generally showed the chine hull to be inferior in windward sailing. Where performance is a major consideration, the chine hull should be of light displacement and the rocker of the chine and keel kept as flat as possible; in effect, a vee bottom sharpie rather than a "yacht"-type hull. For offshore use where good displacement is necessary to carry the weight of ballast, stores, and gear, the deeper vee hull is a necessity. Some performance must be sacrificed to gain seaworthiness and the accommodation space essential for extended cruising, but this is true of round bilged vessels as well.

☐ 24

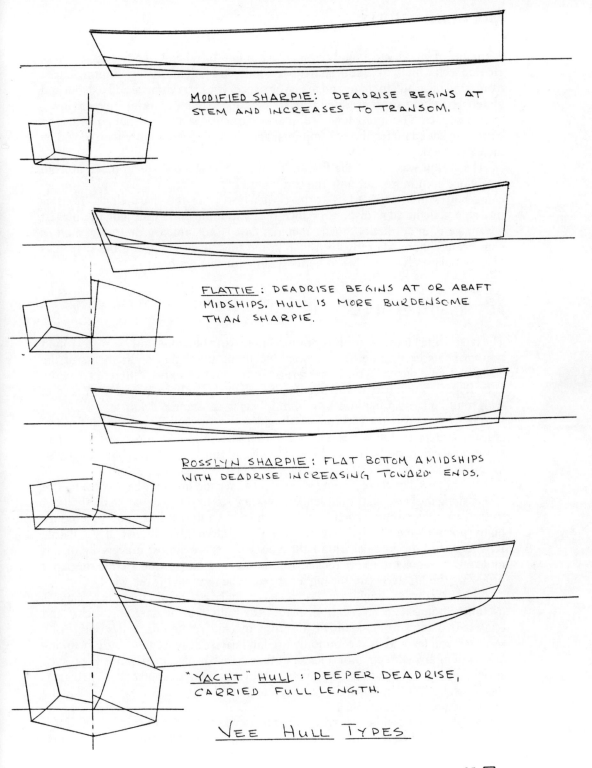

MODIFIED SHARPIE: DEADRISE BEGINS AT STEM AND INCREASES TO TRANSOM.

FLATTIE: DEADRISE BEGINS AT OR ABAFT MIDSHIPS. HULL IS MORE BURDENSOME THAN SHARPIE.

ROSSLYN SHARPIE: FLAT BOTTOM AMIDSHIPS WITH DEADRISE INCREASING TOWARD ENDS.

"YACHT" HULL: DEEPER DEADRISE, CARRIED FULL LENGTH.

VEE HULL TYPES

25 ☐

MULTICHINE HULLS

A number of sailing yachts and certain types of low-speed powercraft (tugs, trawlers, etc.) are seen with two or more chines per side. Such a hull more closely approaches a true round bilge hull in shape and in performance. The extra chine(s) add to labor and material cost but pay off in added performance due to reduced turbulence and lower wetted surface. The multichine hull makes particular sense in metal construction where the added material cost is minimal and the added labor more than repaid by increased resale value.

The author was one of the first to use the radius chine shape in metal hulls to reproduce even more faithfully the true round bilge vessel. This is simply a single-chine hull with a large radius at the corner instead of the sharp chine. There is probably a slight edge in performance over the multichine hull, but the biggest advantage is in aesthetics. Again, material cost is not much greater, but there is considerably more labor involved than in the single-chine hull, and the shape has been popular only on yachts of better quality for this reason.

ROUND BILGED HULLS

The type is often termed "round bottom," but this can be a misnomer as many round bottom boats have quite flat bottoms depending upon the requirements of the design. "Round bilged" is the better term. The form falls into two different types, the U or dinghy section with round bilges and a relatively flat bottom, and the Y section with round bilges fairing into a vee'd hull having substantial deadrise.

The U section is used in canoes, dinghies, and daysailers and also in fin keel cruisers and racers of the largest sizes. In powercraft it is most often seen in semidisplacement hulls such as the well-known Maine lobster boats but is also used in displacement hulls of the lighter type and in a few planing motorboats.

On low-speed craft (i.e., sailing yachts), the U section hull may have considerable rocker along the keel, but the tendency in recent years has been to flatten this in order to increase the prismatic coefficient, straighten the buttock lines, and so produce higher potential speeds when it breezes up. The modern International Offshore Rule (IOR) racer and the popular ultra-light cruiser-racers are almost universally of this mold—U section, little keel rocker, fine bows, and fairly wide sterns, the latter providing the lift necessary for higher speeds when sailing off the wind.

Its appearance in dinghies and ocean racers makes it obvious that the U shape is usefully employed in fast, light-displacement hulls. For ocean-going yachts and cruisers that carry heavy loads of furniture, machinery, liquids, and stores, the Y section is still favored. It is commonly used in heavier displacement craft including larger sailing auxiliaries, motorsailers, and slow-speed displacement powerboats such as tugs, fishing vessels, and ocean-going motor yachts. A derivation of the Y section is the "wineglass" hull in which the bottom lines fair into the lines of the ballast keel by means of a well-rounded tuck.

Back in the good old days, when the *America* was showing her colors around the Isle of Wight, all the yachts were of Y section, and the original Baltimore clipper ships

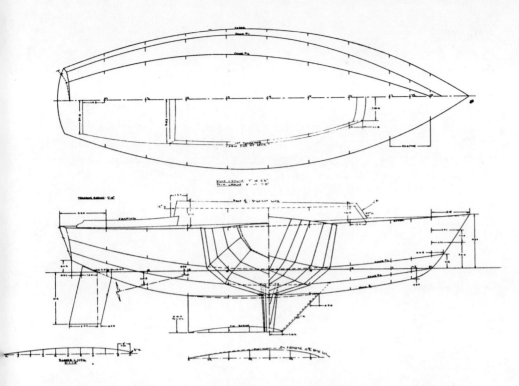

The Murray 33 shows how a double-chine hull approaches the true round bilge shape.

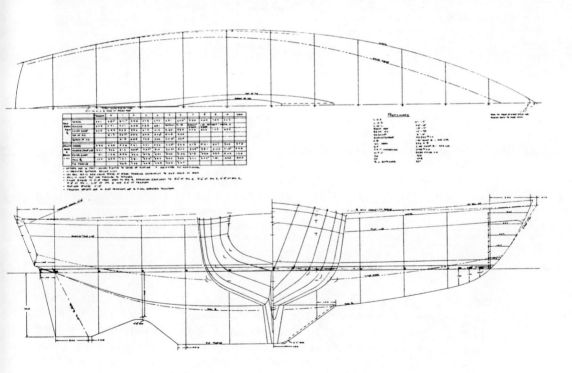

A radius chine hull is difficult to tell from a true round bilge. The Northeast 47.

27 □

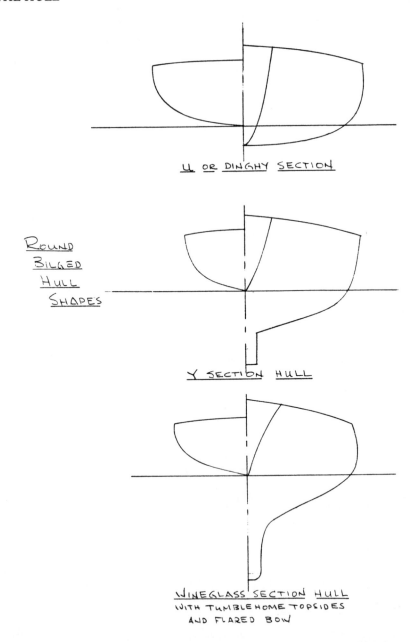

U OR DINGHY SECTION

ROUND BILGED HULL SHAPES

Y SECTION HULL

WINEGLASS SECTION HULL WITH TUMBLEHOME TOPSIDES AND FLARED BOW

used this hull form as well. The wineglass shape came on the scene when outside ballast began to be employed in the 1880s and has been used on better quality displacement yachts ever since. Its main advantage is a slight reduction in wetted surface and possibly in turbulence compared to the true Y shape. However, things have a habit of running full circle, and the modern fin keel yacht shows little wineglass in its sections; typically, a tight radius fillet is all that is used to fair the hull proper to the fin.

Generally, we can say that U-shaped hulls are used with yachts ranging from d/l ratios of 60 to 270 or so and that the Y-shaped sections find their place in vessels from the ultra-heavies of over 400 d/l ratio down to average cruising auxiliaries in the 250-to-300 range. However, there are exceptions to every rule, as we know. One fine example is the pre-World War II 30-square-meter sloop *Waterwitch* with a displacement of 6,160 pounds on a waterline length of 28.5 feet. This is a d/l ratio of only 118.8 yet she was a very shapely wineglass section hull. Ultra-light displacement is certainly not a brain child of modern designers, or perhaps it's simply that Knud Reimers was 50 years ahead of his time.

STABILITY

The speed of a sailing yacht in any given wind is determined to a large extent by the amount of sail she carries. In light breezes this may be limited by the design itself or the handicap rules. In heavier weather, the amount of sail that can be carried is governed by the ability of the hull to remain on its feet; in other words, her stability. Stability can be defined as the tendency of a vessel to return to the upright position when it is inclined by external forces (wind, shifting of crew weights, seas, etc.). There are, of course, two directions of this inclination; athwartship or fore and aft. Our prime concern in the sailing yacht is with athwartship stability as this is the one that affects the driving power of the sails.

Consider the advantages of a "stiff" or "powerful" sailboat reaching to windward in a good breeze. Obviously, the heel angle will be less than that of its tender sister so the sails will operate more efficiently and the boat will move faster. But the keel or fin is more upright as well so it too is working to its maximum potential, and that results in less leeway and probably in pointing a degree or two higher. When you have a boat that is going faster, pointing higher, and making less leeway than the competition, then you have a winner.

The drawing illustrates the basics of athwartship stability. If a boat is heeled from her normal upright waterline (LWL) through an angle ϕ to a heeled waterline (WL 1), there is no change in her displacement. The upward thrust of buoyancy still acts vertically to the water, but the shape of the heeled hull moves this upward thrust (the heeled CB) from its normal position on the centerline (B) to a point outboard of the centerline (B1). In the case of a sailing yacht heeled by wind, this point is to leeward of the centerline.

The center of gravity (G) does not change position as the boat heels, barring unforeseen circumstances. The horizontal distance from G to a vertical line drawn through B1 is termed the righting arm, or righting lever, abbreviated GZ. We know that the buoyancy of the hull is acting upwards through B1 and the weight of the boat is acting downwards through G. These two forces form a couple, called the righting moment, which is equal to the displacement times the length of the righting arm (displacement × GZ). To illustrate, if our boat weighed 2,000 pounds and the GZ distance was 1.25 feet, the righting moment would be 2,000 × 1.25 =2,500 foot-pounds. It would take that much force of wind on the sails to heel the boat to that angle.

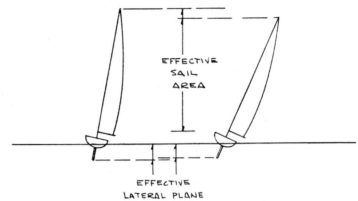

EFFECTIVE
SAIL
AREA

EFFECTIVE
LATERAL PLANE

THE STIFFER BOAT WINS RACES!

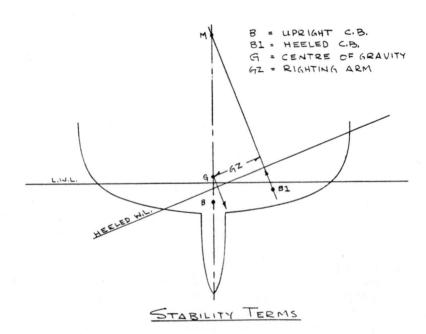

B = UPRIGHT C.B.
B1 = HEELED C.B.
G = CENTRE OF GRAVITY
GZ = RIGHTING ARM

M

L.W.L.

G

GZ

B1

B

HEELED W.L.

STABILITY TERMS

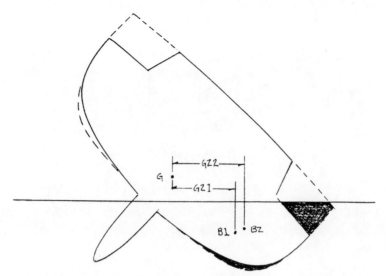

INCREASED BOUYANCY TO LEEWARD (BY HARDER BILGES, HIGHER FREEBOARD, WIDER BEAM) MOVES THE HEELED C.B. TO LEEWARD (B2) AND INCREASES THE LENGTH OF THE RIGHTING ARM.

Obviously, the stability (or the sail carrying power) of a yacht is directly related to two simple factors, her displacement and the length of the righting arm. In turn, the length of the righting arm depends on the location of the center of gravity and the location of the heeled center of buoyancy. The lower the G, the longer the righting arm. The farther to leeward the heeled CB, the longer the righting arm. It's that simple.

Thus, we can carry more sail (or reduce heeling) if we increase displacement, bearing in mind that the added weight must be at or lower than the center of gravity in order not to raise the CG and thus shorten the righting arm. We can also carry more sail if we increase the length of the righting arm, and we can do this by shifting weights to lower the center of gravity or to move it to windward.

The stability created by the shift of the heeled CB to leeward is called "form" stability as it is derived from the actual shape of the yacht. Given equal displacement and beam, the flat bottom scow will have the greatest form stability, so if we are designing a new yacht, the closer the vessel's shape approaches that of the scow, with hard, tight bilges and flat floors with little deadrise, the greater the form stability it will have. Carrying the beam well aft to a wide, flat counter that will begin to immerse as the boat heels will also add to form stablity.

Factors that decrease form stability are a soft bilge, deep deadrise angle, large radius garboards joining the hull to the keel, and a fine stern. These are also the general characteristics of an ocean-going yacht, though, as many designers and owners feel that excess form stability is not desirable for serious offshore work; it can create a harsh, snappy motion that is hard on the crew and the gear.

Reasonably high freeboard is also important to form stability at higher heel

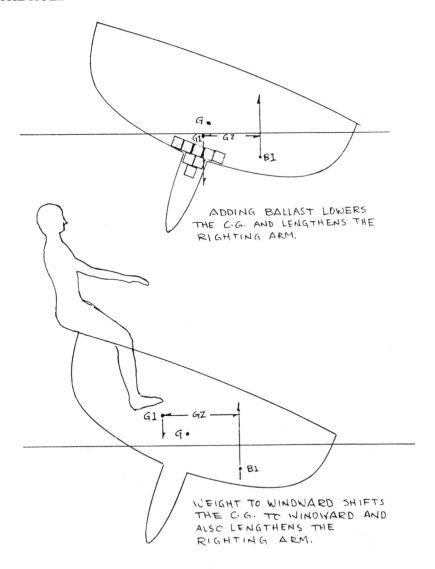

G
G1 — G2
B1

ADDING BALLAST LOWERS
THE C.G. AND LENGTHENS THE
RIGHTING ARM.

G1 — G2
G
B1

WEIGHT TO WINDWARD SHIFTS
THE C.G. TO WINDWARD AND
ALSO LENGTHENS THE
RIGHTING ARM.

angles. Once the deck edge is awash, further heeling will move the CB inboard, shortening the righting arm. In open daysailers, immersing the deck edge allows water to pour into the hull. This rapidly moves the CG to the leeward side, shortening the righting arm to the point where a capsize results if the sail pressure is not relieved immediately—as no doubt many readers have found out to their dismay. Of course, having the deck edge awash is not disastrous on a decked cruising yacht, but it does create considerable added resistance, and a few inches more cruising freeboard might well eliminate this.

☐ *32*

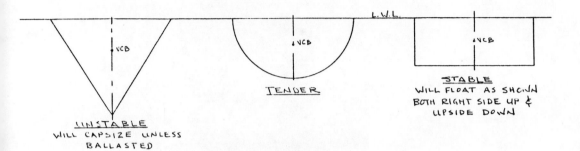

THE BASIC HULL SHAPES

YACHT HULLS WILL RESEMBLE ONE OF THESE.

DISPLACEMENT: HEAVY VS. LIGHT

Over the years, displacement/length ratios have been slowly dropping due largely to the change from the Cruising Club of America (CCA) to the IOR rule for rating racing yachts. The CCA rule actually weighed the boats and gave a large handicap penalty for light displacement. Thus, d/l ratios of 350 to 400 were common. In addition, the CCA rule penalized long waterlines (it was quite common to see a yacht with over one-third of her length in overhangs) so the displacement had to be carried on a relatively short DWL and naturally, this meant larger d/l ratios. On the other hand, the IOR rule measures the hull instead of weighing it so the designer can work to the measurement points and more or less ignore the displacement. Lighter displacement is not penalized as long as the hull fits into the measurement formula. Lower d/l ratios are the result.

The differences are not quite as great as one might think, though. For example, a 1983 Cal 39 displaces 19,000 pounds on a 32'1" DWL (a d/l ratio of 256.9) but her short ends mean that she will not pick up a great deal of sailing length as she heels. Bill Luders's famous 39-footer *Storm*, of pre-1960 vintage, displaced about 17,500 pounds on a 27-foot DWL (a d/l ratio of 396.9) but was probably sailing on a waterline of close to 30 feet when she was laid over in a stiff breeze. The new 39-footer is actually heavier than the older boat but the added 5 feet of waterline reduces the d/l ratio substantially.

The big advantage of the modern boats is not that they are lighter; it is that they carry their displacement on a much longer DWL. This means that their lines are finer with less rocker to the hull profile and a flatter angle to the run at the stern, and this translates into higher top speeds when the wind is right. The long DWL yachts of today have another advantage, and that is accommodations. The longer waterline simply provides more room inside the boat so most modern 32- and 33-footers have space and comfort that would be unheard of in boats of less than 40-foot LOD in the 1950s.

Storm, *rigged as a ketch in 1962. That's me by the lee shrouds with one hand on the "pepper-grinder" winch. The boat's designer, Bill Luders, is by the mizzenmast in a dark shirt. Photo courtesy of Peter Barlow.*

Lower d/l ratios do reduce wave-making resistance and so contribute to speed. At d/l ratios of 100 or less, the yacht may well be able to maintain planing speeds if her hull shape and rig are up to the job. In effect, other things (stability, sail area, wetted surface, etc.) being equal, light displacement equals performance. However, heavy displacement provides motion comfort. If two boats have the same waterline area and one has twice the displacement of the other, the former will receive only half the motion of its lighter sister in a rough sea. Heavy displacement also allows the yacht to carry larger supplies of stores, water, fuel, spares, and gear for extended voyages plus such amenities as generator sets, air conditioners, and heating systems.

In this regard, it must be pointed out that the heavier displacement yacht will be much less affected by the weight of stores required for a long voyage than will its light-displacement sister. Four people setting out from the Pacific Northwest to cruise through the Panama Canal to the Caribbean could well add two tons of displacement to their vessel. Consider their own weights (600 pounds); food for four weeks (400 pounds) plus a week's safety factor (100 pounds); extra water (300 pounds); beer (100 pounds); spare anchors and line (200 pounds); dinghy, outboard, and gas (250 pounds); portable generator (50 pounds); spare parts, oil, grease, paint, etc. (200 pounds); heavy-duty fenders (50 pounds); life raft (100 pounds), and we're up to the first ton, to say nothing of the fishing gear, barbecue, reading material, foul-weather gear, spare sails, clothes, extra battery, portable radio, folding bicycles, and other goodies that so many cruising couples take along.

Add that weight to a light-displacement hull, and suddenly it is not light displacement any more. If we take two 33-foot WL yachts, one with a d/l ratio of 270, the other with 150, and add a modest 3,500 pounds of cruising gear to each, the d/l ratios increase to 313.5 and 193.5 respectively, a jump of 16 percent for the heavier yacht and 29 percent for the lightweight. Assuming both start life with a sail area/displacement ratio of 16.5, the ratio on the loaded boats will drop to 14.9 on the heavier yacht and 13.9 on the lightweight. It is obvious which will suffer the greatest performance loss.

Heavy displacement, the hull shapes being similar, also means greater stability since stability is a product of the displacement times the righting arm. Thus, the heavy-displacement boat can be given a larger sailplan and so may be faster than its sister in light airs. The tradeoff here, of course, is that the larger sailplan means a stouter mast, stronger rigging, and larger sails, and that all costs money.

Contributing to today's lighter displacement yachts is modern boatbuilding technology. Cored fiberglass, laminated wood, and aluminum hulls can be built lighter than the carvel plank-on-frame hulls of yesteryear's ocean-going cruisers and racers. The d/l ratio can be reduced, yet neither the strength nor the amount of ballast is affected. In the days of wood yachts, light-displacement boats were considered vastly more expensive due to the careful workmanship necessary. Today that is not the case unless one gets carried away with the use of carbon fibers, Kevlar, and titanium in an attempt to save every possible ounce. Standard materials can produce boats of quite light displacement and high performance without resort to extremely costly materials or craftsmanship.

Generally, d/l ratios of 250 to 300 can provide the cruising sailor with comfortable accommodations, reasonable storage capacity, and all-around good performance. Above those ratios the owner must decide how much performance under sail he is willing to sacrifice for added comfort; below, the decision is how much comfort will be sacrificed for added performance.

BEAM

Beam is one of the major considerations in the design of a sailing yacht as it affects the performance of the vessel in several ways. First, wider beam increases the wetted surface of the hull and so reduces speed in light airs due to greater drag. However, we should consider that the beamier, more stable hull will probably have a larger rig than its finer sister and so may well have the added sail area needed to overcome the increased resistance in light airs.

Next, wider beam increases the wave-making resistance. This would adversely affect performance in moderate to strong breezes except for the fact that the added beam also increases the stability of the hull, allowing the vessel to carry more sail and/or reducing the heel angle. The reduced heel angle improves the driving force of the

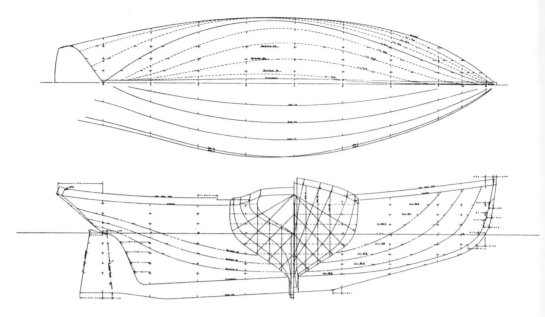

The Sophia Christina, *a heavy displacement schooner, has proven to be fast.*

sails, cuts induced drag, and also enhances the ability of the yacht's keel to resist leeway. The interaction of these factors, resistance, stability, driving force, and leeway, forms an intriguing puzzle that must be solved anew by the naval architect for each design.

Beam/LWL ratios of sailing yachts have varied widely but have been influenced by the handicap rule more than any other single factor. As the rule changes so does the general beam ratio, from the British plank-on-edge cutters of the Gay Nineties with ratios as low as .16 to the chubby CCA keel-centerboarders of the 1960s with ratios approaching .4. The IOR rule has carried on where the CCA left off, encouraging wide beam. It is now common to have deep keel yachts with beam/LWL ratios that would have been seen only on a keel-centerboard hull 20 years ago. This wide beam combined with deep draft and a high ballast ratio has made the modern ocean racer an extremely powerful hull indeed.

A point to note: If all the dimensions of a yacht are doubled, the new vessel will have eight times the displacement and, due to doubling the length of the righting arm, 16 times the stability of the original. The sail area, on the other hand, will be only four times that of the original and the heeling moment eight times the original due to doubling the length of the heeling arm. Similarly, if we halve the size of a yacht in all dimensions, it will have only one-sixteenth the stability of its larger sister but one-eighth the heeling moment and so may well be too tender to carry her sail. Thus, the larger yacht can carry its sail effectively on comparatively less beam than its smaller sister can and still have adequate stability to stand up to a stiff breeze. For this reason, the larger yachts will generally have a lower beam/LWL ratio than will a smaller craft, which of necessity must have a beamier hull in relation to its length in order to have sufficient sail carrying power.

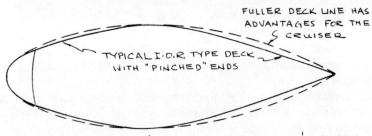

FULLER DECK LINE HAS
ADVANTAGES FOR THE
CRUISER

TYPICAL I.O.R. TYPE DECK
WITH "PINCHED" ENDS

COMPARING I.O.R. & CRUISING BOAT DECK LINES

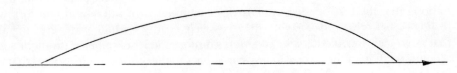

COD'S HEAD & MACKEREL TAIL
TYPICAL 1800s W.L.
WOULD SAIL BETTER BACKWARDS!

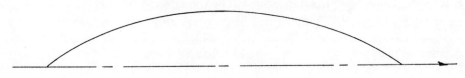

"BALANCED" HULL

BETTER, BUT STILL TOO FULL FORWARD

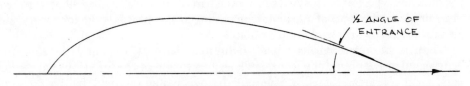

½ ANGLE OF
ENTRANCE

ASSYMETRICAL HULL

THE MODERN FORM. ½ ANGLE OF ENTRANCE
IS UNDER 25°, USUALLY WELL UNDER.

Added beam gives extra interior space for cruising accommodations, of course, but there is another factor for the cruising sailor to consider. The wider beam means greater waterline area and added form stability so the beamier boat will have a quicker motion in a seaway and could be less comfortable than a narrower hull of the same general size.

There is no hard and fast rule to determine the correct beam for a yacht. Charts have been published in many articles and design books showing general proportions over a range of size, but these are usually based on current practice, which is too often a result of the latest handicap rule change. Then the trend changes long before the book is out of print. The value of such charts is more historical than practical. More useful to the student designer or potential buyer is a study of successful designs of the past. These will show the proportions that have passed the test of time and, more importantly, the test of successful voyages completed in safety and comfort. My feeling is that present day yachts are excessively beamy for blue water cruising and that most yachts would be safer and more comfortable at sea (albeit with slightly less accommodation) if they were slightly narrower. On the other hand, I also feel that the modern beamy cruiser is fine for coastal use and provides a good blend of stability, performance, and accommodation at a slight loss in motion comfort and perhaps a greater sacrifice of ultimate safety. However, few of us will cross oceans in our yachts and so need not concern ourselves with inverted stability. The offshore cruising man should give this serious consideration as his life may depend on it. In that case the narrower, deeper, and heavier yacht will be the safest.

BALLAST

Keel sailing yachts will carry a large percentage of their displacement in ballast to provide the stability necessary to carry sail in a stiff breeze. The ballast may be all inside as seen on a few motorsailers and heavy cruising boats generally of the "character" type, but normally a substantial part of the ballast (75 to 99 percent) will be outside in the form of a lead or iron casting as this provides the lowest possible center of gravity and maximum stability.

Lead is the preferred ballast material due to its density (710 pounds per cubic foot compared to 470 pounds for iron). Thus, a given weight can be fitted lower in the hull and so provide greater stability. Some say that, when used as outside ballast, the softer lead also provides a cushion effect in case of grounding. Opponents of this theory claim that this softness lets the lead conform to the shape of the rocks or coral and so makes it more difficult to get the boat off again. I don't buy either argument and feel it is much better to keep the boat off the bottom in the first place.

Many metal and fiberglass yachts have their ballast inside the hull but, due to the hollow fin shape, the ballast is in roughly the same position as if it were fitted outside. This type of ballast is often called "inside" ballast, but "encapsulated" is a more descriptive term. Reserve the term "inside" for the ballast that is within the hull proper and so is not as effective as if it were set down into a deep fin. Where the ballast is encapsulated in a fiberglass hull, the skin takes up some volume so the ballast will be forced up a bit higher than if it were a metal hull or a bolted-on unit. The difference is slight, however, and not significant except for highly competitive racing yachts. On a design for a new 55-foot fiberglass fin keel auxiliary, I found that encapsulating the ballast reduced the righting moment at a 30-degree heel angle by less than 1.9 percent compared to fitting the ballast outside. The average yachtsman would never notice the difference.

The amount of ballast carried will range from 20 to 30 percent of the vessel's displacement for a motorsailer, 30 to 45 percent for an auxiliary cruiser, 45 to 65 percent for an ocean racer, and up to 75 percent for a racing yacht for America's Cup competition. In the mid-1960s the 5.5-meter yachts often carried 3,600 pounds of lead ballast on a total displacement of 4,520 pounds, close to an 80-percent ratio. That means that the hull and rig on these wooden 30-foot sloops weighed just over 900 pounds. Careful construction was a necessity!

One point to note is that steel yachts may seem to have a low ballast ratio compared to vessels of other materials. However, what may not be considered is that the entire weight of the steel keel, floors, and plating at the height of the ballast top and to some degree above it is effective ballast. I calculated this for one of my steel designs and found that when this weight of construction steel was added to the ballast weight it raised the ballast ratio from a seemingly light 30 percent to 36 percent, a much more acceptable figure. The same is true of fiberglass and aluminum yachts with encapsulated ballast, although these lighter materials will not be as effective as ballast as the heavier steel.

A good ballast ratio is desirable for the stability that it provides, increasing sail carrying power and thus performance. However, stability can be obtained by other means—increased beam, increased displacement, hull shape, or deep draft, as we have previously discussed. I have seen successful vessels with ballast ratios as low as 25 percent. Indeed, *Finisterre* had a ballast ratio of under 30 percent, and while she would not show well in today's extremely competitive ocean racing circuit, she is still a fine, fast, weatherly cruiser.

Today's yachtsmen have been educated by Madison Avenue advertising to regard a high (40 percent or over) ballast ratio as essential to a good performing yacht. That is not the case. The essential thing is stability. Achieving a high ballast ratio at the expense of the accommodations and amenities that make for comfort at sea is an easy solution to obtaining stability. But it can also take all the pleasure out of cruising.

DRAFT

Draft is a controlling factor in performance. Deeper draft gives better windward ability, all other things being equal. It is as simple as that. The designer can reduce draft for any given boat by lengthening the keel or fitting twin keels, but he knows at the same time that weatherliness will suffer.

Draft does two things. It increases the aspect ratio (and thus the efficiency) of the keel, and it enables the ballast to be carried lower to increase stability. Fitting a centerboard to a shoal hull increases the aspect ratio of the lateral plane but does nothing to improve stability. The deep draft fin keel of proper shape is still the most effective way to get maximum windward performance.

Of course, deep draft also restricts the yacht owner and keeps him out of many pleasant cruising grounds that are accessible to shoal-draft vessels. This is the main reason that designers still create shoal-to-moderate-draft full keel and long fin keel yachts. Top-notch performance is nice, but the excitement loses its sheen if you have to row a mile to shore every time you anchor or waste long hours waiting for the tide to rise that last six inches to float you off a mud bank.

In recent years, there has been considerable development in ballasted, shaped daggerboards or drop keels. These provide some of the advantages of deep draft fin keels but at the cost of increased complexity and maintenance. Another disadvantage to the shaped hinged boards is the width of centerboard slot required. This creates undesirable turbulence, not of vital importance to the cruising sailor, but for the racing yachtsman necessitating troublesome flaps to close off the slot in order to reduce drag.

There is no easy answer to the draft problem. If you prefer gunkhole cruising or if you want to trailer your boat and launch it from a ramp, then you must have an extremely shoal centerboard or drop keel boat. If your cruising grounds are areas such as Florida or the Chesapeake where the bottom is always close to the surface, then you may want a keel-centerboarder or a shoal-draft keelboat. Otherwise, buy all the draft your waters can handle and you will be repaid by better performance. Bear in mind what one experienced owner told me: "With 6-foot draft, you stay outside the one-fathom line and know you are safe. With 4-foot draft, you can go inside it and tear your bottom out."

INTERPRETING THE LINES

THE WATERLINES

The waterlines of a sailing yacht are formed to one of three general shapes: the "cod's-head-and-mackerel-tail" form with a full bow and fine stern lines, the "symmetrical" form with more or less balanced ends, and the "wedge" form with a fine bow and full afterbody.

The cod's-head type was long favored in British yachts, but the overly full bows created added resistance particularly to windward in any kind of sea. In the early 1960s, the 12-meter challenger *Sceptre* was derived from this shape but showed poorly against the American defender. The full bows react more to the oncoming seas while the fine stern lacks adequate damping effect as the rising bow pushes the stern down. The result is excessive pitching and a slower boat.

The symmetrical shape was advanced in the 1930s as an answer to problems of weather helm. The more balanced ends were assumed to provide a balanced boat and to result in easier steering, in particular a helm that did not develop greater weather helm as the yacht heeled. Certainly, the shape was an improvement on the cod's head; the bows were finer and the stern was fuller so pitching was reduced. Still tests conducted in the mid-1960s at the University of Southampton showed that the steering of the wedge-shaped hull was as good as a symmetrical model and that the former pitched considerably less and so was faster on all points than its even-ended sister. The wedge-shaped or assymetrical hull has other advantages. The wider waterlines at the stern provide greater reserve stability as the yacht heels so that she heels to a slightly lesser degree in any given wind strength. Also, the center of buoyancy of a wedge-shaped hull is farther aft so the ballast can be carried farther aft. This results in a lower center of gravity.

Modern yachts are normally of wedge-shaped form for the above reasons, and in the field of ultra-lights the stern waterlines are often very wide indeed in order to provide lift for planing speeds when off the wind.

The bows of modern yachts are fine, and a half-angle of entrance of 20 degrees or less is common. Certainly, anything over 24 degrees could be described as bluff by present standards. The waterlines forward should be straight or very slightly convex; hollow is to be avoided wherever possible. Hollow waterlines forward mean greater angles aft where the waterline swells out to the maximum beam, and this will increase resistance in the long run. Certain yacht types with relatively plum stems and deep forefoots (i.e., catboats, clipper-bowed craft, etc.) will require some hollow forward in order to avoid overly full diagonals, but these are exceptions to the rule. The entry of such craft should be quite fine so that the diagonals can be kept fair without resorting to excessively deep hollow in the waterlines.

As the waterlines above the LWL approach the deck level, they are given increasing fullness. On IOR racers, this increase in fullness is very slight indeed and the deck line is narrow, often a pinched straight line from the stem to where it fairs into the point of maximum beam. This fits the measurement rule and does reduce the weight of the deck in the forward part of the hull. Such a fine shape is well suited to a racing yacht since the weights on these vessels are concentrated amidships, and the ends are kept as light as possible to lift with oncoming seas.

The same fine bow shape on a cruiser that is loaded forward with anchors, chain, windlass, bosun's stores, spare sails, and maybe a crew member catching a nap in one of the forward vee berths is a mistake. There are benefits for the cruiser in having a moderately full deck line. These include greater working space on deck, more room in the forward cabin, and greater flare to the bow sections. In heavy seas the boat may be slowed slightly as she will tend to pitch a bit more, but she will also lift her heavier forward weights better with each sea that rolls under her and be drier on deck. I feel this is more important than that last twentieth of a knot under heavy weather conditions.

The half-angle of the load waterline at the stern is subject to much more variation than at the bow. Generally, designers are in agreement that the half-angle of entrance should be fine, but it is obvious that they do not agree about the stern ending. A range of angles of 30 to 60 degrees is not unusual. I like to keep the angle fairly full to provide buoyancy aft, but frankly, I never measure it. Yet I am always measuring the bow angles and trying to keep them as fine as possible.

Some modern motorsailers, such as the Lancer line, have quite full sterns in order to provide support aft so that the vessel can reach semiplaning or even planing speeds under power. This full stern does not seem to hurt the boat's sailing performance downwind; indeed, Lancers have done well in downwind races and surprised more than one hot ocean racer. However, the wide, flat stern creates added turbulence and wetted surface when hard on the wind at larger angles of heel, so the shape is not desirable.

BUTTOCKS

First, it must be understood that in discussing buttock lines we are concerned with the buttocks that are about 25 percent of the yacht's beam out from the centerline. Buttocks inboard of this will reflect the shape of the centerline and can develop some odd humps and hollows aft if the yacht is of full keel, wineglass-section type, or has a prominent bustle. Also, the forward end of the inner buttocks will reflect any knuckle in the bow of the vessel, and there will be a "hard spot" where they turn from the run of the bottom to rise toward the sheerline.

Sailing yachts generally should have easy, fair buttocks without excess rounding up in the quarters. Double-enders of the Colin Archer type too often have heavily rounded buttocks aft, and this produces a slow hull, dragging a large quarter wave along with it. The modern racing yacht with its shallow canoe hull has long, fairly straight buttocks. These are ideal for speed both on the wind and off.

The heavier, deeper cruising yacht must of necessity have more rounding in the buttocks. Still the run should be reasonably straight for one-eighth to one-quarter of the waterline length forward of the stern ending and then fair gradually into an easy, rounding amidships before rising to the sheer forward.

BUSTLES

The water flow at the stern tends to separate from the hull at a point where the angle between the hull and the direction of water flow is approximately 15 degrees. As it separates from the hull, the water becomes turbulent and creates considerable resistance. It is obvious that if the point of separation can be moved farther aft, this turbulence and its related drag will be lessened, and the hull will have a higher potential speed in stronger winds.

To this end, the bustle was designed to carry out the after waterlines, flatten the buttocks, and move the 15-degree point aft. In effect, the bustle makes the water think that the hull is longer than it actually is. Another effect of the bustle is to add displacement aft. This moves the center of buoyancy aft, which in turn allows the designer to locate the ballast a bit farther aft and usually a bit lower. To picture the shape of a good bustle, think of the stern lines of an Old Town canoe, with all the waterlines running right to the stern and the profile then turning quickly up to the waterline. Above waterline, the stern shape may be double-ended as in the canoe or faired out into a transom or counter.

One of the earliest yachts to sport a bustle successfully was the 12-meter yacht *Intrepid*, and it was finally carried to extremes on the 12-meter *Mariner*, which, though unsuccessful, showed a great deal of imagination and courage.

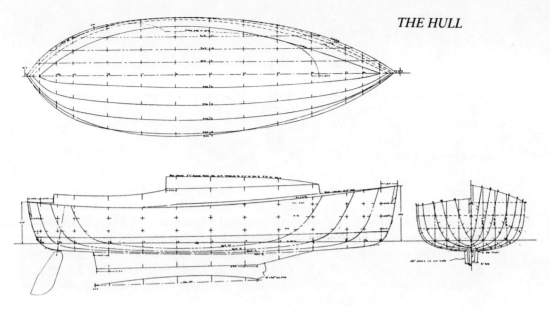

The canoe yawl stern ends in a natural bustle. The Rob Roy 23.

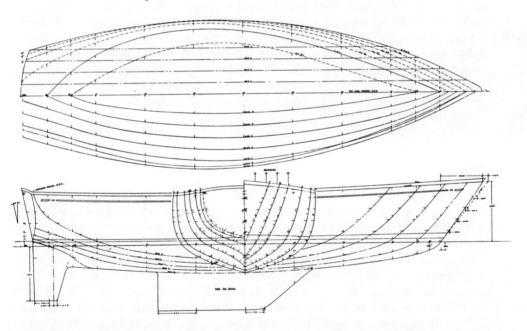

A bustle on a modern auxiliary. Note how the waterline below the LWL is pulled out aft. The Brewer/MT 42.

While the bustle has significant advantages at higher speeds, it does little at low to medium speeds, although on some fin keel/skeg rudder types it may reduce wetted area slightly by filling out the hollow between the skeg and the hull. The bustle is of no advantage on the light, shallow-bodied, fin keel/spade rudder racing yachts that are common today as their buttock lines are already flat. A bustle would only add extra drag as the yacht was trying to surf or plane in a stiff breeze. The bustle's prime benefits emerge when it is used on fin keel/skeg rudder cruisers with d/l ratios in the 250-to-300 range and moderate deadrise in the sections. Obviously, the presence or absence of a bustle should not be a major consideration in the selection of a cruising yacht.

DIAGONALS

Diagonals are predominantly fairing lines for the designer and builder. The shape of diagonals will vary widely depending on their angle and their location in the hull, and as a result they reveal few clues as to potential performance. Generally, diagonals should be smooth, fair lines without humps, bumps, or hollows.

It should be noted that, like buttocks, diagonals that are located vertically and close to the centerline will reflect all the humps and hollows of hard knuckled forefoots or prominent bustles. The shape of such diagonals can be disregarded since they do not affect the performance.

Some designers do not use diagonals at all when fairing the lines, but I believe this to be an error. I find that in the forward sections the run of the diagonals often causes me to change the waterlines and buttocks slightly if all is to turn out sweet and fair. Without this extra check on fairness, the builder could well have problems resulting in humps or hollows in this area. Knud Reimers often faired his hulls with only closely spaced diagonals, and while this worked well on the types of hull that he produced, it would not work on modern yachts with their hard stem knuckles and great change of line direction in the forward end of the hull.

SECTIONS

Beam is a major item to consider when looking at a lines drawing. The beamy hull has more interior space, of course, but there are many other factors to take into account, some of them detrimental to safety at sea if the beam is excessive.

As we have discussed, increased beam adds to stability and to resistance. On the sailing yacht, the added stability means that the boat will heel less in any given wind. This increases the driving power of the sails and also increases the efficiency of the keel as a lateral plane. The net result is that the boat will make better speed under most conditions despite the added resistance. If the beam is truly excessive, then the boat might be slowed to windward in a choppy sea or light air as the wide beam will also be increasing the wetted surface compared to her narrower sisters.

Since stability is a product of displacement times the righting arm, today's lighter displacement yachts require generous beam in order to develop the same sail carrying ability as their older, narrower, and heavier predecessors had. This added stability is not without its problems, though. The lighter yacht has form stability, and her big dinghy-type hull will fight to keep itself upright on the surface of the water at all times. This is fine until a big sea comes along and the surface of the water is suddenly tilted to a 30-degree angle. Immediately, the powerful, beamy hull will adapt itself to the new surface angle, slowed only by its ballast and the wind pressure on the sails. It will heel with the wave and then snap to another angle as the wave passes beneath it. Such a motion is anything but comfortable.

Unlike its fat, hard bilged sister, the narrower slack bilged yacht does not possess great form stability. Indeed, some of the more extreme examples would roll over on their sides at anchor if not held upright by the ballast. In a beam sea this type of hull has less tendency to conform to the angle of the water's surface; its angle of heel will remain more constant due to wind pressure, and its motion will be slower and more comfortable even though its average heel angle may be greater.

The narrower hull provides motion comfort in other ways as well. The acceleration of any floating body in an upward direction as a sea passes beneath it is determined by the weight of the body and its waterline area. The lighter the weight and the greater the area that the sea has to work on, the faster the motion. Thus, the older, narrower hull with its heavier displacement and smaller waterline area will ascend more slowly than modern, beamy, long-waterline yachts. This easier motion translates directly into comfort at sea and can reduce the tendency of tender tummies to refuse food. Of course, a yacht can be so heavy and have such a narrow beam and short waterline that it goes to ridiculous extremes; you could wind up with a boat akin to a half-tide rock, one that lifts so slowly that green seas wash over it in any kind of heavy going. The motion would be smooth but wet, and there is a happy medium.

One point of sail where the modern beamy hull has the advantage is when running downwind, particularly with a spinnaker, as its form stability dampens the roll. The narrow, slack bilged yachts often develop an oscillation under spinnaker that can be truly unnerving at times. On the other hand, when pressed hard in a stiff breeze the narrow hull tends to "roll in" as it heels, keeping the rudder in the water where it should be, so a serious spinnaker broach is rare. The beamy hull "rolls out" as it heels, lifting its windward side well out of the water and, as seen in many action photos of racing yachts, exposes the bottom down to the fin keel. In this position, the rudder can be lifted up into turbulent, aerated water where it loses its effectiveness. Then rudder control is lost, and the result is a spectacular and dangerous broach.

A final point to consider: Boats with light-displacement hulls and super-wide beam may be almost as stable upside down as they are right side up. If they are rolled over 180 degrees in extreme conditions of wind and sea, they may right themselves so slowly that the hull fills with water through the hatches, vents, and other openings. When the boat finally does right itself, if it does, it will be in a dangerously swamped condition. Many authorities feel that this was the major problem in the Fastnet Race a few years ago when 15 lives were lost.

Unfortunately, it is not possible to determine what constitutes "moderate" beam or to draw the line where "extreme" beam begins because so much depends on hull shape, displacement, draft, and other factors. Beam/LWL ratios of yachts have ranged widely through the years, and the ratios also vary with length, larger yachts having generally lower beam/LWL ratios due to the added stability conferred by size, as noted earlier. Too, a heavy-displacement boat will have less inverted stability than a light-displacement yacht of equal beam as the heavier boat, assuming similar draft, will be carrying more weight of structure and ballast in her upside-down keel and so will tend to right more quickly. In essence, light-displacement boats should not have excessive beam.

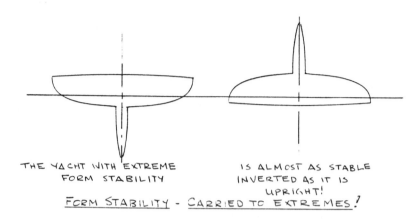

THE YACHT WITH EXTREME
FORM STABILITY

IS ALMOST AS STABLE
INVERTED AS IT IS
UPRIGHT!

FORM STABILITY - CARRIED TO EXTREMES!

THE BEAMY, HARD BILGED HULL REACTS MORE TO WAVE MOTION
THAN DOES ITS NARROWER, SLACK BILGED SISTER SHIP.

Though stability increases with beam, it must be pointed out that yachts with the same beam can vary widely in form stability. The vessel with her maximum beam at the deck, narrowing to the LWL, will have less form stability than her equally beamy sister if the latter carries her beam out at the waterline. Similarly, two yachts of equal waterline beam can have quite different form-stability characteristics. The U-shaped yacht with a relatively flat deadrise and hard bilges will have greater form stability than her wineglass-shaped sister with deep deadrise and slack bilges if both have the same beam at the LWL.

In effect, displacement added well below the LWL by means of a deep V or slack garboards detracts from form stability while displacement added up close to the LWL in the form of hard bilges or wide waterline beam increases stability. This is not to say that boats of either type are good or bad; both can make successful yachts if the other factors are properly designed.

Another point to consider in comparing section shape and stability is "reserve" stability. This is the increasing stability picked up as the hull heels down to a decks-awash condition. If the topsides show considerable tumblehome, the stability will

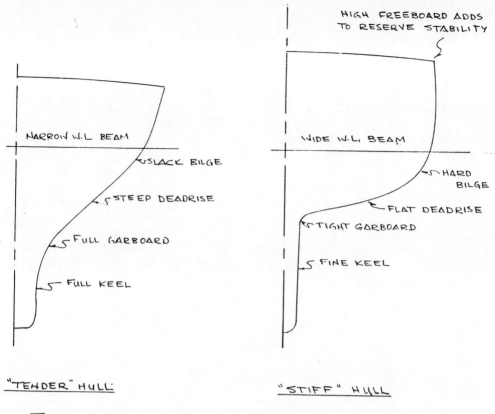

HIGH FREEBOARD ADDS
TO RESERVE STABILITY

NARROW W.L. BEAM

WIDE W.L. BEAM

SLACK BILGE

HARD BILGE

STEEP DEADRISE

FLAT DEADRISE

FULL GARBOARD

TIGHT GARBOARD

FULL KEEL

FINE KEEL

"TENDER" HULL

"STIFF" HULL

FACTORS AFFECTING FORM STABILITY

increase only until the point of maximum beam (say, halfway up the topsides) submerges. With greater heel angle, the form stability will not increase as fast or may even decrease as the area of tumblehome is immersed and the heeled WL beam becomes slightly narrower. On the other hand, a hull that increases her beam to the deck line will be continually putting more beam and more volume into the water as she heels farther and farther. Such a hull is said to have reserve stability; her form stability increases with each degree of heel until the decks begin to submerge. Of course, once the deck edge is underwater, the stability of any vessel will decline substantially.

As usual, there is another side to the story. Given equal beam, the boat with tumblehome will have less deck area and so less weight in the deck. This will lower her center of gravity and increase her righting arm length. She may have less form stability at extreme heel angles but more true stability at normal sailing angles. Another advantage of tumblehome is that by reducing volume high in the topsides the tendency for the boat to roll out as it heels is lessened, and this may lead to better steering at higher angles of heel. The cruising sailor should not be too concerned about tumblehome, or lack thereof, when considering a new yacht. Its effects one way or the other are not too significant unless it is carried to extreme.

3

□
□
□
□
□
□
□
□
□

Appendages

LATERAL PLANE

Sailing yacht underwater profiles have changed drastically since the 1920s and equally drastically since Bill Lapworth reintroduced the fin keel/spade rudder combination with his successful Cal 40 in the mid-1960s. The fin keel had been pioneered by Nathanael Herreshoff, the Wizard of Bristol, and became popular in large racing yachts around the turn of the century. However, the boats were carried to extremes, received a bad reputation, and fell out of favor.

By the twenties, the accepted shape for an ocean-going yacht, whether a racing or a cruising yacht, was the long, deep keel developed from sailing fishing boats. The faithful hailed it then and many still do for its good directional stability, ease of steering, and ability to heave-to. Its faults were slowness in tacking, excess wetted surface, and a relatively inefficient lateral plane to resist leeway considering the area involved.

After Olin Stephens's *Dorade* paved the way in the late twenties by showing that the full keel and deep forefoot were not necessary for seaworthiness, the keel was progressively shortened. The cutaway forefoot increased handiness and reduced wetted area at the same time and with variations this was the standard fast keel boat profile until the Cal 40 era. The "moderate" keel is perhaps a good name for the type. Directional stability is quite adequate as long as the rudder is not located too far

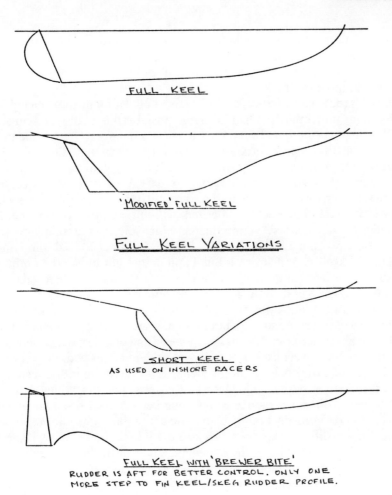

FULL KEEL

'MODIFIED' FULL KEEL

FULL KEEL VARIATIONS

SHORT KEEL
AS USED ON INSHORE RACERS

FULL KEEL WITH 'BREWER BITE'
RUDDER IS AFT FOR BETTER CONTROL. ONLY ONE
MORE STEP TO FIN KEEL/SKEG RUDDER PROFILE.

forward or the keel shortened to extremes as was done on a few ocean racers and many of the 5.5 meters in an attempt to reduce wetted surface to a minimum.

A variation on the "moderate" keel is shown. The rudderpost is more vertical than usual and separated from the keel proper by a cutout. Directional stability is improved slightly while the cutout gives some of the advantages of the fin: a higher aspect ratio and a pivot point for quicker turning when required. I have used this shape on a number of yachts since the early 1970s with good success and still use it when a client asks for a "full keel" cruiser. Even this idea is not new; L. Francis Herreshoff was using a cutout aft in the mid-1930s on his *Tioga* and *Bounty* designs. With modern full keel yachts having their rudderposts so far aft and relatively vertical, this cutout keel is simply common sense. Otherwise, wetted surface would be excessive and the handling very slow.

Inshore daysailers and cruisers as opposed to the heavy offshore racing yachts of the earlier years were always more adventurous in reducing lateral plane. The fin keel

Star has been a popular class since before World War I, and the international class boats, the Square Meter yachts, and one-designs such as the Dragon class had keels that were very much cut away both forward and aft, although with few exceptions the rudder was still hung on the keel.

In the 1950s the keel-centerboard type became popular for offshore racing due to a favorable rating under the CCA handicap rule as well as the successful racing career of the Olin Stephens-designed *Finisterre*. Keel-centerboarders were built in sizes ranging from Bill Shaw's perky little 24-foot *Trina* yawl right up to the largest ocean racers but were forced out of racing when the IOR rule took over as they no longer had the benefit of the favorable handicap of the old CCA rule and could not compete with the new, lighter, fin keeled designs. The type still has definite advantages where a stable, beamy shoal-draft yacht is desired without sacrifice of weatherliness. (Incidentally, do not confuse weatherliness, which means the ability to sail to weather, with seaworthiness. The two can be worlds apart.) Indeed, the Hinckley Block Island 40 keel-centerboarder, a Bill Tripp design not unlike the *Finisterre* in many respects, has been in production for close to 20 years, and these yachts have made many long voyages including several circumnavigations.

Then in the mid-1960s came the Cal 40. Keel yachts and keel-centerboarders continued to race with some success, but by 1970 it was almost 100-percent fin keel yachts in the new cruiser-racer designs. Many weird and wonderful fins were tried— fins with tremendous sweepback, fins faired into the hull, fins with bulbs on them, fins that looked like they belonged on a shark, and everything in between.

Today the ocean racer (it's no longer a cruiser-racer, just a racer) will have some form of the "Peterson" fin as pioneered by Doug Peterson in 1973: a fairly vertical, high aspect ratio fin hung on a canoe body. The cruiser has more choice; we see fin keel hulls of many different kinds as well as the full keel, moderate keel, and keel-centerboarder all in production at the same time. The cruising boat buyer who is not interested in competing in club races probably has a greater selection of underbody shapes to choose from today than ever before.

FIN KEELS

The properly designed fin in conjunction with a skeg hung rudder can provide excellent directional stability, ease of maneuverability, reduced wetted surface, and improved windward performance. These are the reasons we see fin keels on cruising boats; they are not simply a fad. There are good fins and bad fins, of course, so let's consider the factors.

The cruising yachtsman does have to consider ease of haul-out; a very narrow, deep fin can create problems. Boats with such fins are difficult to haul on marine railways so a crane or travel lift is the safest method, but they're not always available. There is also the danger of damage to the shaft or strut when slings are improperly positioned. Still the major problem is that of structural strength because the deep racing-type fin imposes severe strains at the point of attachment to the hull. It is a very weak link in case of an accidental grounding, and I know of at least one case where men have died as a result of a deep fin tearing off when a boat took the bottom.

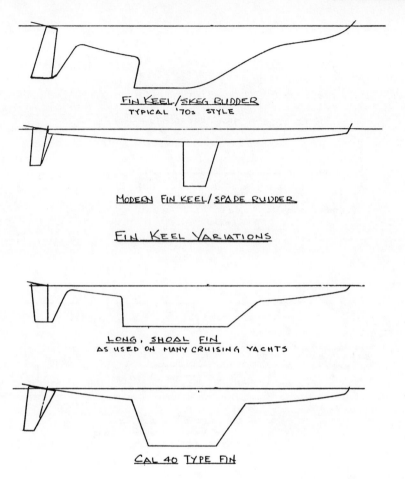

FIN KEEL/SKEG RUDDER
TYPICAL '70s STYLE

MODERN FIN KEEL/SPADE RUDDER

FIN KEEL VARIATIONS

LONG, SHOAL FIN
AS USED ON MANY CRUISING YACHTS

CAL 40 TYPE FIN

For reasons of ease of haul-out and structural strength, then, the cruising boat fin should be longer and shallower, of lower aspect ratio, than the racing boat fin. This works out well in practice as the cruising hull, being of heavier displacement, is deeper, and at the same time its draft is often less than that of its racing sister. There simply is less height available between the bottom of the hull and the point of maximum draft so a longer, low aspect ratio is the only feasible solution. Conversely, the racing owner wants as high an aspect ratio fin as the rule draft will allow. It is more efficient so that the area can be reduced and wetted surface eliminated. The cruising yacht's low aspect ratio fin is not as effective and needs more area to do its job of resisting leeway. In *Aero-Hydrodynamics of Sailing*, Marchaj states that four percent of the sail area is a good guide for fin area. For the cruising yacht it is best to err on the high side as a small increase in resistance is much to be preferred over excess leeway, particularly if the boat is clawing off a lee shore in a gale.

For those not technically inclined, the "aspect ratio" is the ratio of the span squared to the area; i.e., a fin of 20 square feet in area by 4 feet in depth would have an aspect ratio of 4^2 divided by 20, or .8. Without knowing the area, one can determine

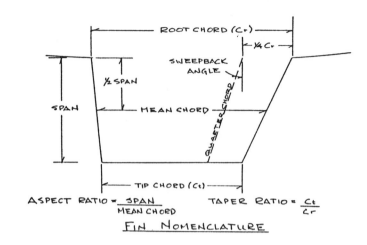

ASPECT RATIO = $\frac{SPAN}{MEAN\ CHORD}$ TAPER RATIO = $\frac{Ct}{Cr}$

FIN NOMENCLATURE

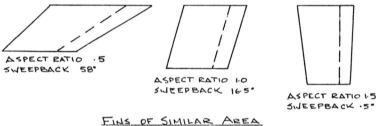

ASPECT RATIO ·5
SWEEPBACK 58°

ASPECT RATIO 1·0
SWEEPBACK 16·5°

ASPECT RATIO 1·5
SWEEPBACK ·5°

FINS OF SIMILAR AREA
SHOWING DIFFERENT ASPECT RATIOS AND
CORRECT SWEEPBACK

the aspect ratio by dividing the depth by the mean chord, the mean chord being the length of the fin at a depth halfway between the root chord (where the fin meets the hull) and the tip chord (at maximum draft). If our 20-square-foot fin had a mean chord of 5 feet, the aspect ratio would be 4/5, or .8.

One of the reasons that the high aspect ratio fin is more efficient is that it has less resistance. A large part of the resistance of a fin keel comes from the vortices created by the pressure differential between the windward and leeward side of the fin. As the water flows from the leeward to the windward side across the bottom of the fin, it creates vortices, like miniature whirlpools. It is apparent that the high aspect ratio fin with its shorter tip will create lesser, or weaker, tip vortices and so drag will be reduced. Tests have shown that rounding the toe of the fin reduces drag as well and this may well be the result of weaker vortices.

For a few years it was common to see "racy" looking fins with great sweepback angle, resembling the tailfins on a 1960 Cadillac. These looked fast when the boat was sitting in slings but were not as efficient as they would have been if the fin was more vertical in the Peterson fashion. The correct sweepback angle of the fin is related to its aspect ratio; the lower the aspect ratio, the greater the sweepback required for efficiency. Most cruising boat fins are of low aspect ratio and should have greater sweepback than the extreme racing fins. Correct sweepback angles have been established by tank testing, and the following data show the relation.

ASPECT RATIO	SWEEPBACK ANGLE
.5	58 degrees
.6	47
.7	37
.8	29
.9	22
1.0	16.5
1.1	11.5
1.2	7
1.3	4.5
1.4	2
1.5	.5

Unfortunately, considerations of sweepback angle are often secondary to locating the ballast at the right spot to trim the boat and to fixing the center of lateral resistance to balance the sailplan. Still it gives the designer an aiming point.

The second consideration in the fin profile is the taper ratio (the tip chord length divided by the root chord length). Tests on one series of fins with a 20.5-degree sweepback showed that the fin with a taper ratio of .32 was over 1 percent more efficient and had .003 percent less drag than an untapered fin. The differences are slight but cannot be ignored. Marchaj also relates taper to sweepback angle, showing that for minimum resistance the fin should have a smaller taper ratio as the sweepback angle increases.

Again, the cruising yachtsman must consider haul-out and grounding situations so the very low taper ratio fins, efficient as they may be, are not the best solution for a cruiser. The tip chord should be long enough that the yacht can be handled on a railway with no major problems and take the odd grounding without major damage. Also, on a moderate draft yacht the extremely tapered fin does not allow the designer to get the ballast as low as desirable, and stability can suffer as a result. This is a more important consideration to the cruiser than to the racing yacht, strange as it may seem, as the latter is working with deeper draft and a much higher ballast ratio to begin with and so can afford to locate the center of gravity of the ballast slightly higher in the fin.

Another consideration in the profile of the fin is whether the tip chord should parallel the waterline or have its deepest point at the trailing edge as was popular a few years ago. From the viewpoint of ease of haul-out and blocking the boat on a railway, the parallel tip chord makes sense. Fortunately, it is also superior in performance to the raked tip chord. Tests have shown that the effective depth of the fin is, essentially, that of the leading edge. Having the trailing edge deeper has no

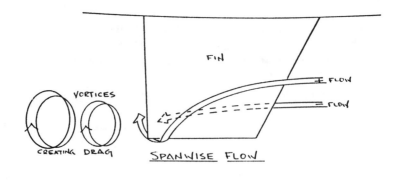

FIN

VORTICES

FLOW

FLOW

CREATING DRAG

SPANWISE FLOW

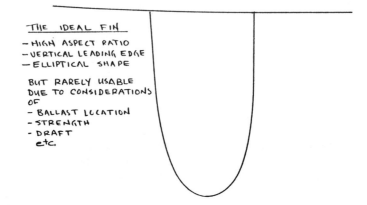

THE IDEAL FIN

— HIGH ASPECT RATIO
— VERTICAL LEADING EDGE
— ELLIPTICAL SHAPE

BUT RARELY USABLE
DUE TO CONSIDERATIONS
OF
— BALLAST LOCATION
— STRENGTH
— DRAFT
etc.

practical effect on aspect ratio and the keel develops less lift and more drag than its parallel bottom mate.

In sum, the fin keel on a cruising yacht should have its bottom parallel to the waterline, be of moderate length for ease of haul-out, and have a moderate tip chord ratio to obtain sufficient area to resist leeway. The racing fin can go to all the extremes of aspect ratio that the rule draft will allow but, of course, both the cruising and racing fin should have a sweepback angle as close as possible to that determined best for its aspect ratio. There is simply no excuse for a designer or builder to turn out a poor fin with what we know today.

FIN WATERLINES

The reader has undoubtedly read of various yachts claims that the keel waterlines are developed from a NACA shape. It sounds scientific and expensive, but the shapes along with the offsets needed to reproduce them are readily available in a paperback book, *Theory of Wing Sections*, by Abbott and Von Doenhoff. NACA, the National Advisory Committee for Aeronautics (now NASA), tested a variety of streamlined shapes for lift and resistance at various speeds.

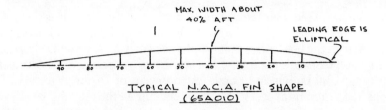

MAX. WIDTH ABOUT
40% AFT

LEADING EDGE IS
ELLIPTICAL

TYPICAL N.A.C.A. FIN SHAPE
(65A010)

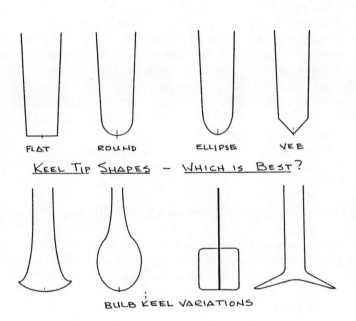

FLAT   ROUND   ELLIPSE   VEE

KEEL TIP SHAPES — WHICH IS BEST?

BULB KEEL VARIATIONS

   Generally, the shape selected will be similar to NACA 65A010. The nose will be elliptical as a sharp leading edge would promote stalling and loss of lift while a blunt leading edge would increase drag. The point of maximum width will be about 40 percent of the length aft, and the shape will be streamlined to a fairly, but not razor, sharp trailing edge. Normally, the favored shapes range in thickness from 8 percent to 12 percent of the chord length (although some experts feel that thicker sections, up to 15 percent, are advantageous). It is not necessary that the maximum thickness be at the same relative point down the whole span of the fin, and it may move forward as it approaches the tip chord. The thickness ratio may also increase gradually toward the tip chord. Indeed, there are advantages in having the thickness ratio increase from the root to the tip chord, not the least of which is the greater concentration of ballast down low as the tip thickens. This is not to say that the tip is bulbed (more about bulbs later), but rather that a fin that is 8 feet long at its root chord and 5 feet long at its tip chord may have a thickness of 10 percent at the root (.8 foot) and 15 percent at the tip (.75 foot). It is still slightly thinner at the tip than at the hull, but the thickness ratio has increased.

It is not unusual to see keels fatter than 10 percent of their length as the designer may have to go to a greater width in order to fit the desired amount of ballast in the correct place to trim the boat. Also, shoal-draft boats may have wider keels to get the ballast as low as possible for stability, but the extra width will add to resistance. Twenty years ago, Bill Luders and I tank-tested dozens of 5.5-meter models. These racing sloops had a minimum keel width of 4 inches under the rule, and whenever we tried to widen it to get the ballast lower we wound up with more resistance and a slower boat.

For a similar reason, bulb keels never proved out in tank tests, although we tried several different shapes. Placing the ballast deep in the bulb improved stability but not sufficiently to overcome the increased drag under average sailing conditions. In the late 1970s, we tested the model of the Morgan 38 at Stevens Institute, first with a normal NACA fin and then with a patented bulb fin. There was no question which was superior so the boat went into production with the conventional fin shape.

The shape of the tip of the fin in section may be flat, rounded, elliptical, or vee'd. Tests have shown the flat, squared-off tip to develop more lift to windward and the rounded (and presumably the elliptical) tip to have less drag on a run. The differences are very slight, amounting to one-fiftieth of a knot or less, and are not significant to the cruising sailor.

CENTERBOARDS, BILGEBOARDS, AND LEEBOARDS

One answer to obtaining performance with shoal draft, as pointed out earlier, is the centerboard, and boards are fitted to every class of craft from dinghies to ocean-going cruisers. Like fin keels, boards come in all types: long shoal boards (typical of that fitted to sharpies); deep, narrow boards; slab-sided boards; streamlined boards; etc. The drop keel seen on many trailer sailboats is simply a shaped centerboard, either ballasted or made of solid metal, and is usually a deep, narrow, high aspect ratio type for better weatherliness.

The efficiency of a centerboard, like the fin keel, depends upon its aspect ratio and its shape. Streamline-shaped, high aspect ratio boards provide the most lift for their area and are the choice where maximum performance is required. Slab-sided boards are simpler and less costly but not as efficient for their area, although probably the great majority of centerboards are of this type. Long, shallow boards also lose efficiency due to their low aspect ratio, but again, there are good reasons to use them. They create less strain on the centerboard trunk and can usually be operated with much simpler mechanisms than can the high aspect ratio boards.

The centerboard boat has always posed maintenance problems. It is difficult to paint the board as the boat has to be raised in slings, and even then you cannot get at the part of the board inside the trunk where all the barnacles grow. The inside of the trunk itself is even harder to paint. On wood boats it's a fine place for worm damage and can wind up being a continual weeping point for minor leaks and eventually a site for major repairs.

The centerboard has its drawbacks, but these can be partly overcome with intelligent design. Look for a positive stop so the board cannot swing wildly if the pennant breaks at sea, along with generally sturdy construction of the board, the pin,

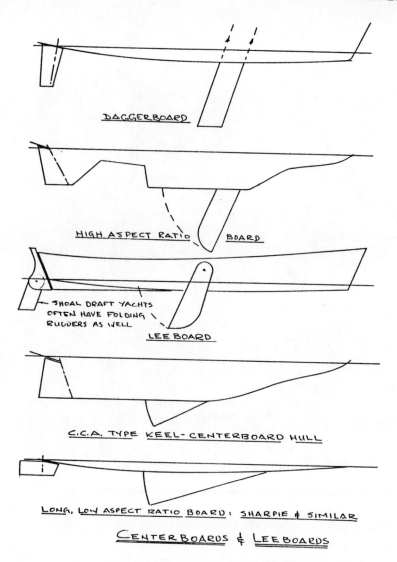

DAGGERBOARD

HIGH ASPECT RATIO BOARD

SHOAL DRAFT YACHTS
OFTEN HAVE FOLDING
RUDDERS AS WELL

LEE BOARD

C.C.A. TYPE KEEL-CENTERBOARD HULL

LONG, LOW ASPECT RATIO BOARD: SHARPIE & SIMILAR

CENTERBOARDS & LEEBOARDS

the trunk, and indeed, every part of the assembly. A pennant that can be easily replaced is desirable, and there are advantages to having a board that can be removed without having to lift the boat (or dig a deep hole). It is difficult to get all of these features in any one design, but the more the merrier.

A simple way to eliminate the headaches, though, is to use leeboards. These have never been popular in North America but have long been used in Holland and other shoal-water areas of the world. L. Francis Herreshoff's *Meadowlark* is one of the few U.S. leeboard designs to achieve any popularity, and Phil Bolger is the only contemporary designer who is using leeboards to any great extent, but the device certainly warrants attention as it has many advantages.

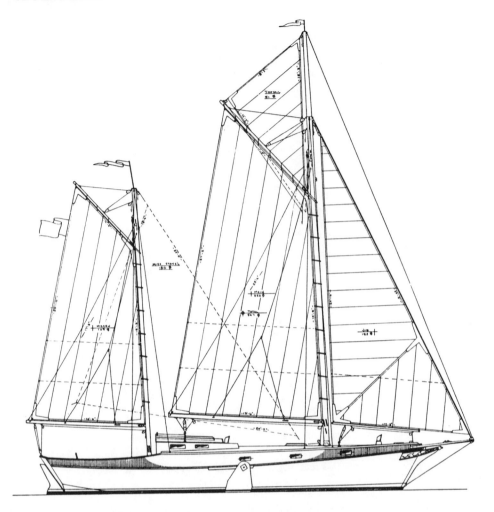

Centennial, *a gaff rigged leeboard ketch.*

The initial cost is low compared to a centerboard and its trunk; there is nothing to leak, jam, or create added drag; the boards can be painted easily and the pennant can be inspected and replaced conveniently. Performance does not suffer greatly either since the boat does not really care if the board is on the centerline or on the side, and unlike the centerboard, the leeboard can be installed at an angle so that it works vertically and more effectively when the boat is heeled under sail. Indeed, if the board is angled out 15 to 20 degrees from the vertical, it will increase its draft as the boat heels, unlike the centerboard, which reduces its draft and effectiveness with increasing heel angle. Leeboards are also made assymetrical (a flat side outboard and a streamline shape on the inboard side), adding to the lift developed. Then they can be toed in a few degrees to the centerline to increase the angle of attack, which also improves efficiency.

So why is my little yawl a centerboarder? Aesthetics! The main drawback of the leeboard is that it breaks up the clean lines of the yacht, and unlike the Dutch, we in America have not had 300 years of getting accustomed to seeing them. The boards need to be shifted whenever the boat tacks, but the average yachtsman who thinks nothing of tacking a 130-to-150-percent genoa should see no reason to complain about that.

Bilgeboards are simply leeboards stuck in two centerboard trunks each side of the centerline. They have all the disadvantages of the centerboard as regards maintenance—double that since there are two of them—but they are not so likely to be jammed in place by mud or rocks if the boat grounds out. Like the leeboard, they are assymetrically shaped and angled to be more or less vertical when the boat is under sail. Still they double the initial cost and the maintenance so their advantages are not sufficient that they have ever become popular.

TWIN KEELS

Twin keels, or bilge keels, have not caught on on this side of the pond either. Despite the fact that they can be assymetrically shaped, angled to be vertical under sail, and toed in, they do not show as well as a normal fin in average sailing conditions as the wetted surface is increased substantially and the bilge keels are usually of very low aspect ratio. Also, bilge keels are fitted with an eye to shallow draft so the ballast center of gravity is raised and stability suffers.

The advantages of being able to ground the boat out on a tide and clean the bottom without haul-out fees should be considered, particularly by the cruising man who pokes his nose into remote areas. Another advantage rarely mentioned is that if the bilge keelboat grounds while under sail, she will reduce her draft once the sail pressure is removed and may be able to kedge or motor off easily once she is upright. Of course if she grounds upright, while running free or under power, you cannot easily heel her to reduce draft and get her off again.

A bilge keelboat with a pair of moderately high aspect ratio fins might be a pleasant surprise as to performance and have some solid advantages for the serious cruising sailor. To my knowledge, no one has ever produced such a boat.

RUDDERS

There are three basic types of rudders: keel hung, skeg hung, and spade. Needless to say, whichever type is fitted, it must be strong in itself, strongly mounted, and for the cruising sailor somewhat protected against grounding damage.

SPADE RUDDERS

Spade rudders are common on small cruising yachts, daysailers, and dinghies, and are *de rigeur* on racing yachts of all sizes. The reason for this is their efficiency, of course.

The spade rudder gives the best combination of minimum resistance and maximum lift, or turning moment, for its area. The spade has its drawbacks, too. It does not have the directional stability of a skeg or keel hung rudder so it requires constant attention at the helm. It is relatively easily damaged and is particularly vulnerable in a serious grounding. And obviously, it is an effective snag that seems to attract every pot warp, mooring line, and kelp frond in the area.

Like the fin keel, the efficiency of the spade rudder increases with aspect ratio. Tests have shown that at a rudder angle of five degrees, increasing the aspect ratio from one to four will almost double the lift for a given area while at the same time reducing the resistance. However, as the aspect ratio increases, the angle at which the rudder will stall, or lose lift, decreases. A rudder with an aspect ratio of two was shown in tests to stall out at about 20 degrees while another with an aspect ratio of eight stalled at 13 degrees. Rudders with aspect ratios of four to five, which tend to stall out at about 15-to-16-degree helm angle, seem to provide the best combination of efficiency and control.

The profile shape of the good spade rudder should show a chord width at the bottom about 33 percent of that at the hull as this gives the least drag. The tip chord, again like the fin keel, should be parallel to the waterline as this appears to increase efficiency also. Early spade rudders often showed great sweepback as did the early fin keels, but these are not as efficient, despite their speedy appearance, as a spade with its quarter chord set at an almost vertical five-degree sweepback. Tests showed increased drag as the sweepback was increased either aft or forward.

The rudder section will also resemble the fin keel, being a NACA section with elliptical leading edge, streamlined shape, and fairly sharp trailing edge. Thicknesses of about nine to 10 percent of the chord length seem to work best. Thinner shapes develop less resistance at zero degrees helm angle but a higher resistance when the normal weather helm of four degrees or so is cranked in. Moreover, the thinner shape lowers the stall angle, and this is also undesirable.

One important point with regard to efficiency is that the gap between the rudder and the hull should be very slight, about the thickness of a well-worn dime. Even a gap of half an inch will reduce efficiency close to 10 percent and increase drag about four percent due to crossflow over the top of the rudder. This is particularly important to the racing sailor, of course.

Since with a deeply vee'd hull the gap between the top of the rudder and the hull will open up as the blade is turned, many designers use a "princess fairing," moving the rudder top below the surface and fitting a fixed fairing above it. This reduces the chance of ventilation (sucking air down the low-pressure side), moves the rudder out of the turbulent water near the hull, and reduces drag at smaller rudder angles by preventing crossflow over the top of the blade.

Much tank testing has been done on spade rudders due to their use on racing yachts, and much more will be done. In 1995 the rudders of today may look as strange to us as some of the 1970 spade rudders do now.

SKEG HUNG RUDDERS

The benefits of using a skeg ahead of a rudder are numerous. The skeg raises the stall

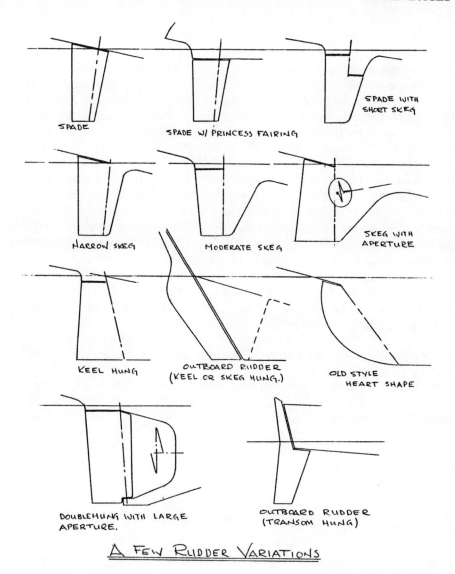

SPADE

SPADE W/ PRINCESS FAIRING

SPADE WITH SHORT SKEG

NARROW SKEG

MODERATE SKEG

SKEG WITH APERTURE

KEEL HUNG

OUTBOARD RUDDER (KEEL OR SKEG HUNG.)

OLD STYLE HEART SHAPE

DOUBLEHUNG WITH LARGE APERTURE.

OUTBOARD RUDDER (TRANSOM HUNG)

A FEW RUDDER VARIATIONS

angle at which the rudder will lose its lift; it provides a greater control surface area, thereby adding to directional stability; it offers better control than a spade rudder when there is a high flow angle of attack, i.e., in case of a serious broach. The skeg does add to resistance so it has gone out of fashion on racing yachts, but it makes great sense for a fin keeled cruising yacht.

Skeg hung rudders come in all shapes and sizes, and much depends on the type of yacht. Indeed, you will even see skegs on outboard rudders on some designs; I used this form on the Aloha 28 a decade or more ago. Skegs may be narrow and deep or shoal and wide, but in either case that area of the skeg ahead of the rudder, amounting to about 10 percent of the rudder's width, is actually contributing to steering and may be considered as effective "rudder" area. The skeg forward of that point may add to directional stability but is not helping to steer the yacht.

For this reason the skegs used on racing yachts were quite narrow (as previously noted, few modern racers use skeg rudders) while cruising yachts generally use a wider skeg for its benefits of easier helm and directional ability as well as extra strength. In this regard, I must add that a fin keel yacht with a skeg hung rudder of adequate size can have all the directional stability of a full keel cruiser and yet be more quickly tacked or maneuvered when the necessity arises.

Like the spade rudder, the skeg hung rudder should be squared off in profile at the bottom, have the top of the rudder close to the hull (or be fitted with a princess fairing), and be of a streamlined NACA shape. One point on shapes is that the low-drag NACA shapes, with their maximum thickness at 50 percent of the chord length aft, are not as suitable for rudders as the higher lift, higher drag shapes with the maximum thickness 30 to 35 percent aft. The low-drag foil is not as efficient and will have higher resistance at the normal rudder angles.

Skeg hung rudders are not as vulnerable as spade rudders since the skeg adds to strength and also permits a second bearing to be fitted. I prefer to see this lower bearing part way up the skeg as it reduces the chance of it being damaged in a grounding. And the rudder may still be operable even with part of the skeg and blade chewed away. The low aspect ratio skeg rudders normally seen on cruising yachts have a reasonably swept-back leading edge so they are not as prone as a spade rudder to picking up lines and debris.

On several yachts, the Morgan 38 being one of them, I designed the skeg large enough to take a propeller aperture. There is no doubt that this adds extra drag and reduces lift, but I feel it makes sense in the added protection it gives to the shaft and propeller. The problems of lifting the boat with slings are minimal as the skeg eliminates the chance of damage to the shaft or strut. It is simply another in the many compromises that designers make between the sturdiness of the full keel cruiser and the efficiency of the out-and-out racer.

KEEL HUNG RUDDERS

The keel hung rudder can be one of two types: with an inboard rudder stock emerging through the hull, or with an outboard rudder mounted on the transom or on the stern of a canoe hull. The inboard type is slightly more efficient if put over hard when the boat is at a great heel angle as it is less likely to ventilate and lose lift, or turning ability. Still the difference is slight, and many outboard rudder boats have made long and successful voyages. The Laurent Giles Venture class and the Scandinavian Folkboat are two well-known examples, and many of Tom Gillmer's delightful little double-enders have sported outboard rudders.

The profile of the rudder should be squared off at the bottom as this shape is more efficient than the old-style rounded or heart-shaped blades. Like the other rudders, the gap between the hull and the top of an inboard rudder should be as small as possible, and again, a princess fairing can be fitted. The shape will carry out the streamlines of the hull and keel, of course, and the rudder should be faired down the leading edge to reduce the gap between the rudder and the keel to a minimum to prevent turbulence.

Protection against grounding is achieved easily if the bottom of the rudder and its vital heel bearing are raised well above the keel's maximum draft. Then if the boat does go aground there is less chance of damage to critical parts. Where possible, the fitting of an intermediate bearing is desirable as it will strengthen the assembly and perhaps permit partial operation of the rudder even if the heel bearing is damaged.

In considering damage to such an essential piece of the yacht as the rudder, it might be well to point out that the outboard rudder has the advantage that it is the most easily inspected and repaired of all the various types. For this reason it has always been a favorite of the serious cruising skipper.

4

AESTHETICS OF YACHT DESIGN

THE BEAUTY AND THE BEAST

The well-known English yachting writer Douglas Phillips-Birt once said, in effect, you can go away for a weekend cruise and have everything go wrong. The decks leak, your blankets are wet, the weather is miserable, the engine won't start, and you run out of whiskey. But then you drop the boat at her mooring and row ashore, and if she is beautiful all is forgiven. I can agree with that.

Certainly, there are different forms of beauty. The stark, purposeful racing machine; the graceful yacht with sweeping sheer and long overhangs; the traditional boat with its reminder of the working days of sail—all have their place, if the design is balanced and true.

Beauty is in the eye of the beholder, of course, and I have seen some ghastly little pots (I'm not too proud of some I've done myself) that are, obviously, objects of beauty to their owners, if not for their appearance then for their function. In that regard, we must remember that the World War II jeep was chosen as one of the most beautiful vehicles in the world by the Museum of Modern Art. It certainly was a functional machine.

For myself, I am not at all fond of the sleek "European look" that attempts to make sailing yachts resemble rocket ships, but that is my own opinion. On the other hand, I do not care for the overdone character boat either. There is nothing wrong

The Cape Carib 33, designed in the early 1970s, has a timeless style.

with clipper bows and sweeping sheerlines if they are well done; indeed, then they are beautiful. It is when such features are overdone or badly done, turning a traditional yacht into a "cartoon" yacht (as Bob Perry terms them) that they turn me off. I like a yacht to look like a yacht.

PROPORTIONS

The old standards for yachts in the late 1930s up to the mid-1960s were given to me by Bill Luders as follows:

65 □

Bow overhang to stern overhang	3:4
Bow angle to stern angle	4:3
LWL to LOA	2:3
Bow freeboard to stern freeboard	8-9:6

Freeboard to be the same height at the transom as at amidships and the low point of the freeboard to be 80 to 85 percent of the LWL abaft the bow.

These proportions produced the graceful yacht hulls of yesteryear with their long ends and sweet sheerlines. One of my favorite Luders designs was the 54-foot sloop *Julie*. She seemed to epitomize the long, low, and handsome cruiser-racer that was popular in those bygone days. However, times have changed, and modern yachts are short-ended in order to obtain as long a waterline as possible for ultimate speed and to spread the displacement out to reduce the displacement/length ratio.

SHEERLINES

Certainly, the feature of the yacht that first catches our eye is the sheerline. The conventional concave sheer has the advantage of distributing the buoyancy to the ends where it is needed in heavy seas, but more important, it looks "right." A good concave sheer should be fairly flat forward with its curvature gradually increasing to the low point and then rising to the stern. Perhaps the most common fault is placing maximum curvature forward of amidships as this makes the flatter sheer aft look weak and timid. One designer has advocated using the arc of a circle as a sheerline (perhaps because it is easily described to a computer and computer fairing is all the rage these days), but such a sheer would have too much curvature forward to look good. In any case, the circle is a monotonous and unimaginative line best restricted to life rings and portlights.

The amount of sheer will vary with the type of yacht; racing craft habitually employed less sheer than cruising yachts, and this trend is still with us. Today we see many out-and-out cruisers with very flat sheerlines, emulating the racing yacht, perhaps, in the hope that this will give buyers the idea that the boat is particularly fast. One sheer to be avoided is the true straight-line sheer. It may look reasonable on paper but rarely shows well in fact. The ends of the yacht are farther away from our eye than the midship point so that optical illusion will make the ends appear to droop. If a sheer is to look "straight," it should have a very slight amount of curve. The ancient Greeks knew that when they built the Parthenon, but the principle seems to get rediscovered from time to time.

Also for reasons of optical illusion, the lines of the guards, cove stripe, paint lines, and toe rails should not be parallel to the sheer or they will look closer together at the ends than at midships. A toe rail should be highest forward and reduce in height gradually to the stern; a cove strip or paint line should be farthest below the sheer at the stem, rising gradually to a slightly lesser distance below at the stern. If the lines are truly parallel, they may not appear parallel on the boat, and the result will not be as intended by the designer.

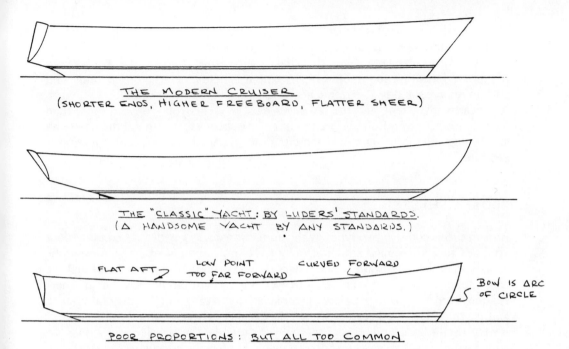

THE MODERN CRUISER
(SHORTER ENDS, HIGHER FREEBOARD, FLATTER SHEER)

THE "CLASSIC" YACHT: BY LUDERS' STANDARDS.
(A HANDSOME YACHT BY ANY STANDARDS.)

FLAT AFT →   LOW POINT   CURVED FORWARD
       TOO FAR FORWARD   ↳   BOW IS ARC
                                    OF CIRCLE

POOR PROPORTIONS: BUT ALL TOO COMMON

CONVENTIONAL SHEERS

Freeboard is an important part of beauty, too, Earlier we pointed out that good freeboard adds to reserve stability, prevents the deck from being immersed at too low a heel angle, and in turn eliminates the added resistance that occurs when the deck edge and its associated fittings (life rails, cleats, genoa track, etc.) are dragged through the water at speed. This must be qualified by stating that the amount of freeboard acceptable for any given design depends to a large degree upon the type of boat; a flat sheered, IOR-type racer can have generous freeboard and still look good. The same applies to a flush decked yacht as we expect higher freeboard in order to obtain the necessary headroom in a flush decker. The same high freeboard would look out of place on a character boat with generous sheer, particularly if the design was trying to emulate a type, such as the sharpie or a Boston pilot boat of the Gay Nineties, where low freeboard was both functional and traditional. The boats that truly upset me are the small 20-to-25-footers that try to retain "character" through the use of sweeping sheerlines, even clipper bows, and yet obtain standing headroom by high freeboard and even higher (in proportion) cabinhouses.

Thirty years ago, it was considered impossible to obtain standing headroom or four berths in a boat smaller than 30 feet. We know that it can be done today, and the boat can turn out handsome if serious consideration is given to proportions. Still there is a lower limit, and my feeling is that this limit is about 25 feet. Below that, the designer and owner should accept generous sitting headroom in order not to burden our already overcrowded waters with atrocities faintly disguised as sailboats.

Where the freeboard is high it should be disguised by use of cove stripe, paint line, or rubrail running the length of the yacht in order to reduce the apparent height.

The reverse sheer is a shape that makes sense since it moves the windage aft, places the maximum room amidships where it benefits the accommodations, and adds to reserve stability at extreme heel angles. Still it has never caught on in North America to any extent, and the few reverse sheer yachts you see were, more than likely, imported from Europe. Owners of reverse sheer yachts can sail them with an air of smug superiority over their more traditional neighbors, as regards function at any rate.

BROKEN SHEERS

Broken sheers come in two types: with a raised foredeck or with a raised poop deck aft. The Crocker-designed Stonehorse sloop is to my mind one of the prettiest of the raised foredeck boats. Some of the others are just plain ugly, but I will add that the raised foredeck boat is not an easy one to design. There should be a "main" sheer running from stem to stern below the broken sheer to carry out the line of the yacht, and as a rule this main sheer looks best if the distance between it and the broken sheer is widest at the break and reduces gradually to the ends. The raised foredeck does put added windage where it is most objectionable but has the advantage of extra room below and a cleaner working area on deck. These can be important to both comfort and security on a small yacht.

The raised poopdeck is usually seen on larger craft with great cabins or full-width owner's cabins aft. This type of yacht is, typically, a character boat with clipper bow and pronounced sheer. The stern overhang should be small as long, overhanging counters look out of place with a high poop. Nor does the high poop combine well with a spoon bow forward. A clipper bow is almost a necessity if the boat is to appear harmonious.

Less often seen today is the low poop as used on the Gloucester fishing schooners. Often on yachts in particular this is really just a break in the rail height; the deck line itself is unbroken. This low poop or rail, often just a few inches in height, can be used with longer stern overhangs and look good indeed when combined with the fisherman's heart-shaped transom as on some of L. Francis Herreshoff's master-pieces.

Again, with the raised poop, the main sheerline must be carried out from stem to stern by the use of rubrail, paint line, or other contrivance if the boat is not to look ungainly and boxy aft.

DECK STRUCTURES

The shape of the deckhouses can make or break a yacht, and many a sweet hull has been spoiled by a cabinhouse that is not in harmony with the lines of the hull. Generally, the line of the cabin side at the roof edge should resemble the sheer but be flatter. The line should not parallel the sheer as then it will rise too much forward and

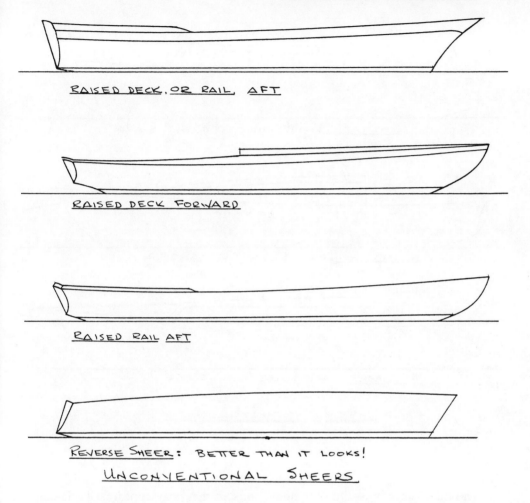

RAISED DECK, OR RAIL, AFT

RAISED DECK FORWARD

RAISED RAIL AFT

REVERSE SHEER: BETTER THAN IT LOOKS!

UNCONVENTIONAL SHEERS

make the house appear boxy. As a rule, a nice effect is achieved if the lines of the cabin are aimed in the general direction of the stemhead, neither pointing up in the air above the stem nor drooping to die weakly in the rise of the sheer forward.

Some boats with normal concave sheers will have a reverse, or convex, sheer in their cabin sides. Occasionally, this seems to come off alright, but the style is really more at home on the modern, flat sheered cruiser-racer vessel. I have to believe that boats with conventional springy sheers look best with a concave line to their cabin roof edge as it compliments the sheer and does not force the eye to travel in two directions at the same time. As to convex cockpit coamings on a concave sheered hull—ugh!

Excess height of the cabin sides is another feature that can spoil the appearance of a yacht. There is no hard and fast rule for cabin height, but anything over half the freeboard at its low point is excessive. If a high cabin is desirable for headroom on a small boat, the height should be achieved by a generous roof crown and not by high cabin sides.

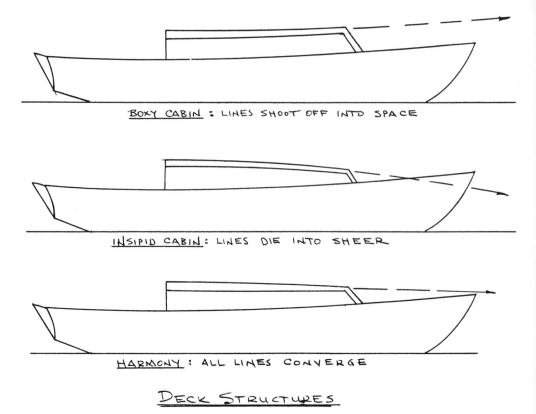

BOXY CABIN : LINES SHOOT OFF INTO SPACE

INSIPID CABIN: LINES DIE INTO SHEER

HARMONY : ALL LINES CONVERGE

DECK STRUCTURES

The cabin sides must "tumble home" or else they may appear to be falling outboard. Again, there are no set rules, but one-quarter inch per foot of height is the minimum, and this can be increased to good effect if the cabin sides are high. On recent pilot house yachts, I have set the cabin sides at angles of between 12 and 15 degrees and it does not appear excessive on these yachts. Modern cruiser-racers often have their house sides at equal or even greater angles, although the sides are quite low. One problem with these steeper angles is the dollop of water you get in the face every time you open a portlight. Some of the newer ports will drain themselves at quite steep angles, but every smart sailor has a towel in hand when he opens a port in any case.

While on the subject of portlights, I'm firmly convinced that round portlights belong on merchant ships and perhaps on very large yachts where there are enough ports to give the effect of a line when seen from a distance. Three or four round ports on a small yacht simply looks like dull design to me, and I cannot help but think that such yachts would look better with oval or rectangular ports. Also, I do not care for rectangular ports that are less than three times as long as they are high. The standard 5"x12" port always seems too boxy to my mind; I much prefer a 4"x12" size. Three-to-one seems to be the minimum length-to-height ratio for good appearance, particularly on a modern yacht.

The ports should be set on a line centered halfway between the roof edge and the deck. All too often they are all set the same distance below the roof edge, and since the cabin sides become lower as the sheer rises forward, the line of the ports appears to droop into the sheer. If the ports are centered on the cabin side, they will be aiming at the stemhead, along with the lines of the sheer and cabin, giving a most harmonious appearance.

Contemporary performance cruisers and cruiser-racers sport quite flat sheers, though still usually convex, and have very low trunk cabins that often fair gradually into the foredeck instead of having a distinct end. Some of these yachts can be very beautiful indeed (e.g., the 1984 C&C 42), and some of them are gassers (the late, unlamented US 25).

In truth, there are beautiful yachts of every type, modern, traditional, or character; but each type of hull needs a well-designed cabin to match if the overall picture of the yacht is to be one of beauty and harmony.

THE LIVING ENDS

The ends of a yacht contribute to her beauty and to her performance. Modern yachts have short ends, giving them a maximum waterline length for their length overall. This, as noted previously, reduces the displacement/length ratio and thus increases the potential speed, plus adding to accommodation space. Unfortunately, such short ends, though purposeful, are rarely beautiful, bow overhangs being straight lines on many designs, while the chopped-off reverse transom does little to add to appearance either.

THE BOW

Over the years, there have been many variations of bow shapes—clipper bows, spoon bows, plumb bows, and even the tumblehome bow as seen on many older Cape Cod cats. The spoon bow was popular for many years and has several advantages. It provides reserve buoyancy forward in a seaway. It picks up waterline length as the boat heels, thereby adding to potential speed. And when the yacht is upright running downwind or heeling only slightly in light air, the long spoon bow reduces wetted surface with a resultant gain in performance.

The long spoon bow went out of favor for several reasons. A Madison Avenue approach to advertising in the 1960s stressed the length overall rather than the more traditional (and better guide to size) LWL. Once the LOA was accepted as the size criterion, then the gray-flannel-suit boys put the accent on accommodations, and the best way to get more accommodations into a given LOA is to lengthen the LWL by shortening the ends. Now we have boats boasting six berths in 26-foot LOA on a 24-foot waterline, and they are sold to people who would be a lot happier if they owned a

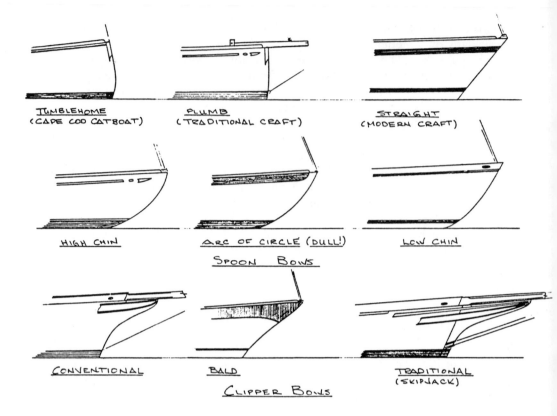

TUMBLEHOME
(CAPE COD CATBOAT)

PLUMB
(TRADITIONAL CRAFT)

STRAIGHT
(MODERN CRAFT)

HIGH CHIN

ARC OF CIRCLE (DULL!)

LOW CHIN

SPOON BOWS

CONVENTIONAL

BALD

TRADITIONAL
(SKIPJACK)

CLIPPER BOWS

yacht that was 28-foot LOA on 22-foot waterline and had two less berths. When you consider that the Luders 27 of the late 1950s was about 40 feet overall, it is easy to see that times, and truth, have changed.

In addition, the changeover from the Cruising Club of America rule, which favored long ends and short waterlines, to the IOR rule was a large factor in altering the proportions of our yachts. And even though 90 percent of the yachts built are never raced, the manufacturers felt that they had to follow the trend.

Spoon bows come in many shapes depending on the length of the overhang. A few are illustrated. The one important criterion is that the bow shape should never be the arc of a circle as this is, in my view, dull and ugly design. Obviously, the lower and shallower the line of the bow, the more waterline the yacht will pick up as she heels, but the long, low bows can lead to excess pitching by providing too much reserve buoyancy. It is fine for inshore racers but out of place on an offshore cruiser. Fortunately, it is now out of style as well and seen only on meter-type boats today.

The clipper bow is another old favorite that has made a small comeback in recent years. Unfortunately, it is obvious that some designers have never studied the proportions of traditional clipper bows or the words of wisdom in the writings of

Chapelle and Herreshoff and do not have the faintest idea of the original purpose of trailboards or how to design them. There is no doubt that a well-designed clipper bow is beautiful, but it is all too easily spoiled by bad design (and I've done some that I don't like to look back on) or execution.

The bald clipper bow, as used by Philip L. Rhodes on *Thunderhead* and other designs, is also beautiful and a refreshing change from today's straight-lined stems. Such a bow can lengthen the yacht sufficiently, as on *Thunderhead*, that the need for a bowsprit is eliminated, and the added deck area is welcomed by the foredeck crew. The bald clipper bow should not have trailboards as they look out of place without a bowsprit. A small scroll might be used, but the Rhodes designs looked beautiful without any such embellishment.

The clipper bow is probably the hardest shape to design properly, and careful attention to the rules of tradition is necessary if it is to look right on the yacht. This is definitely a part of yacht design where art wins out over science.

There is not much to say about the modern straight stem. It makes sense—it is easy to design and hard to muck up. It fits in with today's short-ended yachts, particularly if the sheer is moderate. Often the "straight" stem looks best if it is given a bit of shape, either a very mild spoon or clipper curve. On yachts with a pronounced sheer, the true spoon or clipper bow will fit more smoothly into the overall design as they blend better with the line of a generous sheer.

STERNS

Like bows, sterns come in many different styles. The plain transom stern can be raked aft or forward. The overhanging counter stern can be short, long, or intermediate, and the transom may be set raked aft, raked forward, or vertical. Then the double-ender can be of the Scandinavian type with outboard rudder, of canoe-stern type with little or lots of overhang, or the more rounded cruiser stern. There is ample variety for every taste.

The long stern overhangs of 25 to 40 years ago had the same advantages as the long spoon bow: added waterline when heeled under sail, reduced wetted area when upright, plus increased buoyancy aft to reduce the chance of being pooped when running before heavy seas. Plus, they were beautiful. Unfortunately, they also added weight in the ends so they probably added to pitching more than the increased buoyancy aft dampened it. As well, the weight was high up in the hull where it was detrimental to stability.

Modern sterns are shorter, of course, giving reduced weight in the ends and a longer LWL for a given LOA. This is all to the good, but I think it has been carried too far as regards the cruising yacht. Possibly the first reverse transom yacht of any fame was the 12-meter *Weatherly*. In 1962, when we were preparing her for the America's Cup defense at Luders's shop, we were trying to save every ounce of weight and Bill came up with the idea of sawing off her lovely, long counter and fitting a reverse counter. I cannot recall how much weight was saved, but it was in the neighborhood of several hundred pounds, up high in the hull and aft. Between that and other changes, she was fast enough to defend the Cup successfully and apparently set a trend for reverse transoms that is still with us over 20 years later.

73 ☐

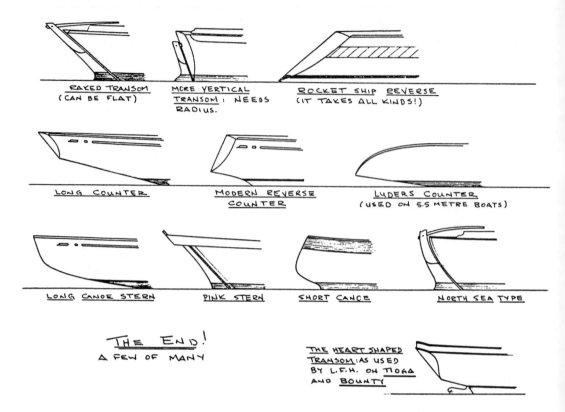

RAKED TRANSOM
(CAN BE FLAT)

MORE VERTICAL
TRANSOM: NEEDS
RADIUS.

ROCKET SHIP REVERSE
(IT TAKES ALL KINDS!)

LONG COUNTER

MODERN REVERSE
COUNTER

LUDERS COUNTER
(USED ON 5.5 METRE BOATS)

LONG CANOE STERN

PINK STERN

SHORT CANOE

NORTH SEA TYPE

THE END!
A FEW OF MANY

THE HEART SHAPED
TRANSOM: AS USED
BY L.F.H. ON TIOGA
AND BOUNTY

The reverse transom does make sense for racing yachts where every ounce is important, but the cruising yacht can benefit by the extra cockpit length and added lazarette storage given by a vertical or aft raked transom. This is particularly true in those yachts with a quarter berth. This feature destroys one good cockpit locker so that the extra stowage space of a roomy lazarette is often more desirable than the added twentieth of a knot given by the chopped-off reverse stern.

The Colin Archer type of double-ender, long favored by many cruising men, suffers from a short, nonbuoyant stern and is prone to being pooped when running off in heavy weather. There are arguments that this stern "splits" the seas, but I doubt this is the case. What probably happens is that when running before it, particularly in breaking inlets, the nonbuoyant stern does not lift with the sea. Thus, the rudder remains deeper in less turbulent water and so the yacht has less tendency to yaw and broach than a vessel with a more powerful stern shape. The problem with this form of double-ender is that the buttocks may become steep and heavily rounded aft below the waterline, creating added resistance and a slower boat, particularly when combined with the very heavy displacement common to such craft.

Double-enders with inboard rudders and longer sterns, such as Bob Perry's Valiant 40 or Herreshoff's beautiful little canoe yawl, *Rozinante,* tend to shift the rounding of the buttocks aft and up so that extra drag is minimal. The overhang does add some buoyancy and reserve stability of a normal counter stern while keeping a nice, easy run to the buttocks under water.

Possibly one of the prettiest sterns ever developed is the long, overhanging canoe stern, but it has fallen out of favor along with all other long stern forms today. Too bad.

TRANSOM RADIUS

Transom stern yachts will usually have an athwartship radius to the stern as it greatly improves appearance, taking away the flat, sawn-off effect. There are no rules to transom radius. Indeed a narrow transom, or one set at a great angle, can get by nicely without a radius. The dory-type hull and the Folkboat are two examples of a flat stern used intelligently. As the transom becomes wider and/or more vertical, the radius should increase.

One of the prettiest sterns is the type that Bill Luders used on many of his 5.5-meter designs. The reverse transom was curved in both a fore-and-aft and an athwartship direction. The long stern overhang of the 5.5 sloops made this particularly effective and handsome.

The radiused transom does add more work and cost to the lofting and construction of the yacht, but it is money well spent in almost every case. Nothing looks more like a barn door than a big, wide, flat, and ugly transom on an otherwise handsome vessel.

OVERHANGS AND SEAWORTHINESS

As noted previously, the trend today is toward light to moderate displacement and short ends. This combination produces the most boat for the money, and, as a rule, the best performance. Luckily, it also makes sense as far as seaworthiness is concerned.

Consider a heavy-displacement boat with short ends. In a seaway she does not have enough reserve buoyancy in the short ends to lift her weight and so will tend to be very wet. As each wave comes along the boat remains steady and the wave sweeps over it. The worst case would be the boat with a plumb bow and a long stern overhang. The buoyancy aft tends to depress the bow so she will dive into the oncoming seas and be very wet indeed. The heavy-displacement hull needs moderately long ends for reserve buoyancy to allow her to lift with the seas. Phillips-Birt said that overhangs of up to one-third the length were not unreasonable. While I think that may be a bit extreme, I do believe that overhangs totalling a quarter of the length overall are quite within reason and will rarely fail to produce a handsome yacht. Longer ends make particularly good sense if the overhang forward will eliminate the need for a bowsprit and permit an all-inboard rig.

The modern lighter and longer hull does not need a great deal of reserve buoyancy in the ends as her large waterline area will lift her more modest weight with each sea. This is one case where form follows fashion, and the moderate end overhangs of today are both in style and practical, even if they're not as beautiful as the longer bows and sterns of the past.

5

□
□
□
□
□
□
□
□
□

RIGS AND RIGGING

SAILING RIGS

THE FORE-AND-AFT RIG

The history of the fore-and-aft rig makes fascinating reading. Surprisingly, two of the earliest types developed, the lateen sail of the Mediterranean and the junk sail of China, are still in use in the areas where they originated. On the other hand, the fore-and-aft rig in Europe underwent constant development.

The first fore-and-aft rigs in northern waters were the sprit rig, probably adapted from the lateen, and the lug rig, a descendant of the square sail of the Vikings. The dipping lug rig was used on fishing boats in the North Sea and English Channel waters right into the early part of this century. An interesting point about the efficiency of the dipping lug rig is that it was outlawed during the Napoleonic wars as the luggers could outpoint the gaff rigged revenue cutters and were too widely used as smugglers to suit the authorities. Unfortunately, the rig is slow to tack and requires a large crew or it might have still been in use.

The gaff rig was seen in Holland around the 1500s, the first sails being loose footed as the boom was not developed for another hundred years. The Bermudan rig was another innovation of the period, possibly first developed in Holland but not favored until reports about the performance of the small sloops of Bermuda reached

Europe in the late 1600s. In any event, the Bermudan rig (also known as the leg o'mutton rig in Europe and the marconi rig in America) could not become useful for larger craft until the invention of wire rigging, turnbuckles, and sail track in the late 1800s and the first part of this century.

Today we see both gaff and Bermudan rigs in our waters, some lateen rigs on sailboards, and junk rigs on a few cruising yachts. It is rare to see a lug rig today, although I received my first sailing lessons on a lug rigged craft, the 27-foot whaleboats and 32-foot cutters of the Royal Canadian Navy. Those interested in learning more about the history of the fore-and-aft rig are referred to Phillips-Birt's *Fore and Aft Sailing Craft*, to Leather's *Gaff Rig*, and to March's *Sailing Trawler* and *Sailing Drifter*.

GAFF VS. BERMUDAN

The gaff rig has definite advantages besides its picturesqueness, of course. With its two halyards the gaff can be adjusted to trim for poorly fitting sails; not as important in this day of long-lived and relatively nonstretch dacron sailcloth as it was in the days of cotton sails. Then the peak halyard can be dropped in a squall to "scandalize" the sail and immediately reduce its area by 35 to 40 percent.

While not as efficient to windward as the Bermudan rig, the gaff sail is more efficient off the wind because the gaff swings off to leeward to present a flatter sail to the breeze. The rig has a lower center of effort than the Bermudan and so less heeling moment, although the weight of the gaff and the often heavier spars may mean more weight aloft. But the weight of the gaff does come down as the sail is reefed. Also, the rig itself is less sensitive to bad tuning, simpler, and cheaper to set up, and repairs at sea are generally more straightforward if something does go wrong. The mast for the gaff rig can be supported more simply. It does not require the complexity of shrouds and spreaders that made early yachtsmen name the Bermudan rig after a Marconi wireless mast.

Though rarely seen except on a few small production boats such as the Herreshoff Eagle catboat, a modern gaff rig with aluminum spars is entirely feasible. Unfortunately, the gaff rig has fallen out of favor and has not had the advantages of the development that has gone into the Bermudan rig over the past 70 years. If it had, we might see gaff rigged craft with the sail on a track, the gaff itself traveling either on a track or in the slot of the aluminum mast, and the rig supported by spreaders in the same manner as a marconi spar. This would save weight aloft and increase the efficiency of the sail compared to the old-fashioned hoops and lacings still in use.

There is no denying that the Bermudan rig has advantages of its own, of course, The higher aspect ratio of the rig gives it better windward performance while its weakness off the wind has been eliminated by the parachute spinnaker. The spars and gear are lighter. And a major advantage of the rig is that a permanent backstay can be set, thus adding to safety and simplicity.

There is no real choice between the two rigs as they operate on different planes. The racing sailor and the cruising sailor who puts efficiency above romance will opt for the Bermudan rig. The gaff rig will continue to be favored by those who love character boats and want their yachts to retain as much flavor of the past as possible. Fortunately, there are such souls. Over the years I've been commissioned to design a number of gaff rigged yachts, including a catboat, a sharpie, a Quoddy sloop, a Friendship sloop, and four schooners, ranging in size from 32 to 45 feet. The gaff rig is still alive, and our waters will be very dull if it ever dies out completely.

MISCELLANEOUS RIGS

The sprit rig has made a comeback in recent years. The original sprit rigs were low aspect ratio leg o' mutton sails with a sprit (boom) set part way up the sail and lashed to the mast or held with a "snotter." The sprit remained on the one side all the time so that on one tack the sail would press against the sprit and its shape would be deformed. The rig was popular only on small working craft.

Modern sprit rigs use a wishbone boom, curved to the sail shape and made of laminated wood or aluminum. The boom fits on both sides of the sail. Because of its shape it does not touch the sail on either tack and so is much more efficient than the original sprit rig. Netting hung between the two sides of the sprit boom, loose enough to clear the foot of the sail, is used to gather the sail when it is lowered.

The advantage of the rig is that the sprit boom forms a strong vang and prevents the sail from lifting and losing efficiency when the sheets are eased. The rig is seen on many modern catboats and periaugers today, the sails being of higher aspect ratio and more powerful to windward than the original leg o' mutton rig. One problem with the rig has been that of reefing. It is not as fast or simple as the slab reefing used with conventional booms. However, designers have come up with various solutions, and the prospective buyer would do well to look at this aspect of any particular boat rather closely.

The sliding gunter rig is either a Bermudan rig with a reefing topmast or a gaff rig with a vertical gaff; take your choice. Its primary use is on daysailers and small craft as it shortens the mainmast so it can be stowed inside the boat and raised more easily due to its lighter weight. It is similar to the Bermudan rig in its general characteristics but has the advantage that the weight of the gunter spar is lowered as the sail is reefed.

The junk rig is a fully battened sail similar in shape to the old European lug rig. The sail remains on the same side of the mast on both port and starboard tacks. The advantages are in easy reefing as the battens obviate the need for reef pennants. The luff, being clear of the wind shadow of the mast, also adds to efficiency, but still the rig will not sail with a Bermudan rig to windward. Its use has been restricted largely to husky cruising boats and has never been popular on this side of the Atlantic. Several variations of it have been developed in Europe but are only rarely seen here.

Fully battened Bermudan sails are also seen, of course. The battens allow a large roach to be built into the sail so that generous area can be spread or the heeling moment lowered. Reefing is simplified, again no pennants to tie off, and the sail does not shake itself to death while luffing as the battens keep it lying quiet even when head-to-wind. The disadvantage is that the large roach prevents the use of a

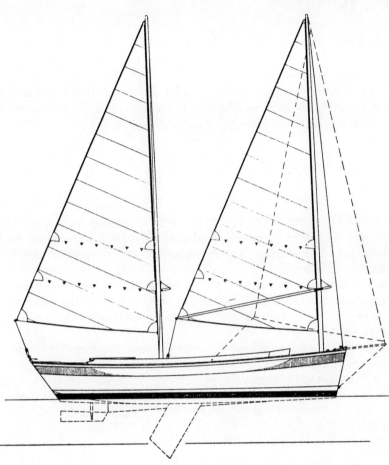

Above: *A small periauger with sprit rig.* **Left:** *A junk rigged 33-foot "schooner." Rig design by A. Boswell of England.*

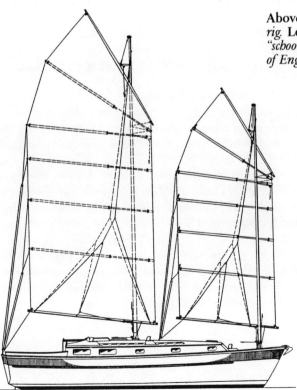

79 □

permanent backstay, but the modern boats on which it is seen (catboats and cat ketches, the latter more properly termed periaugers) usually have freestanding spars so this is not a problem. The fully battened sail is not permitted in most racing rules but I expect it will be used on a few cruising yachts as sailors become more familiar with it. It is certainly more weatherly than the junk rig, less complex to set up, and a more familiar shape to North American yachtsmen.

HEADSAILS

The modern Bermudan rigged yacht is slightly undercanvassed as a general rule and has to rely on a large variety of overlapping headsails to make up for its lack of working sail. The cruising boat is better, in my opinion, if she is somewhat overcanvassed by present standards. It is easier and faster, and often safer, to tuck in a reef when the wind pipes up than it is to change headsails on a wet, heaving foredeck. It is also cheaper to buy the slightly larger suit of sails in the first place than it is to go into hock for a wide variety of genoas, drifters, reachers, spinnakers, and other light weather sails.

Still there is a limit to sail size. An area of about 500 square feet in one sail is about the maximum that a cruising couple can reasonably handle. An area of 450 square feet is even better. Fortunately, modern developments in roller furling/reefing headstays, jiffy reefing, and even the roller masts and booms have taken much of the effort out of sailhandling, albeit at the expense of greater mechanical complexity and extra cost.

The large genoa jib with a LP (longest perpendicular measurement from luff to clew) of 150 percent of the foretriangle base is a necessity on racing yachts as the rules rate the rig for that size sail. Not to carry one is to give your opponent an unnecessary advantage. The racing yachts will also carry a wide selection of smaller genoa jibs, reaching jibs, spinnakers ranging from 160-percent heavy weather sails up to the maximum allowable 180-percent foot length, plus an assortment of bloopers, cheaters, and other rags.

The cruising man should settle for a smaller genoa in 125-to-130-percent-LP range and will be rewarded by easier handling at the cost of a bit of light air performance. Also, the sail should be cut a tad on the high side. Deck sweeping jibs are good for efficiency (the deck acts as an end plate) but a nuisance as regards restricted visibility from the helm. The cruising man might also select the simple pole-less spinnaker, as now available from most good sailmakers, over the more complex, and dangerous, spinnaker set on a pole. Twin jib rigs are also safe and easily handled in comparison to a spinnaker and find their place on long downwind legs where they can be trimmed for self-steering. They are truly blue water, tradewind sails, but they are very effective.

Much has been written about the efficiency of large genoa jibs, with the explanation that this is a result of the slot effect that such sails create in combination with the mainsail. The fallacy of this theory is well illustrated by the fact that sailboat racing classes in which the entire sail area is measured and the overlap is not free

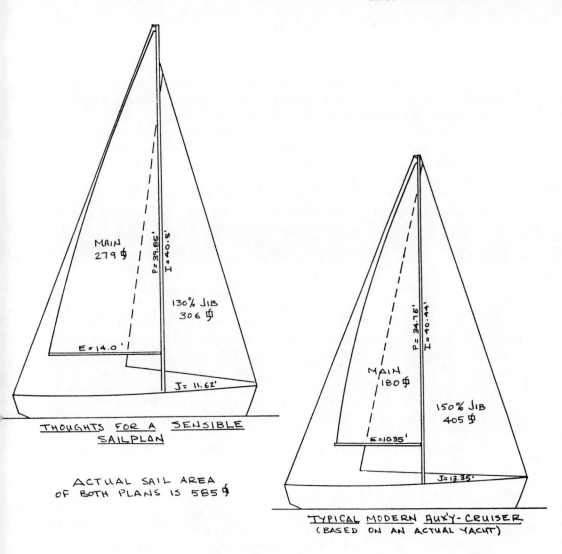

MAIN
279 ☐

P = 39.85'

I = 40.5'

130% JIB
306 ☐

E = 14.0'

J = 11.62'

THOUGHTS FOR A SENSIBLE SAILPLAN

ACTUAL SAIL AREA OF BOTH PLANS IS 585 ☐

P = 34.75'

I = 40.44'

MAIN
180 ☐

150% JIB
405 ☐

E = 10.35'

J = 13.35'

TYPICAL MODERN AUX'Y - CRUISER
(BASED ON AN ACTUAL YACHT)

quickly evolved into using nonoverlapping jibs. The 5.5-meter racing yachts are one example of a class that showed that the genoa jib does not pay its way unless the overlap is not measured into the yacht's handicap rating. Unfortunately, it would not be feasible to change the rules to measure the largest headsail. If this were done, then the boats measured with small headsails (and lower ratings) would always win in heavy air, while those that chose large headsails, and the devil with the rating, would win in the light stuff.

The cruising sailor is not locked into a rule, though, so he should realize that in average conditions he will have added performance along with easier handling if his boat is set up with a large main and 125-percent genoa instead of having the same sail area spread in a small main and 150-percent genoa.

RIG TYPES

Arguing the merits of the various rigs with another sailor is like arguing the choice of hats with your wife. The end result is the same; you get nowhere. Each rig has its advantages and its place so we'll examine them one by one.

First, the cat rig: A few years ago cat rigs were limited to small daysailers, class racers and character cruising boats of the Cape Cod model. Today they are seen in chubby fin keel cruisers up to 36 feet or so, spreading almost 750 square feet in one high aspect ratio Bermudan sail.

In the small sizes the cat rig is an easy rig on which to learn to sail. It is simple and has good downwind ability, although larger Cape Cod cats can be a bit of a bear with the wind astern. The rig is handy as long as the boom is not overly long, as it was on some of the older cats where you had to stand on the rudder to tuck in a reef and needed the strength of a gorilla to handle the weather helm.

The drawback of the cat rig has been that it is not as efficient as a sloop to windward. This was particularly true of the gaff rigged, centerboard cats. The new crop of Bermudan cats features shaped dagger boards or even NACA fin keels, along with spade rudders. Windward performance has improved as a result—but not so much that some of the builders are not fitting jibs on their "cat" boats to improve light air performance and weatherliness. This was done on some of the traditional Cape Cod cats, of course, as their "summer" rig, to gain area in light weather.

While suitable for coastal cruising with an eye on the weather, no single-masted cat rig, even the most modern, can be a true blue water cruiser. Someone will cross an ocean in one for sure, but oceans have been crossed in folding canoes, too. Just not with me aboard.

Periaugers (often termed cat ketches) have gained popularity since Gary Hoyt reintroduced the rig in his Freedom line. The rig is an old one and was used by the Dutch in the 1600s and in America into the early part of this century on Block Island boats, sharpies, and other fishing craft. Periaugers are a better choice for offshore use than catboats and have made extensive voyages without problem.

The sloop and cutter: In the late 1700s, the sloop was a burdensome vessel with a single mast set well aft; a fixed, sharply steeved bowsprit; and a fixed topmast. It was used as a cargo carrier. The cutter was a finer lined vessel intended for speed in the revenue and military services and had a reefing bowsprit and topmast. Both vessels set a gaff mainsail, squaresails, staysails, and several jibs; but the cutter, with her crew of 40 to 50 men, had a much larger sail area than the sloop.

Unfortunately, there are no true cutters left today, and in any case it is not easy to differentiate between a modern cutter and a sloop with a double-headsail rig. If the vessel has its mast located almost amidships and sports a bowsprit and double headsails, it is certainly a cutter. If there is no sprit and the mast is located much less than 40 percent of the LWL aft, then it is a sloop. In between these two extremes it is whatever the owner wants it to be. To add to the confusion, even with a long bowsprit and two or three jibs, the boat is a sloop if the mast is set well forward as in the famous Friendship sloops.

The sloop and cutter are the most weatherly of all rigs, with the single-headsail

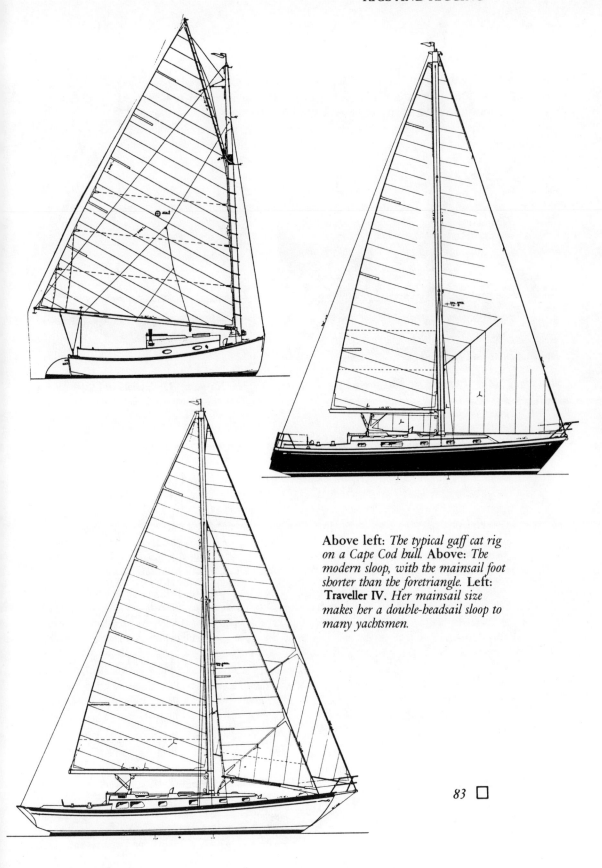

Above left: *The typical gaff cat rig on a Cape Cod hull.* **Above:** *The modern sloop, with the mainsail foot shorter than the foretriangle.* **Left: Traveller IV.** *Her mainsail size makes her a double-headsail sloop to many yachtsmen.*

The Hong Kong skyline is the background for the Cape Carib sloop.

The Kaiulani 38: a modern cutter with bowsprit.

Blue Jeans, *a cutter with all-inboard rig.*

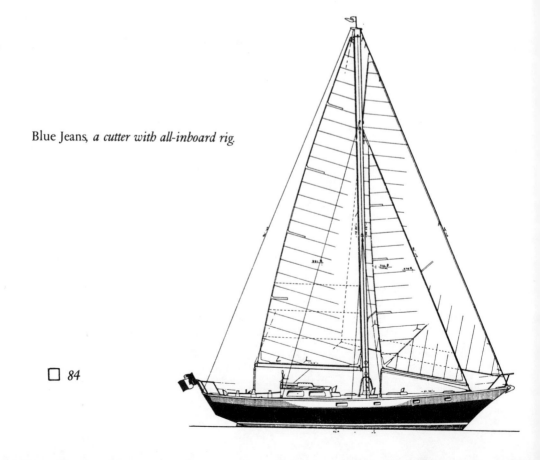

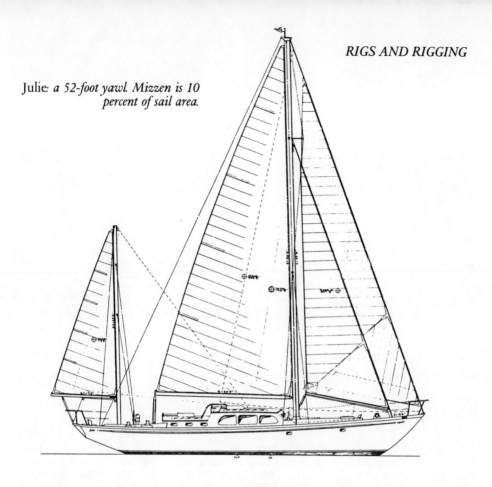

Julie: *a 52-foot yawl. Mizzen is 10 percent of sail area.*

sloop having the edge over the double-headsail rigs. Properly set up, either rig is simple to handle and well suited to any yacht up to 40 feet or more. Indeed, a sloop with self-tending jib would be as easy to handle as a catboat or periauger and a great deal better all-around performer.

The yawl: The true yawl has its mizzenmast located abaft the rudderpost and the mizzensail area is about 10 to 15 percent of the total. It is a useful rig with some of the advantages of both the sloop and the ketch. It is almost as weatherly as the sloop but like the ketch, can set a mizzen staysail in light air or can job along under jib and mizzen if it gets dusty.

The rig was popular in the 1960s for racing under the old CCA rule as the mizzen staysail was free sail area and the mizzen itself was rated very lightly. However, in too many cases the mizzen was too small to be a useful sail in itself and was carried simply as an excuse to set the mizzen staysail for racing. Today the yawl has fallen out of favor for cruising and has been handicapped out of racing. This is unfortunate as a well-proportioned yawl, one with more than a token mizzen, combines the advantages of both the sloop and ketch. It is more versatile than the sloop and more weatherly than the ketch. It is certainly more suitable than the ketch for boats under 40 feet.

To be effective, the yawl must have a decent-sized mizzen, at least 10 percent of the total area, and the mast must be strongly stayed so that the sail can be used in heavy weather to balance a jib with the main reefed or under storm conditions to

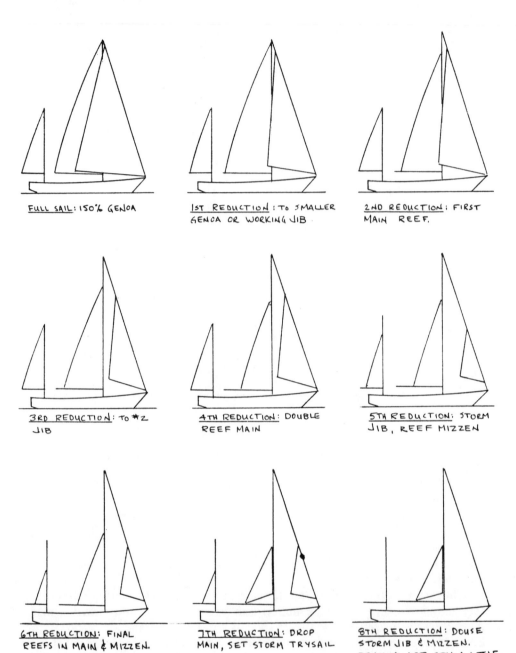

FULL SAIL: 150% GENOA

1ST REDUCTION : TO SMALLER GENOA OR WORKING JIB

2ND REDUCTION: FIRST MAIN REEF.

3RD REDUCTION: TO #2 JIB

4TH REDUCTION: DOUBLE REEF MAIN

5TH REDUCTION: STORM JIB, REEF MIZZEN

6TH REDUCTION: FINAL REEFS IN MAIN & MIZZEN.

7TH REDUCTION: DROP MAIN, SET STORM TRYSAIL

8TH REDUCTION: DOUSE STORM JIB & MIZZEN. PRAY A LOT. CRY A LITTLE.

SOME STEPS IN REDUCING SAIL ON YAWLS & KETCHES

keep the yacht head-to-seas with a sea anchor off the bow. It is not easy to design a yawl on a modern hull, though. The definition of the yawl places the mizzenmast abaft the rudderpost, and today's yachts have the rudder so far aft and the stern overhang so short that fitting a mizzen and staying it properly is difficult, if not impossible.

The ketch: The ketch has its mizzenmast stepped forward of the rudderpost (the only possible place for a mizzen on modern, short-ended yachts), and the sail is larger than that of the yawl—up to 20 percent of the total sail area. It is not as weatherly as the yawl, due to the larger proportion of sail in the mizzen, and is also slower as the mizzen is partially backwinded by the main when beating to windward. Nevertheless, the ketch is a popular cruising rig and rightly so, as it is very versatile. It can be balanced nicely under a wide variety of reduced sail combinations and it also performs very well off the wind. To many cruising couples, the ketch's handiness in heavy weather and its good performance in the breezes that most of us go cruising for anyway more than offset the loss of a knot to windward.

Recently when asked for ketch designs I have compromised somewhat. The mast is located forward of the rudderpost, of course, but the sail is smaller, closer to yawl proportions. I feel that this makes a good rig with some of the advantages of both ketch and yawl. The mast can be properly stayed for strength, and the mizzen sail is not so large that efficiency is unduly compromised.

The ketch and the yawl can be built in any size. I've owned a 22-foot ketch and 22- and 23-foot yawls and had fun with them all. Still it is generally considered that 40 feet and up is their proper place. Below that, the cutter is best for ocean going and the sloop for coastal use as far as efficiency is concerned. With only a couple for crew I would not dismiss either the yawl or ketch in sizes of 30 feet or over, particularly for extended blue water cruising. The versatility and handiness of the rigs can make up for an extra day's time on the voyage if you are not in a mad rush to get there.

The schooner: Probably no single rig better represents the North American sailing vessel than the schooner. Though originated in Holland, the schooner was most widely used and developed to perfection in the Americas. Today it is rarely seen, and to my knowledge there are only two fiberglass schooners in production: the 32-foot *Lazyjack* built by Ted Hermann from my design, and the Cherubini 44.

The standard schooner that first comes to our minds when we hear the term is set up with one or two jibs, then a gaff foresail set on the foremast, and either a gaff or Bermudan main. The staysail schooner replaces the foresail with a staysail between the masts, and the main is generally of Bermudan cut, but not always. The famous *Nina* was a staysail schooner, winning her first transatlantic race in 1928 and her final Bermuda Race in, as I recall, the late 1960s. In her career she set a racing record that was the envy of many sloop and yawl skippers.

A few schooners have been built with Bermudan sails on both the fore and main masts. My *Ingenue* design was of this type and had an excellent racing record; indeed, she is still winning schooner races 20 years after her launching. I do feel that this rig has possibilities for further development and would be my choice for a modern schooner. *Ingenue*, with a knowledgeable owner at the helm, certainly beat many larger yachts boat-for-boat yet was easily handled by the owner and his wife for coastal voyaging.

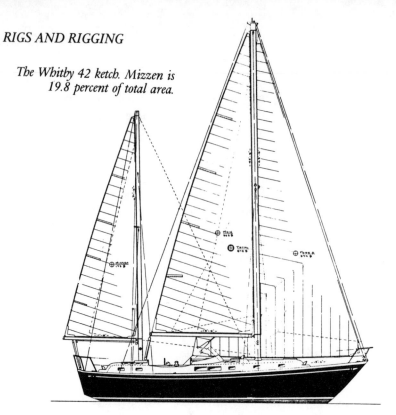

The Whitby 42 ketch. Mizzen is 19.8 percent of total area.

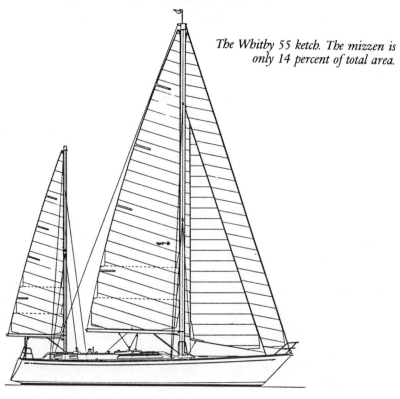

The Whitby 55 ketch. The mizzen is only 14 percent of total area.

The Whitby 55 ketch beating up a narrow channel.

Lazyjack, *a modern fiberglass schooner with Bermudan mainsail.*

89 ☐

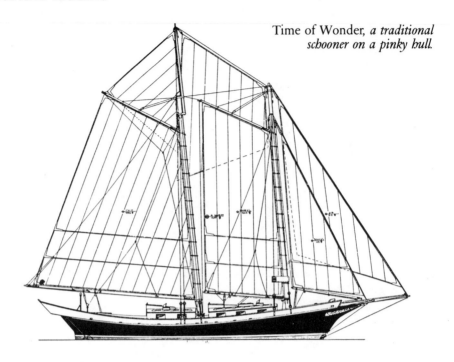

Time of Wonder, *a traditional schooner on a pinky bull.*

The Arden 60: a "tern" (or three-masted) schooner.

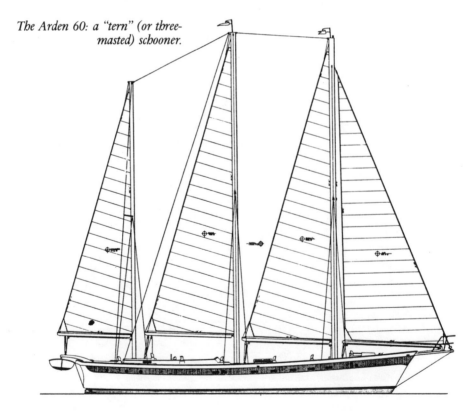

The schooner rig is fast off the wind but not the best to windward for obvious reasons. A well-designed schooner can beat to windward in a blow with just her foresail up, though, so it can be a handy rig for cruising. Moreover, she can set a lot of light air sails between her masts and need not be slow in the zephyrs.

Though schooners have been built as small as 20 to 22 feet, the rig is really more suited to larger craft.

SIZE AND RIG

There are no well-defined limits, either upper or lower, to the size of yacht that can be fitted with a particular rig. For racing, the sloop is the choice even in the 70-foot-plus maxi-boat sizes, although in these larger craft the ketch (with yawl-sized mizzen) may run a close second.

The "rules" are much more flexible when it comes to the cruising yacht and depend to a large degree on the anticipated voyage as well as the size of the normal crew. Long voyages or two-person crews tend to make one consider a cutter instead of a sloop or a ketch instead of a cutter, according to the size required. The cruising man should bear in mind that ease of sailhandling and versatility of rig may well be more vital than the added efficiency of the sloop rig.

The cruising yacht may be fitted with sloop rig to 45 feet or so, often with double headsails. Larger than that, the cutter with its smaller main is a bit easier to handle for the shorthanded cruising crew, as are the yawl and ketch. For a two-person yacht, I would start to consider the cutter at about 33 to 35 feet and the two-masted rigs at 40 to 42 feet, and I would drop those size limits a few feet if I intended long blue water passages. The schooner rig is in a class by itself; either you want one or you don't. If you do, size does not enter into it.

RIG EFFICIENCY

The Royal Ocean Racing Club (RORC) handicap rule of the 1960s gave allowances for rigs according to the following table. It is a reasonably good guide to the efficiency of the various rigs but says nothing as to their handiness, of course.

RIG	HANDICAP
Bermudan sloop or cutter	100%
Bermudan yawl	96%
Bermudan schooner and gaff sloop	92%
Bermudan ketch and gaff yawl	88%
Gaff schooner	85%
Gaff ketch	81%

In effect, RORC was saying that a Bermudan ketch had only 88 percent of the performance of a sloop, all other things being equal. Of course, they are not always equal, and a gaff ketch rig on a good hull with a well-polished bottom could undoubtedly sail circles around a sloop rigged Colin Archer hull or similar chunky, slow vessel.

The cruising yachtsman must still bear in mind that efficiency is not necessarily safety. Certainly, a cruising yacht must have a hull-and-rig combination that has sufficient weatherliness to enable it to beat to windward off a lee shore under storm conditions. That is safety, but only if the rig is capable of being handled by the crew. If a sloop's sails are too large for a small cruising crew to set and reef properly, then you may have efficiency but not safety, and would be better off with a divided rig with its smaller sails and easier handling.

SAIL AREA

The amount of sail that the designer will load onto a hull depends on several factors: the handicap rules, the stability of the hull, the rig type, and the use of the boat, whether for coastal or offshore cruising or intended primarily for a light or heavy weather area.

Obviously, character boats such as Friendship sloops, catboats, pilot schooners, etc., will not be setting 150-percent genoa jibs and 180-percent spinnakers and should have more area in the working sails than a modern IOR sloop with its huge selection of overlapping jibs and spinnakers. Similarly, the two-person cruising yacht is better off with a generous sail area as it reduces the need for the large and unhandy light air sails. It is simple common sense to realize that a generously canvassed yacht will sail well in light winds and can be readily reefed as it breezes up. Ocean-going yachts will be more lightly canvassed than their coastal cruising sisters as they would expect to meet steadier and stronger winds, but there are no hard and fast rules.

The designer must also take stability into account, of course, as a powerful hull can spread a larger sail area than its tender sister. The type of rig also enters into it. A two-masted rig with bowsprit will spread its area fore and aft and will have a lower heeling moment than the same area in a tall, all-inboard Bermudan rig. The lower rig can effectively carry more sail in the same wind strengths. There is no way to say that any given amount of sail area is too much or too little as too many other factors are involved. Relating sail area to displacement as described earlier in the book is a reasonable guide, but the sail area/displacement ratios given must be modified according to the stability, rig type, boat use, sailing area, and general common sense.

HELM BALANCE

Proper balance on a sailing yacht is an elusive but highly desirable quality. Ideally, a perfectly balanced hull-rig combination is one that will develop three to four degrees of weather helm and retain a light, easily managed feel under all conditions, from zephyrs to gales.

Weather helm of three to four degrees is desirable for two reasons. First, if the helm is let go accidentally, the boat will turn into the wind and luff rather than turn away from the wind and either get knocked down or jibe; so weather helm is a safety feature. Second, the rudder serves two purposes: It both steers the boat and aids the lateral plane in developing lift to offset leeway. If the rudder has a slight weather helm, it will provide lift; so having the correct weather helm is a performance feature.

On the other hand, excess weather helm adds unnecessary resistance, is tiring to the helmsman, and may make it difficult if not impossible to jibe the boat when such a maneuver is required. Conversely, a lee helm gives negative lift, thereby increasing leeway, and can make tacking difficult or impossible.

Perfect weather helm in all conditions is not always possible but is certainly a target to aim at. It is common to find boats with a neutral or slight lee helm in light airs increasing to a moderate weather helm as it breezes up. This is acceptable as leeway in light air is not a serious problem. This combination is certainly preferable to having moderate weather helm in light air and a very strong weather helm in a breeze.

The amount of weather helm is governed by the "lead" of the rig, lead being the distance that the center of effort of the sails is forward of the center of lateral resistance (CLR) of the hull, and it is expressed as a percentage of the LWL. If the center of effort is too far aft (insufficient lead), the result will be excess weather helm. If the center of effort is too far forward (excess lead), the boat will have a lee helm.

The lead we work with is that derived from the geometric center of the sails and the hull, but these centers move when the boat is underway. The center of effort moves forward and to leeward due to the natural shape of the sails, the easing of the sheets, and the heel of the boat. The CLR for a fin keel can be determined, as we know from data on symmetrical airfoils that the hydrodynamic center of lateral resistance for fins of normal form is about 25 percent of the chord length abaft the leading edge (but this does vary with angle of attack). Unfortunately, we cannot pin down the CLR of the hull nor the effects upon the CLR of the fin and hull combined. Tank testing can be a valuable means to determine the true CLR of the hull and fin, but it is costly and even then not infallible. On the *American Eagle*, we had to move the mast forward substantially from the location given by tank testing in order to reduce weather helm. The designer has little choice but to work with the geometric centers and his intuition in the search for good helm balance.

THE PROPER AMOUNT OF LEAD

The designer works with the geometric centers to locate the center of effort and CLR and obtains the horizontal distance between them, and if this is not within the range that he feels is correct he reworks the sailplan or perhaps relocates the fin to suit.

In locating the center of effort it is common to use one-half the area of the mizzen, and in locating the CLR, to use a percentage of the rudder area or even omit the rudder entirely. This practice will vary with designers, and each will interpret the result to suit his own experience in any case. Indeed, even leading authorities do not agree on the correct amount of lead to be given different types of yachts as the following will show.

Chapelle

Keel cruising yachts, long keel	0-10% lead
Higher rigs and short keels	10-16%, average 12%
Gaff rigs	4-16%

Kinney - first revision of Skene's

Sloops	12-16% lead
Yawls	8-11%
Ketches and schooners	5- 7%

Kinney - second revision

Sloops	14-19% lead
Yawls (½ mizzen area)	15%
Ketches (½ mizzen area)	20%
Schooners (all sail)	5%

Baader

Sloop - fine lined yachts	3- 4% lead
Dragon and International yachts	4- 6%
Racing dinghies	4- 6%
Beamy, long keel sloop	7-10%
IOR sloop	5- 8%
IOR yawl and ketch	3- 6%
Beamy, long keel yawl and ketch	4- 6%
Schooner	3- 4%

Henry and Miller - based on original Skene's

Shallow fin keel or centerboarder	5-15% lead
Full-ended keelboats	5-10%
Normal cruising hulls	6%

Of course, in considering the wide disparities between some of these recommendations, we must take into account the amount of rudder area that the designer suggests since this will affect the location of the CLR. Moreover, Chapelle and Skene wrote 40 years ago when yachts were typically narrower than they are today, and beam definitely affects lead. Even so, saying that any boat should have a lead of four to 16 percent is wrong as four percent could give a lee helm and 16 percent a weather helm that would rupture a gorilla. This is far too broad a range.

Still some of these figures are obviously wrong, and I consider Baader's leads on the low side particularly for the split rigs. A few examples from my own design experience: A large keel-centerboard ketch with 22.5-percent lead balanced beautifully. The *Ingenue* schooner, originally with 10.5-percent lead, had to have her bowsprit lengthened to correct excess weather helm; a 35-foot cutter with 17.5-percent lead had her mast moved forward a foot to counter weather helm; a yawl with 10-percent lead had a lee helm; a ketch with 15 percent had excess weather helm. Only Kinney's recommendations are even close to some of these leads, and even they do not take into account the many variables in hull form, beam, rig height, etc., all of which affect the required lead.

Several factors affect the amount of lead, and they cannot be considered in any table that simply says "give a ketch x-percent lead." Consider two yachts, identical in all respects except that one is built of steel and has a 33-percent ballast ratio; the other of light cored fiberglass has 50-percent ballast ratio. The steel boat will be more tender and will heel more in any given wind strength. As a result, the center of effort will move farther to leeward and the luffing moment will be higher with a weather helm greater than that of her stiffer sister. The tender hull will need more lead in order to reduce the weather helm.

Take another pair of identical yachts with the same sail area, but one has a low, broad rig; the second, a tall, high aspect ratio rig. Boat #2 will heel more in a breeze, and the center of effort will move even farther to leeward due to the height of the rig. She will require more lead to eliminate excess weather helm. There are other factors that affect the lead, and these are as follows.

FACTORS SHORTENING LEAD	*FACTORS LENGTHENING LEAD*
Short keel	Long keel
Deep draft	Shoal draft
Narrow beam	Wide beam
Stable hull	Tender hull
Fine forward waterlines	Full forward waterlines
Low aspect ratio rig	High aspect ratio rig
Two-masted rig	Single-masted rig

With all these factors affecting the proper lead, it is obvious that there is no such thing as the "correct" lead for any single rig. Each design has to be analyzed individually and the lead adjusted to suit the above factors and the designer's experience.

CORRECTING POOR BALANCE

If your boat has a poorly balanced helm, there are some things you can do to correct it. Poor helms can be caused by warped rudders, centerboards, or skegs so check these

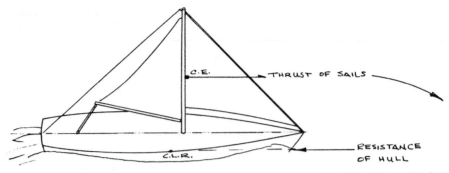

THE THRUST OF THE SAILS IS TO LEEWARD OF THE RESISTANCE OF THE HULL AND THUS FORMS A COUPLE TURNING THE YACHT TO WINDWARD.

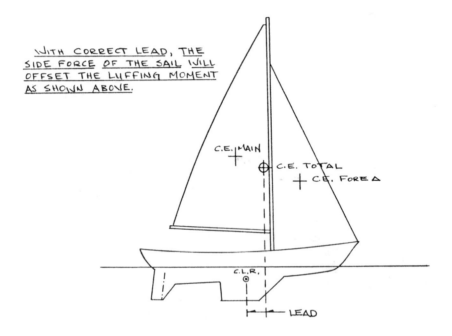

WITH CORRECT LEAD, THE SIDE FORCE OF THE SAIL WILL OFFSET THE LUFFING MOMENT AS SHOWN ABOVE.

out before you start making changes to the hull or rig. If the problem is not in these areas, then it is undoubtedly an incorrect lead. You can alter the lead by one or more of the following changes.

To Shorten Lead (to correct lee helm):
- increase rake of mast by lengthening forestay, shortening backstay
- shorten bowsprit, moving headstay aft
- move mast(s) aft
- move centerboard forward
- increase length of boom to accommodate a larger mainsail
- increase area of mizzen by longer boom and/or taller mast
- adjust mainsail to greater fullness

To Lengthen Lead (to correct excess weather helm):
- plumb up mast, tilt it forward if necessary
- lengthen bowsprit (or add sprit) to move headstay forward
- move mast(s) forward
- recut main shorter on foot
- decrease mizzen area by shorter boom and/or mast
- move centerboard aft
- adjust or recut mainsail flatter

Most boats, fortunately, can be cured of helm problems by simple tuning and adjustment so major alterations are rarely necessary. However the cure is affected, the end result is the same: A weather helm of three or four degrees will turn a cranky, ill-balanced boat into one that is a pleasure to handle, with better performance as an added benefit.

MASTS AND RIGGING

MASTS

The designer's job is to provide a mast that is light and of low windage, yet strong enough to take the loads when the yacht is beating to windward in a gale and clawing her way off a lee shore. Obviously, the needs of strength and lightness are completely opposed. The racing yacht designer will err on the light side (and hope for the best) with safety factors of 1.5 or thereabouts. The cruising yacht designer will work with safety factors of 2.5 and often more and will still say his prayers.

The earliest masts were wood and unstayed, depending on the strength of the mast itself to handle the loads. Such simple spars are still used in small craft, and many Cape Cod catboats are sailing around with unstayed, solid wood masts older than most of us. Recently, we have seen a return to unstayed spars, but the modern yachts use lightweight and low-maintenance aluminum or carbon-fiber masts. The one drawback of the unstayed spar is that it cannot be used effectively with a jib. The load of the jibstay bends the mast forward and gives us poorly setting sails both ahead and abaft the mast, hardly a setup that makes for efficiency.

Stayed solid wood masts are still found in small boats and in character boats of all sizes. The modern "solid" wood mast may be laminated, of course, and this has its advantages. The wood is less likely to check, and the grain can be oriented to the direction of maximum strains. It is difficult to obtain suitable timbers for solid spars in many areas of the country, while smaller material for laminating is usually readily available. The laminated mast makes good sense for most small traditional craft.

The sizes of solid masts may be calculated to suit the loads imposed by the stability of the masthead hull in combination with the spread of the rigging, but generally they are designed by rule-of-thumb methods as outlined in Skene's and Chapelle's books, the diameters at the deck, hounds, masthead, etc., being a percentage of the overall length of the spar. Similar methods are used to figure the sizes of the booms and gaffs.

Hollow wood masts came into vogue shortly after the Bermudan rig became popular. The first ones were round, but later masts were pear-shaped to streamline them and reduce drag. These spars were complex, required great skill, and were costly to build so the rectangular "box" spar became popular for cruising yachts. The box spar is still fairly common, particularly on amateur-built yachts, but the fancier shapes are rarely seen today as aluminum spars do the job better at less cost. Indeed, if one considers his labor into the job, the amateur builder can still purchase an aluminum extrusion and complete the mast for less cost than a good Sitka spruce, glued-up, box-section mast.

The aluminum spar is less costly, lighter (and so contributes to stability), requires less maintenance, and with any reasonable care is more durable. For these reasons, the extruded aluminum mast is almost universal in modern yachts with stayed rigs. The alloy used in the spars is 6061-T6, a heat treated alloy that has excellent strength and is readily extrudable. Another alloy, 6063-T6, has also been used but is not as strong or weather resistant.

The mast is formed by forcing a billet of aluminum through a die under tremendous pressure. The result is a uniform section from heel to masthead, but weight can be saved aloft by tapering the mast. This is done by squeezing the mast until the desired athwartship taper is obtained, then cutting out a long, triangular, pie-shaped piece from each side, holding the aft end straight and bending the forward part of the mast aft to meet it, then welding up the seam. The process is not inexpensive and is usually confined to racing yachts for this reason. The weight saved aloft by tapering is an aid to stability while the thinner mast section offers less obstruction to the air flow to the mainsail than does an untapered mast. Tapering makes great sense for a racing yacht, but the average cruiser would gain more by putting his money into a feathering propeller to save drag when under sail.

The size of the mast is determined by the designer based on the loads that will be required to heel the hull to a certain degree and corrected to reflect the angle that the shrouds make with the spar. The stayed mast is working in compression so that the greater the angle that the shrouds make with the mast, the lower the compression load on the mast itself and the lower the tensile load on the shrouds.

Since the mast metal is aluminum, only aluminum or stainless steel fittings should be used on it. Bronze bolts, winches, or mast lights will lead to quick deterioration unless they are thoroughly insulated from the aluminum with neoprene gaskets. Winch pads should be shaped of stainless steel rather than wood, as was common some years ago, as the acids in the wood affect the mast, no matter how carefully gasketed.

KEEL VS. DECK STEPPED MASTS

Each has its advantages, but the keel stepped mast is the only one to take offshore. Basically, the keel stepped mast is about 30 percent stronger than a deck stepped mast of identical section due to its being fully supported at its lower end. In effect, you can go to a mast section that is lighter and has less windage and still have a stronger mast than its heavier, bulkier, deck stepped counterpart. Since it is supported at the deck, it is also much less likely to go over the side if a shroud breaks. It may bend alarmingly, but it will hold if you relieve the sail pressure quickly enough.

Then, if the keel stepped mast does go by the board, you will usually have a stump left that can be fitted with a jury rig to get you home. The deck stepped mast may go over the side with little or no damage in a similar situation, and if you can lash it alongside and motor home, you can save yourself (or your insurance company) some money. But if you are out in blue water, that mast alongside is worthless. Indeed, if there is any sea running, it is a danger as it may hole the yacht.

The advantage of a deck stepped mast is that its underdeck support takes up little or no room in the accommodations. That's the only advantage. Otherwise, it is weaker for a given section, more likely to fail completely, and harder to fit a jury rig to the remnants than with a keel stepped spar.

Some yachts have the mast fitted in a tabernacle for ease of lowering and raising. This is an advantage to the trailer sailer, but some quite large yachts fit tabernacles as their owners want to cruise in the canals of Europe and other areas where help in stepping and unstepping a conventional keel or deck stepped mast is unavailable. A truly husky tabernacle will give the bottom of the mast some support, and the resultant strength will lie somewhere between the keel and deck stepped spars. The usual trailer sailer tabernacle gives very little support so the strength is the same as if the mast were deck stepped, although setting up a jury rig would probably be easier due to the tabernacle.

SPARS

About the only spars we are concerned with today are booms, gaffs, spreaders, and spinnaker poles. The yards of the old sailing ships are seen on only a few character boats, such as Jay Benford's *Sunshine* pinky. Solid wood spars are still used on traditional craft, long may they grace our waters, but hollow wood booms are a thing of the past—simply too expensive and too much maintenance to compete with aluminum. The modern boom is extruded aluminum, usually with reefing lines run inside it on the larger boats. Spreaders, too, are aluminum and may be of tubular shape (on cheaper yachts), tapered tubular shape (slightly more costly craft), or streamlined teardrop shape on the better yachts.

The streamlined spreader is best if it is set at a fore-and-aft angle of about 15 degrees to the LWL as this will reduce resistance slightly when the yacht is beating to windward. Athwartship, the spreaders should cock up five or six degrees so that the loads are taken in pure compression, without the bending moment that would occur if the spreader paralleled the waterline. Spreaders that appear to droop, and we have all seen them, are simply a broken mast waiting to happen.

SINGLE- AND DOUBLE-SPREADER RIGS

Generally, it is desirable that the shrouds make an angle with the mast of about 12 degrees. Racing yachts can shave this to nine or 10 degrees and blue water cruisers

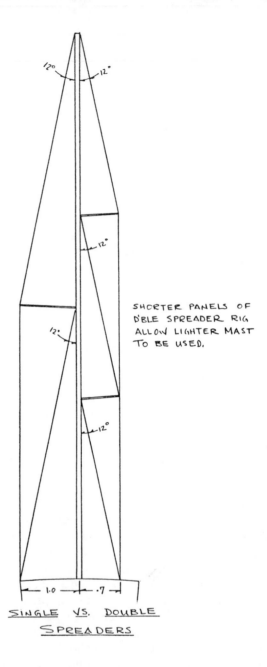

SHORTER PANELS OF
D'BLE SPREADER RIG
ALLOW LIGHTER MAST
TO BE USED.

SINGLE VS. DOUBLE
SPREADERS

may go up to a 13- or 14-degree angle, but we can take 12 degrees as a solid average.

The big advantage of the double-spreader rig is that it allows the designer to maintain a proper shroud-to-mast angle yet move the shrouds inboard on the deck to obtain a narrower sheeting angle for the headsails and so gain an edge in windward efficiency. I did both single- and double-spreader rigs on a 38-foot sloop, and the comparisons are interesting.

☐ *100*

	SINGLE	DOUBLE
Lower shroud/mast angle, degrees	11.5	12
Width of chainplate from CL	63.5"	48"
Angle from jib tack to chainplate, degrees	17.5	13.5
Lower spreader length	59"	46"
Length of unsupported mast panel	25.5'	17.3'

It is obvious that the double-spreader rig with its tighter sheeting angle and narrower spreaders will be more efficient to windward. Equally interesting is the fact that despite the narrower support base the mast needed to be no heavier as the unsupported panel was shorter, and the shrouds are the same diameter as on the single-spreader rig (although, of course, there is one more shroud per side).

In effect, the double-spreader rig is more efficient but at the cost of greater complexity; an extra chainplate, turnbuckle, shroud, and spreader on each side—just that much more to fail. With its extra shrouds, the double-spreader mast may be less likely to go over the side if any one shroud does let go, of course, and with modern rigs and decent maintenance, failures are relatively rare.

Size has little to do with it either. Laurent Giles's 21-foot yawl *Trekka*, in which John Guzzwell circumnavigated the globe, had double spreaders, and I've designed 56-footers with single spreaders and 23-footers with no spreaders at all. It all depends on the chainplate location and the angle that the shrouds make with the mast. If the chainplates are outboard and the shroud angle is about 12 degrees with single spreaders, then going to double spreaders will gain you little, although the mast could be of lighter section. If the chainplates are well inboard, then a double-spreader rig will probably be necessary to obtain a good shroud/mast angle.

HEADSAIL RIGS

There are three basic headsail rigs: the three-quarter or seven-eighths rig, the masthead rig, and the double-headsail rig.

The three-quarter rig was queen for many years but was edged out in the late 1950s by the masthead rig. It has come back into popularity for racing yachts as sailors have learned how to control sail shape by bending the spar aft to flatten the draft of the sail in heavy weather. The three-quarter rig has not made a comeback in cruising yachts, but I believe it makes sense for the cruiser. With modern reefing gear, the larger mainsail can be controlled easily while the smaller jibs of the three-quarter rig mean less work for the shorthanded cruising crew.

The three-quarter rig does need running backstays or jumper struts to maintain a tight headstay. Runners are not the problem that many people believe as they can both be left set up when tacking to windward. They only need tending when off the wind, the lee runner being released to clear the boom. This is certainly a lot easier than tacking a 150-percent genoa. With jumper struts there is no problem at all except for initial tuning.

Still most yachts in sizes to 40 feet or so are masthead rig, carry a relatively small mainsail, and need the area of large, overlapping genoas in light air. The masthead rig is a simple rig to tune and maintain and spreads the maximum area for a given mast height. In addition, it does not require running backstays or jumper struts to keep the headstay taut, and this is the main reason for its popularity, in my opinion.

Put an inner forestay on the masthead rig, and you have the double-headsail rig, popular in blue water cruisers for years. A staysail is set on the forestay and a high-cut or Yankee jib on the headstay to give a versatile setup that can be adjusted readily with various sail combinations to suit any conditions of wind and sea. If the forestay has a quick-release lever at the deck, it can be pulled back out of the way to leave the foretriangle clear. This allows easier tacking with large genoa jibs in light air and eliminates the problem of the sail hanging up in the small gap between the forestay and headstay.

The forestay is also a good place to set the storm jib. The stay is well inboard so the crew do not have to work so far forward as if the jib is set on the headstay, and this contributes both to speed in sail changing and safety. As well, with the storm jib inboard, it will often balance better with the storm trysail.

One problem with the double-headsail rig is that it really needs running backstays or jumpers to tension the forestay when driving to windward. Most owners dislike both of these alternatives so the designers make do with an intermediate backstay that is really set at too shallow an angle to do its job well. A better solution is to fit chainplates at both the intermediate backstay and the running backstay positions and end the backstay in a very strong tackle. Then the stay can be set up and tensioned as an intermediate backstay in light air and still used as a proper running backstay when it breezes up.

I do think that the double-headsail rig is being overdone today. We see it on small cruisers that will never get out of sight of land and indeed may never spend a night at sea. If most of your sailing is in the light-to-moderate air conditions so typical of our coastal waters in summer, then a three-quarter or masthead rig of generous sail area will give you better performance and be easier to handle than a double-headsail rig. The double-headsail rig is more at home on character boats and on those modern yachts that will be making long blue water passages.

STANDING RIGGING

Standing rigging consists of the shrouds and stays that support the mast. On modern yachts it will be of either wire or rod, with wire being by far the most common.

WIRE

The wire used for standing rigging will be of one of two types: 7x7 wire, composed of seven strands, each formed of seven individual wires; or 1x19 wire, composed of a single strand formed of 19 wires. Seven by seven wire is readily spliced and so is commonly used on traditional yachts. The standard commercial end terminals can also be used with 7x7 wire, but 1x19 is preferred for such applications as it is over 20 percent stronger and has considerably less stretch.

END TERMINALS

The thimbles used for spliced rigging should be of solid bronze with a hole drilled through of the correct diameter for the rigging pin. Often the common, formed stainless steel thimbles are used but are apt to deform under load, causing the rigging to stretch. Welding together the two ends of the formed thimbles will help prevent the deformation, but the solid thimble is best if available.

Eyes can be formed in rigging by the use of Nicopress® sleeves, copper sleeves that are squeezed onto the wire. Where the eye is intended for standing rigging, particularly on larger craft where the loads are great, a solid or welded thimble should be used and two Nicopress fittings employed back to back for greater strength. One advantage of the Nicopress fittings is that they can be easily and quickly installed by means of a simple tool and are handy for emergency use at sea.

Hot socketed terminals have gone out of fashion on yachts but have much to recommend them. These are bronze terminals that are attached to the wire by pouring molten zinc into the cone of the socket to form a strong metallurgical bond with the wire. They are relatively inexpensive and reusable but are now difficult to obtain. The Castlok® terminal operates on a similar principle but uses special epoxy resin instead of zinc, is also reusable, and is easy for the amateur to apply. One of the advantages of the Castlok® terminal is that the epoxy seals moisture out of the wire strands inside the fitting, a major cause of corrosion and failure in other types of fittings.

Swaged terminals are the most common type of fitting on modern yachts. The wire is inserted into the terminal and then the terminal is squeezed onto the wire under immense pressure by a special machine. An experienced rigger must handle the job as it is all too easy to ruin a terminal by excess pressure, and once it is on the wire there is no way to get it off. Swaged terminals have withstood the test of time but there have been many failures, generally due to poor swaging. Old terminals should be inspected regularly for hairline cracks, and any that are the least suspect must be replaced immediately. Also, fittings that are slightly bowed, a sign of a bad swaging job, should be discarded. Unfortunately, when you throw away a swaged terminal you also throw away the wire to which it is attached. You can use an upper shroud to make a shorter intermediate or lower, but a lower shroud with a bad terminal is simply junk.

One enemy of swaged terminals is corrosion caused by sea water getting into the terminal. Sealing the end with epoxy or melted beeswax will help keep moisture out and will add to the useful life of the fitting.

In recent years, several types of mechanical terminals (Norseman® and Sta-Lok®) have gained popularity. These fittings can be installed by anyone using common sense and readily available tools and form a strong bond to the wire. While slightly more costly than swaged terminals, they are reusable and also replaceable at sea.

While I would not discard perfectly good rigging simply because it had swaged terminals, I would replace them with Castlok® or mechanical terminals when the time came to discard them. Also, if I were buying a new boat that I intended to keep for some time, I would willingly pay the little bit extra to eliminate the swaged terminals in favor of a reuseable type.

ROD RIGGING

As the name implies, this is a solid rod, but it is available in several types, both round and streamlined. Manufacturers include Navtec and Merriman/Yacht Specialities. The advantage of rod is that it has less stretch than any of the wire rigging and is of smaller diameter, thus reducing windage. Special high-tensile rods are also available for racing yachts and further reduce diameter and windage, while the streamlined rod can reduce drag by as much as 30 percent compared to round rod.

Special end terminals are used with rod rigging. The terminal is slipped onto the rod and then the head cold formed by pressure. The result is as strong as the rod, and the terminal cannot pull off, nor can it retain moisture, the enemy of wire rigging. The rod is less subject to corrosion as a result and will considerably outlast wire, particularly when sailing in warm salt water.

Unfortunately, rod is also much more costly than 1x19 stainless wire and so is usually seen only on racing and better-quality yachts. On these craft, it is an investment in reduced drag and longer life.

CHAINPLATES, TANGS, AND TURNBUCKLES

These fittings must be designed to exceed the strength of the wire to which they are attached. A point to note is that terminals come in two basic types: "marine eyes," which have relatively large diameter pins, and "aircraft" forks and eyes with smaller diameter pins. Only marine eye terminals should be used on yachts. A marine eye for one-quarter-inch-diameter wire will have a half-inch-diameter pin while a forked fitting for one-quarter-inch wire will have only a three-eighths-inch-diameter pin, with less than 60 percent of the strength of the marine eye. The strength of the smaller pin is adequate for the wire strength but does not allow for the wear and corrosion that is so prevalent in marine use or for wear over the years.

RUNNING RIGGING

Running rigging consists of the halyards, sheets, preventers, topping lifts, vangs, and other lines used to control the sails and booms.

Mainsail and jib halyards may be of wire, particularly on larger craft. The wire used is a flexible 7x19 construction and has the advantage of having less stretch than even the best prestretched dacron line. A rope tail is spliced onto the wire so that the rope can be used to haul the sail up most of the way; then the wire is made just long enough to allow three or four turns around the winch. One drawback of wire is that it tends to "fishhook," one strand breaking to form a small snag that will slice open the toughest skin as neatly as a scalpel.

Main halyards may be all wire, with the halyard wound on a reel winch. These winches have probably caused as many accidents on yachts as all other causes combined. If the brake slips, the wildly swinging winch handle can break an arm or crush a skull with equal facility. I have been shipmates with many reel winches of various makes and types but never found one I could love.

Because of fishhooks and bone cracking reel winches, many cruisers are switching to prestretched dacron line for main and jib halyards. In my opinion, it is a change for the better. The prestretched line will let the sail sag a bit after you are underway awhile or if the wind pipes up, but a quick luff and a slight crank on the winch will set things right again.

The stretch of 7x19 wire under a load of 30 percent of its breaking strength will be just under one percent of its length. That of prestretch dacron with a similar load will be about three percent. Regular dacron line will have between seven- and 10-percent stretch under the same conditions. The racing yacht should use wire for its minimal stretch, but the cruiser can manage nicely with prestretched dacron.

If you must have wire halyards, the following is a guide to size for stainless 7x19 wire. Dimensions are the wire diameter in inches.

LENGTH	*MAIN HALYARD*	*JIB HALYARD*	*TOPPING LIFT*
10-18'	3/32"	3/32"	3/32"
18-24'	1/8"	5/32"	3/32"
25-35'	5/32"	3/16"	1/8"
36-45'	3/16"	7/32"	5/32"
46-55'	7/32"	1/4"	3/16"

Prestretched dacron line has its place for spinnaker guys also. In large yachts, these are of 7x19 wire to reduce stretch, but in smaller craft and cruisers the prestretch will do the job nicely—and no fishhooks. Topping lifts are often of 7x19 as well as the smaller wire diameter creates less drag. The wire does cause more chafe on the sail, of course, and it is another job that might better be done by prestretched dacron for the average cruising yacht. Only on the larger yachts do boom and mainsail exceed 100 pounds, and since three-sixteenth-inch prestretch has an 880-pound breaking strength there is ample safety factor. The added resistance is not serious to the cruising sailor.

Nylon line has over 20 percent more stretch than dacron, and though it is stronger, the stretch renders it unsuitable for running rigging. Use it where its stretch is useful as a shock absorber; i.e., anchor line, dock lines, and dinghy painters. The yellow polypropylene line is next to useless on a yacht. It will float, but it is slippery, and this makes it almost impossible to hold a trustworthy knot. Its flotation may make it seem suitable as a dinghy painter since it can keep the line out of the prop, but I would be too afraid of losing the dink to place my faith in it.

The following chart shows generally appropriate line sizes for dacron running rigging for cruising yachts. The dimensions are the diameter in inches. Spinnaker sheets are given in two sizes, for light and average winds. Mizzen sheets and halyards may be same size as for the staysail.

SHEETS (Dacron)

LENGTH	MAIN	JIB/GENOA	STAYSAIL	SPINNAKER
10-18'	⁵⁄₁₆"	³⁄₈"	NA	¼-³⁄₈"
18-24'	³⁄₈"	³⁄₈"	³⁄₈"	¼-³⁄₈"
25-35'	⁷⁄₁₆"	⁷⁄₁₆"	⁷⁄₁₆"	¼-⁷⁄₁₆"
36-45'	½"	½-⁵⁄₈"	⁷⁄₁₆"	⁵⁄₁₆-⁵⁄₈"
46-55'	⁵⁄₈"	⁵⁄₈-¾"	½"	³⁄₈-¾"

Note: It is possible to use lighter than ³⁄₈-inch line on the smaller craft, but thinner lines are hard on the hands. I recommend a minimum diameter of ³⁄₈ inch wherever you may need to give a strong pull.

HALYARDS (Prestretch Dacron)

LENGTH	MAIN	JIB	STAYSAIL	SPINNAKER
10-18'	¼"	¼"	NA	¼"
18-24'	⁵⁄₁₆"	⁵⁄₁₆"	¼"	⁵⁄₁₆"
25-35'	³⁄₈"	³⁄₈"	⁵⁄₁₆"	⁵⁄₁₆"
36-45'	⁷⁄₁₆"	⁷⁄₁₆"	³⁄₈"	³⁄₈"
46-55'	½"	½"	⁷⁄₁₆"	⁷⁄₁₆"

It is useful if the running rigging is color coded, particularly when you have guests or novices aboard. A wide variety of colors is available, and you can have the lines a solid color or white with colored strands running through them. This is especially important if all the sheets and halyards are led aft to the cockpit. Otherwise, with all white line, it can be a frantic guessing game. I suggest using white line for main sheet, main halyard, and reefing gear; white with red insert for port jibsheet; green insert for starboard; yellow for jib halyard; red for spinnaker. It may look a little strange, but it does reduce confusion.

LAZYJACKS

One piece of running rigging that is all too rarely seen is the lazyjack, and I feel this useful gear deserves serious consideration by the cruising sailor. For years, I had only designed lazyjacks onto traditional yachts—schooners, catboats, Friendship sloops, and the like. Then I did a 48-foot performance cruiser for a friend of mine. He and his

MAIN & JIB SHEET LOADS

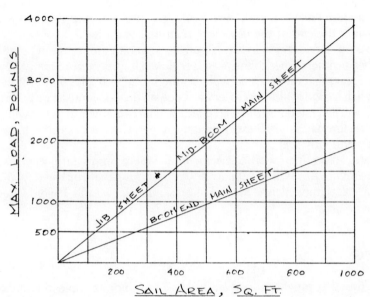

MAX. FORCES EXERTED BY SAILS ON SHEET
LEADS IN WIND SPEED OF 30 KTS.

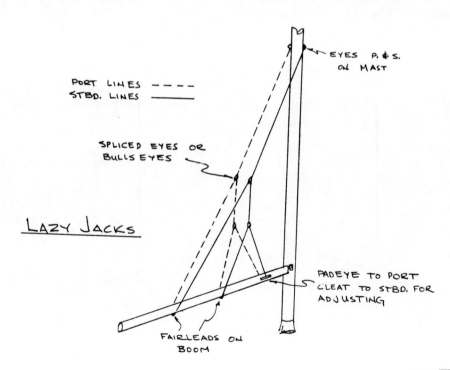

LAZY JACKS

PORT LINES ----
STBD. LINES ——

EYES P. & S.
ON MAST

SPLICED EYES OR
BULLS EYES

PADEYE TO PORT
CLEAT TO STBD. FOR
ADJUSTING

FAIRLEADS ON
BOOM

107 ☐

wife were both elderly and found the mainsail of this large yawl a bit too much to handle by themselves. The answer was a set of lazyjacks. Sure, they slow the yacht by a fraction of a knot when beating to windward, but the convenience when reefing or lowering sail at the end of the day more than makes up for it.

For the uninitiated, lazyjacks are dacron lines running from several points on the boom to a single line, thence to the mast (see sketch for only one of many ways to rig them). The idea is that the lazyjacks will restrain the sail into folds on top of the boom as it is lowered; it cannot blow off to leeward, roll on the deck and get dirty, or fall into the water. Also, when reefing, the reefed area will be contained so that it will not flap around. This eliminates the necessity for tying in pennants or a lace line. It makes the "jiffy" reef a true jiffy reef.

Any craft can be fitted with lazyjacks; I have them on my little yawl. On larger yachts with double-headsail rigs, it may be worth putting them on the staysail as well. They are a great convenience for the shorthanded crew, and I would never sail without them again.

THE VANG

Vangs are lines that provide added control to a spar. For example, the foresail on a gaff rigged schooner might have a vang from the aft end of the gaff to the mainmast so that the sag of the gaff to leeward can be controlled. The most common vang on modern craft is the boom vang. Ordinarily, when the sheets are eased off, the sail will belly and be less effective. However, if the boom is tightly strapped down with a vang, the sail cannot belly, the maximum area is presented to the breeze, and the sail is steadier and gives the maximum drive.

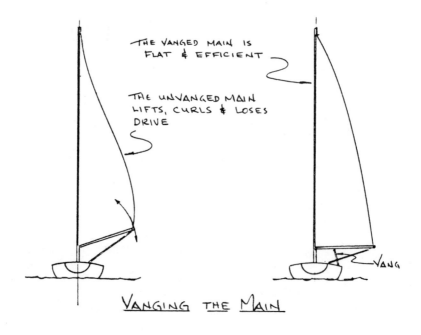

THE VANGED MAIN IS FLAT & EFFICIENT

THE UNVANGED MAIN LIFTS, CURLS & LOSES DRIVE

VANG

VANGING THE MAIN

The most common boom vang is a three- or four-part tackle with snap shackle blocks on each end. One end is snapped onto a bail located on the boom about 25 to 30 percent of its length abaft the mast; the other end snaps onto an eye near the rail or a chainplate, etc. Such a vang must be shifted each time the yacht goes onto the other tack, of course, but while it is in place it does act as a preventer to cut the risk of an accidental jibe.

Alternatively, the lower end of the vang can be fastened to a padeye at the base of the mast. This setup does not give as good a lead and does put a compression load on the boom and gooseneck. Its advantage is that the tackle does not have to be shifted each time the vessel changes tack. With this arrangement, the vang is, more or less, a permanent fixture. And that leads us to vangs made of solid rod with a turnbuckle-type adjustment, or the hydraulic vangs that are standard on so many racing yachts and becoming more common on club racers and other performance types. The hydraulic vangs, in particular, are very powerful and quickly adjusted. Most racers of any size would seem naked without one.

Regardless, whether for a racer or a snooze-and-booze cruiser, the boom vang is an essential piece of gear that will add substantially to performance.

PREVENTERS

Preventers, as the name implies, prevent accidental jibes. The preventer is a single-part line attached to a padeye at the aft end of the boom and led forward to the foredeck where it is cleated. The boom is locked in position by the sheet aft and the preventer forward so an accidental jibe is impossible.

On shorthanded yachts, permanent preventers may be rigged in order to eliminate the need to go forward and switch over with each jibe. Lines will be fastened to the boom end both port and starboard. These lines will be led outside the shrouds to blocks on the foredeck and then run aft to cleats handy to the cockpit. The "lazy" preventer (the one not in use) will have a tendency to get hung up on everything possible so a shock cord rigged to keep it tensioned and out of the way of winches, smokestacks, etc., will pay its freight.

It was mentioned earlier that a vang will act as a preventer, and it will. But the vang is located well forward on the boom, so if the boat rolls and dips her boom end into the sea, you can wind up with a broken boom. The proper preventer, being attached aft on the boom, can prevent broken booms as well as wild jibes and broken skulls.

TOPPING LIFTS

The topping lift is a line fed from the mast to the boom end to support the boom when the sail is furled. The usual topping lift on the modern Bermudan rigged yacht is a light 7 x 19 wire, fixed at the masthead, and with an eye spliced at its lower end. This eye attaches to the boom end with a very light dacron lashing line so that the tension can be adjusted.

Ingenue *shows how a schooner can set a tremendous spread of sail.*

Improvements over this setup can be made by using prestretched dacron line for the topping lift (so there is less chafe on the sails), running it through a block at the boom end to a cleat alongside the boom for easier adjustment. Or, if preferred, the block can be at the masthead and the cleat on the mast near the gooseneck.

On heavy booms, two- or three-part tackles can be rigged to make it easier to top up the boom. On smaller yachts, the topping lift may be just a short wire attached to the backstay with a snap shackle on its lower end that attaches to an eye on the boom end. It is unsnapped just before the sail is hoisted (unless someone forgets to unsnap it, as is often the case) and snapped back on when the sail is lowered. The varieties of topping lifts are only exceeded by those of Heinz catsups.

Then, if you have a solid or hydraulic boom vang, the vang will hold the boom up as well as hold it down so you can dispense with the topping lift completely.

Staysail booms are also good candidates for topping lifts. Indeed, without a topping lift the boom can fall when the sail is lowered and scratch up your expensive Bomar® foredeck hatch. A small block below the staysail stay attachment and a light line will handle the average staysail boom nicely.

SAILHANDLING

On the cruising yacht, the ability to hoist sail quickly and put the boat to bed easily and swiftly after sailing can often mean the difference between taking the boat out for a pleasant evening sail or going to a movie. With many yachts, particularly in the larger sizes, there is so much effort involved in getting the sail cover off, hoisting the main, dragging out a large genoa, hanking it on, and hoisting it (to say nothing of undoing all this work later) that the boat is not used as often as it should be. This is particularly true where the crew consists only of a couple to handle the vessel.

Much of this effort can be avoided with modern sailhandling gear; i.e., roller furling jibs and mainsails. The end result is a yacht that will be sailed more often and will be enjoyable to take out even for an hour or two. Bear in mind that these remarks do not apply to smaller yachts where making sail is no major problem, racing yachts where there is ample crew to handle the job, or ocean voyagers where the sails may be hoisted and, with occasional sail changes, left hoisted for a week or more.

ROLLER FURLING JIBS

The roller furling jib is not new. My history is a little uncertain, but I know that such sails were in use at the turn of the century. These early roller jibs were set on a hollow, split wood roller that was fastened around the headstay and operated in the same manner as our modern furling gears with their grooved aluminum rods. Due to a lack of ball bearing swivels and other modern niceties, the old-time roller jibs were not used on larger craft.

There are several basic roller systems. The simplest has a wire luff sewn into the sail and the sail is wound up around its own luff. The disadvantage of this type is that the wire lacks torsional rigidity so that the top of the sail may lag behind the turning of the furling drum and the bottom part of the sail furl up before the top does. Or when sailing with the system partially furled as a reef, the top of the sail may unwind under the pressure of a strong breeze, and the sail will then set poorly. Another disadvantage is that the yacht must still retain a separate headstay so the furling drum has to be located well abaft the stay or the headstay may wind up with the sail and jam things completely. On the other hand, having the separate headstay allows a storm jib to be hanked on easily if conditions necessitate. These simple roller systems are acceptable on small craft, but on a boat with a jib of over 200 square feet or so, I would consider one of the alternatives.

The heavier duty furling gears, as produced by Hood, Stearns, Hyde, Cruising Design, Famet, and others, use a grooved aluminum rod into which the sail is held by a boltrope. These gears do have the torsional rigidity needed for reefing, although the set of a roller reefed jib is never as good as that of a sail hanked onto the headstay. Still it has proven adequate for the type of coastal cruising that most of us do.

In theory, the large jib can be removed from the grooved rod and a smaller jib sent up in its place. This sounds fine until you realize that by the time you decide to set a smaller jib you will have already rolled up 70 percent of your genoa. Now to set the smaller sail you have to go onto the foredeck in a half gale, unfurl the 140- to 150-percent genoa all the way, get it down and bagged, and then feed the boltrope of the smaller jib into the slot. This is difficult for two people; for one it is virtually impossible as you cannot feed the boltrope and hoist the sail at the same time.

A partial answer is the double-weight sail as pioneered by Herb Hild. This sail has heavier cloth in the foot and leach so that it will hold its shape better as it is reefed. A sensible answer, for the offshore cruiser in particular, is to use the grooved rod system but also to fit a separate headstay, onto which a storm sail can be hanked in an emergency. This may account for the popularity of the cutter rig today as the forestay is a fine place for the storm jib and the genoa can simply be rolled up and ignored.

The sloop without a separate headstay can get by with a special storm jib with a heavy wire luff. This can be set flying alongside or just abaft the furled genoa and, with a strong halyard winch, can be hauled up taut enough to be reasonably effective.

FURLING MAINSAILS

The roller furling mainsail works on the same principle as the jibs, the sail rolling around a grooved rod. This rod can be set just abaft the mast using any of the popular heavy-duty gears or it can be fitted inside the mast, as offered by Hood, Kenyon Spars, Metalmast, etc.

With either system, there is the disadvantage that the mainsail cannot have battens and so it loses its roach area. The rod abaft the mast also loses efficiency as it can sag off to leeward and there is a bit more turbulence due to the gap between the sail and the mast. It is a less costly system than the sail rolled inside the mast, though, and undoubtedly easier to unjam or repair at sea if something does go wrong.

Roller furling mains that stow outside the mast (and all roller jibs, of course) suffer from the necessity of having a shield against ultraviolet rays (Yachtcrillic® or similar material) to protect the dacron sail from the sun. This shield is in the form of a cover sewn onto the leach and foot of the sail, and it tends to make the sail set badly because of the weight and the different stretch characteristic. Also, the heavier cloth does not help the shape of a partly rolled sail.

A new development that looks promising is the Hood roller boom. In this furling system the sail rolls down inside the boom instead of abaft or into the mast. Its advantages are that the main can retain its roach area and battens and needs no ultraviolet guard. Then, as I see it, the system is fail-safe. If anything does jam, you can simply drop the sail and flake it down on top of the boom in the normal fashion. I believe it is the system that I would prefer if I were considering a roller furling main, but I must add that I don't see the point of any main roller system unless the sail is so large that it is just too much effort to take the boat out for an evening sail. Of course, that could be anywhere from 20 to 60 feet, depending on the owner's age, fitness, and enthusiasm.

☐ *112*

The epitome of roller furling: jib, main, mizzen, and mule. Rigged on an Olympic 47 by Hathaway, Reiser and Raymond. Peter Barlow photo.

One other innovation that bears mentioning is the North Zip Stop® system, in which the sail is not rolled but is furled vertically abaft the mast inside a cloth turtle. Again, the sail cannot have battens or roach, but it is less costly than the roller furling inside the spar and is a unique approach to the problem. A similar system is available from North for genoa jibs.

SELF-TENDING STAYSAILS AND JIBS

The jib on a single-headsail sloop and the staysail on a double-headsail sloop or a cutter can be made to be self-tacking, reducing the need to tend sheets when beating to windward in close quarters. There are several ways to achieve a self-tacking headsail, and each has advantages.

The most common setup is to have a club or boom on the foot of the sail. Fitting the forward end of the club to the stay is the simplest and cheapest system, but the sail pressure puts a load on the club in directions that the stay and turnbuckle are not designed to support. A better system is to fit the club to a pedestal attached to the deck abaft the stay. The sail is not held as flat as with the full length club and will take some shape as the sheets are eased. The most common error with this system is to locate the pedestal too far aft; it should not be more than 10 percent of the foot of the sail abaft the stay, or the sail will belly to excess as the sheets are let out, so losing efficiency when reaching.

Rarely seen today except on a few character boats is the club with its forward end fitted on a fore-and-aft rod traveler located on the bowsprit. The club can move forward as the pressure of the wind puts shape into the sail so the sail is never held unduly flat even when sheeted in hard for windward work. This is possibly the most efficient full club setup, but the hardware takes up considerable deck space and is usually only workable where the staysail or jibstay is fitted on a bowsprit.

All full-length clubs require that the sail have a jackline at the lower part of the luff. If this is not fitted, the sail will bind when the halyard is let go, and you have to go forward and unhank the snaps to get it down all the way. Sailmakers are aware of this problem, of course, so they will usually fit the jackline as standard practice if they are advised that the sail is to be self-tending on a club.

Sprit-type clubs have been used to make headsails self-tending also. These run from part way up the luff to the clew of the sail and have the advantage that they also provide a vang effect, preventing the sail from lifting when off the wind. Several types of sprit have been developed, ranging from wishbones to heavy battens inside the sail itself. Berig Sailmakers of Northeast, Pa., offers a Camberspar® jib with a wishbone-type sprit.

The club can be a shin cracker when you are working on the foredeck, though, so a third answer is a partial club, about 30 to 40 percent of the length of the foot of the sail, attached to the sail at the clew and part way along the foot. Being shorter, the club can be of smaller diameter as well and so is much lighter and less likely to cause damage to the crew. Not being held taut as it is with a full length club, the sail can take a better shape when the sheets are eased a bit. It takes considerable experimentation to get the sheet lead just right, though, and my clients have had mixed emotions about this type of jib on the few designs where I've used it. Another problem is that a topping lift is useless with this rig so when you drop the sail the club thumps down on the deck or forehatch and may cause some scratching of the finish.

The short club is not unlike the self-tending jibs with heavy clew battens that are used in some daysailing and racing classes. This type of self-tacking setup can be used on larger yachts but has not proven popular. The sail should be cut fairly low, and this reduces visibility. Moreover, any short club will not hold the sail out when running so it collapses back onto itself and speed is lost unless it is held out with a whisker pole. Indeed, the full-length clubs are no great shakes at keeping the sail trimmed out on a run either as the weight of the club tends to drag the sail back towards the centerline in anything except a half gale. A whisker pole is a definite necessity.

Roller furling has been used on self-tending staysails and jibs, but I have not as yet seen a really workable installation. The problem is that the sheet lead of a headsail alters as the sail is rolled up. With a self-tending jib, the lead is fixed in one place, either at the end of the club or on the track on deck, so that the sail sets poorly in anything but the fully extended position. I suppose there is some advantage in a club jib of being able to roller furl the sail even if you cannot roller reef it as it saves flaking it down on the club and fitting a sail cover when you put her to bed at the end of the cruise.

In sum, self-tending jibs and staysails simplify tacking for the shorthanded crew, but all of them impose problems of their own. One answer that I like is to fit a club jib on a pedestal but cut the sail and fit normal jibsheet tracks so that it can be taken off the club and handled as a regular headsail. This allows a better set and increases efficiency, but you still have the option of switching back to self-tending when you have a long beat to windward in close waters.

TWIN JIBS

Twin jib setups are selected by many blue water voyagers as they have numerous advantages for tradewind sailing. The gear is a bit complex, requiring two sturdy whisker poles, but once set up the operation is simple. Again, there are several variations on the twin jib theme.

One unusual setup is a two-layer jib that acts as a normal genoa when reaching and beating to windward but unfolds to become a twin jib for downwind sailing. This jib is also roller furling and has proven popular with many cruising yachtsmen as it is a good multipurpose sail that can handle a wide variety of wind directions and conditions.

Frederick Fenger and George Gill developed and perfected the twin jib rig named after them. This rig uses two identical jibs that are set flying and tacked three to four percent of their hoist forward of the mast and the same distance port and starboard of the centerline of the yacht. When the twins are hoisted, the after guy is trimmed so that the whisker poles are angled 23 degrees forward of athwartships. A complete description of the setup and hardware is available in the Amateur Yacht Research Society book, *Self Steering*. I have set up this twin rig on several of my designs and admire its simplicity of handling. The owners have reported favorably on it as well. One point in its favor is that the twin jibs are sails of normal cut and can be used as regular high-cut Yankee jibs for windward sailing.

The rig provides self-steering on a downwind course and for a small crew is much more easily handled and much safer than the unseamanlike spinnaker. One enthusiastic owner reported to me that on a voyage to Tahiti from the canal he had not had to touch the helm for a week and was making a steady seven knots or better. I know that if I ever equip a yacht for a long voyage in the trades it will have a Fenger-Gill twin jib rig aboard.

CRUISING SPINNAKERS

These sails started to become popular a few years ago as cruising yachtsmen tired of the problems of the conventional spinnaker. Essentially, the cruising spinnaker is a lightweight, full-cut sail that attaches to the stem fitting at the tack in the normal manner and may have its clew wung out by a spinnaker or whisker pole when the wind is abaft the beam. It is, in effect, a half of a racing spinnaker and is reminiscent of the original spinnakers of the early 1900s.

It is easier to set and handle than a conventional spinnaker and much safer for a small crew. Most sailmakers have their own version of this sail, some with leach, luff, and foot drawstrings so that the shape of the sail can be adjusted for various conditions. Several sailmakers also offer "squeezers," a long cloth tube that holds the sail folded vertically. The sail is hoisted in the tube (nothing to run wild that way), and then the tube is hoisted to release the sail. Dowsing the sail is accomplished by pulling the tube down again, and then the whole thing is lowered to the deck. Simple and safe.

The cruising spinnaker is a more versatile sail for the coastal yachtsman than twin sails. It is less effective than a true spinnaker, of course, but the ease of handling ensures that it will be used more often, and this alone may increase the average speeds on a cruise. I consider the standard 180-percent racing spinnaker a rather dangerous and unseamanlike sail that is inappropriate on a cruising yacht. Its only excuse for being is the speed that it gives to the otherwise moderate downwind performance of the Bermudan rig.

In case the reader may think I am speaking from prejudice rather than experience I will add that I was on the foredeck of Bill Luders's *Storm* for six years and on an 8-meter sloop for two years before that. I've sailed Bermuda, SORC, two Trans-Pacs, and more East Coast races than I can count. I didn't like spinnakers then, and I guess I never will. For racing they are necessary (as long as everyone else has them), but I will never put one on any cruiser that I own.

6

AUXILIARY ENGINES

Having explored the rig and sails in some detail, it is only fair that we give some consideration to the poor, despised engine hiding somewhere in the bilges. Auxiliary engines have always posed a problem in sailboat design. Most owners want maximum speeds under both power and sail, but the two requirements are very much in conflict. Under sail we want a small aperture and a smaller, narrow blade propeller, or even a folding propeller, in order to keep resistance to a minimum. Unfortunately, for maximum performance under power we require a large diameter, three-bladed propeller. The two needs are completely opposed.

The following chart (based on data accumulated by John Thornycroft) shows the power required for various sized auxiliaries at various speeds. It assumes an effective propeller, not some narrow, folding gizmo with 20 percent or less efficiency.

Note that weight is not nearly so critical to performance as is speed. Doubling the displacement increases the power requirement by about 50 percent, but adding two knots to the speed can increase the power needed by several hundred percent. Of course, the table is only a rough guide. Even identical yachts with identical engines may vary greatly in speed due to trim, loading, bottom smoothness, etc.

Enough cannot be said about the efficiency of a large diameter, slow turning propeller either. One of my designs, a 40-foot-waterline 48,000-pound displacement schooner manages to cruise nicely at 6.5 knots with only a 30-bhp engine, but the engine is geared down to turn a 25-inch propeller and so is operating at near peak efficiency. Too many yachts have very inefficient installations with high-speed

BRAKE HORSEPOWER (BHP) REQUIRED FOR SPEEDS AS SHOWN

LWL	TONS DISP.	5 KNOTS	6 KNOTS	7 KNOTS	8 KNOTS	9 KNOTS
20 feet	.5	1.0	1.7			
	1.0	1.8	3.6			
	1.5	2.6	5.7			
	2	3.1	8.0			
	3	3.7	12.0			
		(1.12)	(1.34)			
25 feet	2	2.4	5			
	3	3.0	6.5			
	4	4.0	8.7			
	5	5.0	12.0			
		(1.0)	(1.2)			
30 feet	2	1.9	3.6	6.4		
	3	2.5	5	9.7		
	4	3.0	6.4	13		
	5	3.3	7.7	16		
	6	3.5	8.8	19		
	8	4.0	11	26		
		(.91)	(1.1)	(1.28)		
40 feet	4	2.8	5.2	8.5	13	
	6	3.5	7.0	12	25	
	8	4.0	8.4	15	26	
	10	4.4	9.9	18	33	
	12	4.6	11	21	40	
	14	5.0	12	24	46	
	16	5.2	13	27	53	
	18	5.6	14	30	59	
	20	5.9	14	33	66	
		(.80)	(.95)	(1.11)	(1.26)	
50 feet	8	4.1	7.2	13	19	28
	10	4.6	7.9	15	23	35
	12	5.0	8.8	17	27	42
	14	5.3	9.6	20	30	49
	16	5.6	10	11	34	56
	18	5.8	11	23	38	63
	20	6.0	12	25	41	70
	25	6.5	13	30	50	87
	30	7.0	14	34	57	105
		(.71)	(.85)	(.99)	(1.13)	(1.27)

- Power requirements are expressed in bhp with allowance for engine and shafting losses of approximately 15 percent.
- Propeller efficiency taken at .58. Narrow, two-blade propellers will develop an efficiency of only .35 or thereabouts, so these figures must be increased by about 60 percent for such installations.
- Hull must be of correct form for indicated speed.
- Figures in parentheses are speed/length ratio.

engines, reduction gears that do not reduce enough, and little egg beater propellers that operate above the limits of tip speed and blade pressure. Then the owner complains that the boat does not perform well under power.

Speaking of horsepower, there are several ways to measure it. Brake horsepower (bhp) is the power put out by the engine less the gearbox and may be measured by the SAE (U.S.) or DIN (German) method, the latter being a bit more conservative. Then we have shaft horsepower (shp), which is the output at the shaft abaft the gearbox. As well, every engine should have three power ratings: maximum—the absolute top power output, which the engine cannot maintain for more than a couple of minutes without blowing up; intermittent—the power that an engine can maintain for a given period, usually 30 or 60 minutes; continuous—the power that the engine can put out for long periods of time without developing problems. Only the continuous bhp (or shp) is of interest to the sailor.

Adding to the confusion is the fact that different engine manufacturers may provide different figures for two engines built on the same block. One might claim 50 bhp at 4,000 rpm; another, 40 bhp at 3,000 rpm. Both figures may be true, one maximum and the other intermittent, but if this is not apparent from the brochure then the figures are of little use. Indeed, the continuous rating might be down to 30 to 32 bhp at 2,400 rpm, and that is the rating we need to know as it is the useful power of the engine.

Perhaps a better guide to engine size selection than bhp is cubic inches of engine displacement (the total volume of air displaced by the pistons) per ton of hull displacement. The engine capacity is always readily available from the manufacturer. The following is a guide to engine selection based on the displacement of the yacht.

Power Rating	Yacht Type	Displacement
Light	Blue water cruisers and racing yachts	5- 8 cubic inches per ton
Moderate	Coastal cruisers	8-11
Generous	Heavily powered auxiliaries	12-15
High	Motorsailers	15-20

This is only a general guide, of course. As we have learned, a modern fin keel yacht with its long waterline and low wetted surface will have less drag than a short waterline, full-keel yacht of the same displacement so the power requirement must be modified to suit.

ENGINE INSTALLATION

There are a number of items that must be considered in a good engine installation.

ACCESS

Access for servicing—can you get at the fuel and oil filters, the oil and water filters, the oil dipstick, the gearbox dipstick and filler, the stuffing box? Access for repairs—can you get at the injectors? remove the head without removing the engine? remove the engine without taking the boat apart?

INSULATION

Diesel engines are noisy and tend to vibrate, although the higher rpm and multicylinders of modern engines have reduced vibration substantially. To combat noise and vibration (and it can be very tiring on a long run), the engine must be flexibly mounted on sturdy beds and the engine space well insulated, preferably with a foam that has a thin lead or solid vinyl core. The foam reduces certain types of sound vibrations while the heavier density core tackles those that sneak by the foam.

FILTRATION

The fuel filters on modern diesel engines are basically secondary filters so a good primary filter is needed between the tank and the engine. This filter should have the capacity to handle considerable dirt and water as these spell death to the fuel injectors of the modern diesel. Dual filters are advantageous and should be rigged so that the engine can continue to operate while one filter is plugged or being changed.

VENTILATION

Although the U.S. Coast Guard does not have ventilation rules for diesels as they do for gasoline engines, every engine needs large quantities of air to operate efficiently, making good ventilation a necessity. This should take the form of two vents of ample size; one ducted to below the engine and the other ducted to high in the engine compartment. A blower is not essential on a diesel, but it is handy to get rid of heat and fumes after a long run in warm weather.

COOLING

Most modern high-speed diesels are designed to be freshwater cooled due to their high operating temperature. A few engines intended for raw water cooling have large water passages and run at low enough temperatures that salt build-up is not a problem, but the freshwater cooled engine has its advantages. The higher temperatures make the operation of a hot water heater more efficient, and the enclosed freshwater system can have antifreeze added for cold weather and to prevent corrosion in the block. Generally, the freshwater cooled engine with heat exchanger is to be preferred for average use and will have a longer useful life.

☐ *120*

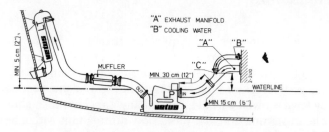

Exhaust system with waterinjectionpoint "C" 15 cm (6") or more above the waterline.

Water lift muffler systems. Courtesy W.H. Den Ouden (USA), Inc.

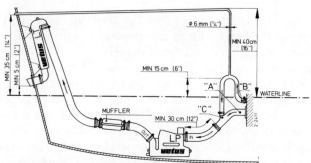

Exhaust system with waterinjectionpoint "C" below or less than 15 cm (6") above the waterline.

EXHAUST

Modern exhaust systems employ a "water-lift" muffler; all the engine salt water is fed into the exhaust line just abaft the engine and then goes into the muffler where the pressure of the exhaust gas forces it overboard. In the older water jacketed systems the exhaust line was a double-wall metal tube with the exhaust gas inside the inner tube, the cooling water in the outer. The system was costly as it had to be custom-made for each yacht and was prone to leaks. The water-lift setup is much cheaper to install, simpler to maintain, and quieter. Correct installation is a necessity, of course. The water-lift muffler must be located well below the engine manifold, and a siphon break must be fitted in the cooling water line well above the waterline, between the engine and the point where the water enters the exhaust pipe.

HAND STARTING

Many smaller engines are offered with hand starting as a standard or optional feature. It can work, but with high-compression diesels you must have a compression release to allow the engine to turn over, and it must be situated so that the person cranking can reach it handily. If it is not conveniently located, hand starting becomes a two-man job. Also, there must be ample space around the engine to swing the crank without barking your knuckles. Finally, the engine must be small enough. Since I can barely start my lawn mower, I would rule out any diesel of much above 15 bhp as a candidate for hand starting unless it was a slow turning unit with a heavy flywheel, such as the Sabb engines.

SAIL DRIVES

Sail drives, in which the engine drives directly down through a shaft to a propeller gear box (similar to the lower unit of an outboard motor), are offered by several manufacturers in both gasoline and diesel models.

OMC (Johnson and Evinrude) manufactures a 15-bhp, electric start, two-stroke gasoline unit that is neat and light, at just under 100 pounds. It is a good choice for auxiliaries under 30 feet and for light-displacement craft of even larger size. My own boat is driven by a 7-5-hp Volvo Penta sail drive powered by a four-stroke Honda engine. It is geared down to swing a 12-inch, two-blade propeller and is an easy starting and strong unit that can drive my one-ton boat at five knots on half throttle. Several diesel manufacturers (Bukh, Farymann, Volvo Penta, etc.) also offer sail drives in the 7-to-20-hp range, and these are suitable for yachts from 24 to 40 feet or so, depending on displacement.

The sail drive units are fairly simple to install; they eliminate the need for shaft, strut, and stuffing box; and are generally well suited as auxiliary power. The disadvantages are the somewhat bulky lower unit, which increases drag, the limited propeller selection available on some models, and the fact that most, perhaps all, are raw water cooled. Also, the aluminum lower unit is not the most compatible metal for some forms of construction, e.g., bronze fastened wood hulls. Further development in sail drive units is possible, so we may see them become more popular.

OUTBOARD MOTORS

Many sail cruisers, up to 28 to 30 feet or more, are outboard powered. The main advantages are low initial cost, ease of taking the motor to a shop for repair, and light weight; also, depending on installation, the unit may be lifted or removed to reduce drag under sail. The disadvantages are that most outboards are geared high for powering small fishing skiffs and so swing a small and inefficient propeller. Then if the engine is mounted on a stern bracket its weight is too far aft and affects sailing

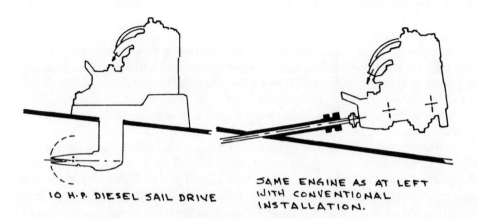

10 H.P. DIESEL SAIL DRIVE

SAME ENGINE AS AT LEFT WITH CONVENTIONAL INSTALLATION.

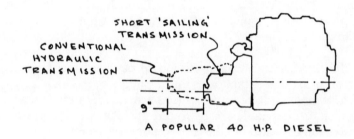

SHORT 'SAILING' TRANSMISSION

CONVENTIONAL HYDRAULIC TRANSMISSION

9"

A POPULAR 40 H.P. DIESEL

SAME 40 H.P. DIESEL WITH HYDRAULIC VEE DRIVE TRANSMISSION.

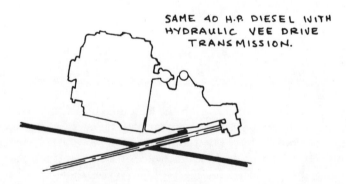

performance, the prop lifts out and races in a seaway, can drown out in heavy following seas, is hard to reach for maintenance, looks ugly, and is easy to steal. On top of that, many outboards exhaust through the propeller hub, so in reverse, the prop works in exhaust gas to some degree, and the thrust in reverse is reduced accordingly, by as much as 50 percent. It can make docking a tricky maneuver with a heavy yacht, sometimes terrifyingly tricky in adverse wind or current.

I much prefer to see the outboard mounted in a proper well where it is accessible for maintenance and is not prone to lift its prop out or drown in a seaway or spoil the appearance of the yacht. A well should have the hull opening just large enough to pass the lower unit and prop with a minimum of clearance. Where space permits, it is best to arrange things so the motor can be tilted up and the well closed off completely when sailing, but this takes up additional length and is not always feasible.

Outboards for auxiliary power should not be the high-speed type intended for runabouts. Rather, they should be geared down to turn a larger propeller at reasonable rpm for low-speed efficiency. An alternator is desirable for battery charging as well, and electric start is handy. OMC, Seagull, and Honda build suitable units for auxiliary use. It should be noted that the older Seagulls use a high oil/fuel ratio and so tend to be smoky and, if installed in a well, will suffocate from their own exhaust unless the well is thoroughly ventilated. Chrysler outboards have been designed specifically for auxiliary use and are geared down to a lower rpm so that they can swing a larger propeller. It is interesting to note that a 6-hp Chrysler swings a 10½-inch wheel while a 9.9-hp Mercury only turns a 8½-inch prop. Both engines develop the same forward thrust despite the 50 percent greater horsepower of the Mercury. (See *Cruising World*, June 1984, for information on outboard auxiliary power).

Most outboard driven auxiliary yachts use standard outboard fuel tanks in a cockpit locker sealed off so that fumes cannot get into the hull proper. This is fine, but one tank is not sufficient for extended cruising, especially in remote areas, as you can easily use up its six gallons in one windless day if you are bucking tides. I feel that one tank is fine for the racer and daysailer, but the cruiser should have provision for two, or even one large built-in tank. Outboards of the two-stroke model are unusually thirsty little beasts so six gallons of fuel will not take you too far. An extra tank of fuel can save the day.

PROPELLERS

A two-blade folding propeller gives the least drag under sail, and a three-blade solid prop provides the most efficiency under power. Several compromises are available for the owner looking for the best combination of powering efficiency and reasonable drag. A fixed, narrow blade, IOR-type wheel in a two- or three-blade model will give much more power than a folding prop in reverse and somewhat more efficiency ahead and will reduce resistance under sail compared to a typically fat, three-bladed auxiliary prop.

The costliest but best all-around installation is a feathering propeller in either a two- or three-blade model, as produced by Luke in the U.S. or Maxi-Prop in Italy. These props have large blade areas for powering, but the blades twist on their base to line up with the water flow when under sail and so reduce drag almost to that of a folding prop. Unlike the folding prop, the feathering wheel gives good stopping power in reverse. The best of both worlds—but of course, at a price. The feathering wheels may have another advantage when used in an aperture as a two-blade prop can be lined up behind the hull and, when feathered, will help reduce water flow and turbulence through the aperture.

Usually seen only on larger yachts and motorsailers is the variable pitch propeller, in which the pitch of the blades can be adjusted while underway for best powering efficiency and, in some models, lined up to feather under sail. The cost is substantial, of course, and involves an expensive retrofit unless installed as original equipment. The husky Sabb diesels are available with a variable pitch prop setup and are worthy of consideration for a new installation on yachts of heavy displacement. I have fitted 30-hp Sabbs to several cruisers in the 40-to-45-foot and 20-ton-displacement range and obtained seven knots due to the efficiency of the slow turning, large diameter wheel.

Barring the price of a feathering or variable pitch prop, the yacht with an aperture might be fitted with a four-blade, narrow-style wheel. Two blades can be lined up behind the hull, the other two exposed but presenting less blade area to create resistance than the two exposed blades of a fat three-blade wheel. Yet under power, the four narrow blades will have almost the same area as a typical three-bladed prop and so will be quite efficient. It is a fairly good compromise for the cruising sailor. Three-blade folding propellers are now offered by at least one manufacturer and would be a good solution, particularly for yachts with the propeller exposed on a strut.

FUEL TANKS

Fuel tanks for diesel engines are generally of "black iron" sheet. If the tank is kept well painted on the outside, the fuel oil will protect the inside, and such tanks will give satisfactory service for many years. Stainless steel tanks are to be avoided; the metal can develop pinholes since it is subject to crevice corrosion. Stainless steel needs oxygen to remain stainless, and where it is deprived of oxygen, as in the folded and welded seams of tanks, it will deteriorate in time.

I prefer fuel tanks of a high-magnesium-content aluminum alloy, such as 5083 or 5086, or fiberglass. These should last the life of the yacht if properly built. In aluminum yachts, the tanks are usually built in, using the hull plate as one side of the tank. One of my designs, built in 1967, has had no problems since that time, a reasonable sign of integrity.

Monel is another ideal material for tanks but is rarely used due to its high cost. Still, in relation to the total cost of a fine yacht, the price of the monel is a small item and well worth its cost in longevity. Galvanized steel tanks are acceptable for gasoline but are a no-no with diesel fuel. The galvanizing will flake off and clog the injectors in a very short time.

Fuel capacity is always a design problem. The designer would prefer to have small tanks that can be removed easily for repair or replacement. The builder wants to advertise a large cruising range under power, and the owners seem to demand this feature for some reason, so we wind up with tanks so large they cannot be removed

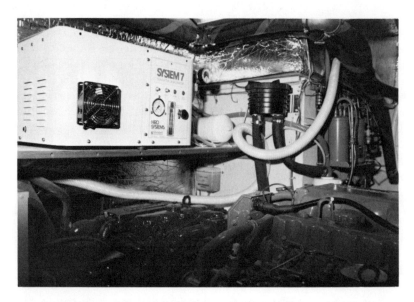

This busy engine room is replete with water maker, auxiliary generator set, and a maze of wiring and piping.

without tearing the boat apart. Long range wins out, yet how many owners actually run a solid 48 hours without refueling?

A reasonable solution, and one that is becoming more popular, is the collapsible tank of PVC or similar plastic. The tanks will not have quite the capacity of a solid tank in any given location but can be larger than "replaceable" tanks as they can be folded when empty to fit through locker openings, hatches, etc. Another advantage of these tanks is that they do not need a breather vent, and this eliminates a major source of sea water polluting the fuel, a prime source of diesel engine malfunction. Indeed, on one trip to Bermuda we spent four days without engine and eventually without electricity, radio, and other niceties of life, all due to water getting into the fuel through the tank vent in rough seas.

It is desirable that a smooth cradle be made to support these collapsible tanks as they are subject to chafe and puncture, and they must be strongly fastened in place so they cannot shift in a seaway. Bear in mind that a 50-gallon fuel tank will weigh about 350 pounds, and you can imagine the havoc if it tore loose from its mountings in rough weather. The same applies to solid metal or fiberglass tanks, of course; they may chafe and puncture to a lesser degree, perhaps, but it can still be a problem. A solid mounting is an absolute necessity.

INSTRUMENTS

Most engines come with a standard instrument panel that has a tachometer to indicate rpm and either gauges or "idiot" lights for oil pressure, water temperature, and battery charging. Gauges are much to be preferred as they will indicate problems before they develop into major repairs. They should be lighted for night use with red lighting and a dimmer switch.

Also highly desirable is an audible alarm that will sound a loud buzzer or horn in case of low oil pressure, high water temperature, lack of cooling water in the exhaust system, or lack of battery charging. The helmsman has other things to do and cannot always keep an eye on the engine instruments. The audible alarm can keep a minor repair from developing into a major overhaul.

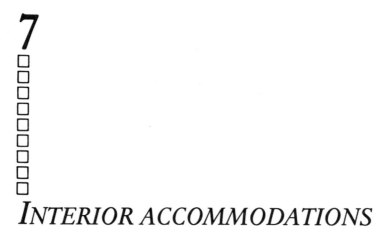

INTERIOR ACCOMMODATIONS

Largely due to Madison Avenue advertising, most cruising yachts have too many berths. They would be better boats for any service (except perhaps chartering to a school band) if one or two berths were given over to a larger galley, a stall shower, added bureaus, a wet locker, or any of the other amenities that make cruising more pleasurable. One of the problems with too many berths is that it tempts you to take too many people on a cruise, and that can sour you on cruising forever.

Generally, one berth for every 6 feet of length is the maximum that can be fitted without sacrificing other desirable features. One berth for every 7 feet is better, and even this may be stretching it for smaller yachts. How many 24- or 25-footers have you seen with four or five berths but no decent head compartment, a minimal galley fit only for making sandwiches, no wet locker, no decent hanging locker, and the cockpit locker space given over to unnecessary quarter berths? Sure, you can cruise four or five people aboard such a boat, but would you want to?

Even the smallest cruisers require certain amenities if they are to be comfortable for more than a weekend, and the smaller the cruiser the more attention that should be paid to comfort and the less given to the number of berths.

THE GALLEY

I have raced over 11 days at sea on a yacht where every meal was a gourmet's delight (avocado salad, roast beef and Yorkshire pudding, vegetables, French bread, fresh baked pies, all washed down with good wine, and that in a 40-knot gale), but that is not essential. Nice, but not essential! What is necessary is that the galley be set up to provide solid, hearty meals in any reasonable weather, reasonable for the size of the boat, that is. You can't expect the cook in a 22-footer to turn out the same quality of food as the cook in a 50-footer, particularly when it's blowing a half a gale outside.

Regardless, reasonable food requires a decent stove on gimbles (one burner on a small boat perhaps, but two is better), a decent-sized sink (7" deep x 10" x 13"), some counter space, and adequate stowage for dishes, utensils, pots and pans, canned goods, cleaning materials, and what-have-you in several drawers, lockers, and racks, plus room for a portable or built-in ice chest. A small, fixed stove, a shallow, round basin, and one or two small lockers is not good enough for serious cruising, even in a 20-footer. Your appetite does not diminish with the size of the boat.

As boat size increases, we can look for a stove with oven, perhaps three or four burners in the over-30-foot size, more stowage, a good trash container, double sinks, and a large, built-in ice chest or electric refrigerator/freezer where the yacht has ample power.

On yachts with standing headroom, the galley counter should be 36 to 38 inches above the sole. On boats with sitting headroom only, a counter top about 12 inches above settee height seems to work well. Ideally, the galley should be arranged so that the chef does not have to stand in line athwartship with the stove in case of scalding spills. Failing that, the cook should wear foul-weather gear in heavy weather as protection against scalds and burns. A barrier rail to keep the cook from being thrown onto the stove in a seaway is very desirable. A safety harness of heavy webbing is fitted to many yachts, but its actual safety is open to question since it may restrain the chef in an emergency and ensure a bad scald from a spill that might otherwise be avoided by a quick hop to one side.

Stove fuel is always a subject for personal opinion. Propane, kerosene, and alcohol have all worked well for me if the burners are clean and properly maintained. Even Sterno® can be a good fuel on small boats in a proper stove, and I regret that the old two-burner Sterno® stove with flame control is no longer made. At the moment I'm using a Swedish Origo® alcohol stove, and I'm very pleased with its performance. Unlike the pressurized alcohol stoves, it needs no preheating and cannot flare up yet still boils a coffee pot full of water in six or seven minutes. A model with oven is now available and would be a good choice for the average 28- to 33-footer.

Alcohol has the advantage that its flame can be put out with water; a very useful safety factor if a pressurized stove flares up on you. Its disadvantage is that it is the most costly fuel and slower than most other fuels (except Sterno®). As well, many people cannot stand its odor. Kerosene is cheaper than alcohol and burns hotter but needs a primer fuel, usually alcohol, to get the stove going. It tends to blacken pots, and the smell of kerosene is not going to win any awards either. Still it is readily available around the world and is the choice of most experienced deep water sailors.

Owners of larger yachts will choose propane as a rule, and I have not heard of many problems, certainly not of any horrendous explosions, if the tanks, line, and stove are properly installed. The tanks must be situated in a compartment that is air-tight to the hull, the lines protected against chafe, and proper valves fitted so that gas cannot leak into the hull proper, including a solenoid switch at the stove that will turn off the valve at the tank. The fuel burns hot, requires no priming, of course, and is widely available.

Compressed natural gas (CNG) is becoming popular as, unlike propane, it is lighter than air and so will rise and dissipate into the air, reducing the chance of explosion. The fuel has not been widely available, but the number of U.S. outlets is increasing, and the coastal cruiser should have no problem obtaining supplies. It would not be a good choice for an ocean voyager as it is difficult to find outside of North America. Although safer than propane, proper installation is a necessity. CNG is a combustible gas, and it is dangerous if handled carelessly.

Diesel stoves have long been favorites in the Northwest as the constant heat is a great blessing in a cool, damp clime. Since a stovepipe is a necessity with a diesel stove, it is not suitable for gimbles, but the stoves have high rails and spills are rare. It is essential that the nongimbled stove be located where spills will not burn the cook, of course. It must be installed so that the cook will stand forward or abaft of the stove, never inboard of it. Diesel fuel burns very hot and is both cheap and available. Still I would not recommend such a stove for any yacht heading for the tropics as it could raise the cabin temperature to an uncomfortable degree in hot weather.

Regardless of the stove type or fuel chosen, it is always nice to have an old, faithful Sea Swing® hung on the bulkhead with a few cans of Sterno® in the locker. The Sea Swing® takes up little space and is handy for keeping a coffee pot on those long night watches. On a small boat it is also a welcome third burner for that rare gourmet dinner when you are trying to impress your guests.

Sinks must be deep for obvious reasons and located as close to the centerline as possible so that they will drain on either tack. If a pressure water system is fitted, an auxiliary hand or foot pump is a must. It can save unbolting the tank top and scooping the water out with a pan, as I had to do on one trip to Bermuda when the batteries went flat. A second manual pump to bring in salt water (or fresh water if you are a Great Lakes sailor) for cooking is also useful as it will save substantially on the supply in the tanks.

Hot water for the galley and shower is supplied from a heater operating off the engine cooling water. Hot jacket water from the engine circulates through coils in a tank and heats the water. The tank is insulated so that running the engine for an hour or so in the morning and evening (necessary to charge the batteries in any case) will heat ample water for dishwashing and showers for several hours. The heater may also have a 110-VAC electric element for use dockside or if the boat has a generator. The hot water heater does take up considerable space (the average tank is over a foot in diameter and several feet long), and obviously, it cannot be used with outboard motors; thus, it is rarely seen on boats under 28 or 30 feet.

Some method of keeping the beer cold and the meats and veggies fresh is essential, of course. On very small craft, up to 24 feet or so, a portable ice chest does the job nicely. On larger yachts, the ice chest will be built in with a fiberglass or metal interior. Insulation should be polyurethane foam (not styrofoam), three inches thick at the very minimum; four inches is better if the ice is to last any length of time. The box should not drain to the bilge as the impurities in the ice can create an unpleasant

The gourmet galley features microwave oven, three-burner gas range with oven, and ice maker (Whitby 55).

odor after a while. It is best if the box drains into a removable container that can be emptied overboard occasionally.

Electric refrigeration is available from many manufacturers in a variety of models. One point I would make is that the machine should be the same voltage as the ship's power. Certainly, a 110-VAC unit or an engine driven unit is more efficient, but it means that the boat cannot be left at a mooring for a day or two when you are cruising unless you can arrange for someone to come aboard and start the engine or generator every day. This is not the height of convenience.

If the yacht is large enough to warrant an electric refrigerator then it is certainly large enough to have an inboard engine that can handle a husky alternator to charge the batteries and large enough to have sufficient battery capacity to run the refrigerator for 24 to 48 hours. Failing this, I would rather have a large, well-insulated ice box as at least it does not tie you to the boat unnecessarily when you would like to do some sightseeing.

SETTEES AND BERTHS

I've already spoken my mind about excess berths on a cruiser so I will go on to my other pet peeve—quarter berths. The quarter berth is almost standard on modern cruisers; indeed, some yachts have two of the things. The problem with quarter berths is that they take up valuable cockpit locker space and leave you with no place to store the crab traps, spare sails, diving gear, stern anchor, fenders, and the zillion other items that are best stored in cockpit lockers. This is particularly true on smaller yachts where cockpit storage is already at a premium because part of the space is taken up with an outboard fuel tank bin.

Quarter berths should be limited to larger yachts where they make a good sea berth for the off-watch crew and where the cockpit is large enough that there is still adequate stowage despite the quarter berth taking up its large chunk of useful space.

Nor am I fond of convertible dinette tables. Most make poor berths and worse tables as they are too often flimsy, hard to set up, and prone to collapse at the most inopportune moment. Solid, good quality hardware for convertible dinettes is available from Zwaardis in Holland but few production boatbuilders take advantage of that fact. The table fiddles should be removable for greater comfort, and the top should lock solidly in position when it is lowered. The dinette generally makes a double berth and so is not useful at sea unless provision is made for a strong lee cloth on the centerline of the berth to keep the sleepers apart when the boat heels.

The standard cabin settee makes an excellent berth if it is at least 22 inches wide; 24 to 26 inches is better. However, these widths are a bit much for comfortable sitting so a back rest is needed. Most designers (I'm guilty, too) forget that the back rest has to be removed and stored somewhere when the settee is used as a berth. A shock cord or velcro-and-webbing sling from the cabin overhead would be very handy and much preferable to the wet cabin sole.

Rarely seen today is the pullman-type pipe berth, yet it is even better than the usual settee. The berth is an aluminum pipe frame with a dacron bottom laced in. It folds down over the settee when in use and during the day swings up to form the seat back. The advantages are numerous: The berth can be triced up level when the boat is heeled under sail; the dacron bottom conforms to the human figure and is very comfortable, almost like a hammock; bedding can be stowed outboard of the berth to provide seat back cushioning; it can be used without a mattress and so is cooler in hot weather; and with a thin foam pad, it is warm when required. There is always a better idea, of course: A client recently suggested making the laced-in bottom of two layers of dacron cloth with a layer of one-inch foam in the middle to get both cushioning and insulation in the one package. It sounds like a winner.

Although I have not seen it done, it would not be difficult to fit two sets of hooks, low and high. Then the pipe berth could be set on the top hooks and used as an upper berth over the settee when you needed space to sleep four. The lower set of hooks would be used for the normal pullman position, of course.

The Root berth is another canvas bottom berth, but its outboard edge is lashed to eyes on the hull and its inboard edge has a metal pipe or wood rod sewn into it that sets into racks fastened to the bulkheads at each end of the berth. The racks have several positions so that the berth can be stretched taut or allowed to sag, somewhat like a hammock. When stowed away, the Root berth takes almost no space, and it makes a fine upper berth when extra sleeping accommodation is needed.

Pilot berths are the best of all at sea. The pilot berth is outboard of the settee and

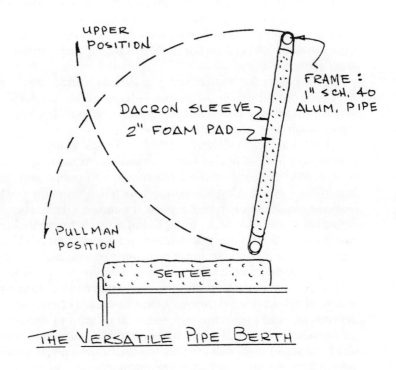

UPPER POSITION

FRAME:
1" SCH. 40
ALUM. PIPE

DACRON SLEEVE
2" FOAM PAD

PULLMAN POSITION

SETTEE

THE VERSATILE PIPE BERTH

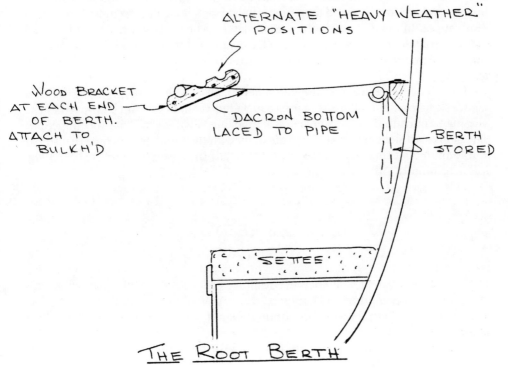

ALTERNATE "HEAVY WEATHER" POSITIONS

WOOD BRACKET AT EACH END OF BERTH. ATTACH TO BULKH'D

DACRON BOTTOM LACED TO PIPE

BERTH STORED

SETTEE

THE ROOT BERTH

133 □

usually raised just enough that the settee back makes a built-in lee board. Being in the saloon, it is located more or less amidships where the motion is least, and the sleeper is out of the way of traffic and secure in a snug bunk. There is a tradeoff as always, since fitting a pilot berth means the loss of a great deal of useful locker and bookshelf space outboard of the settee.

While I like pilot berths, I still feel that the average boat already has too much sleeping accommodation and that the space taken by the pilot berth is best given over to storage. There are always exceptions when that extra berth is vital, and I would take a pilot berth over a quarter berth any day.

The forward cabin is always a problem. For sea-going yachts, it is best if the space is made into a workshop/sail bin combination as the motion so far forward is not conducive to sleeping comfort. For coastal yachts that will spend most nights in harbor, the forward cabin is practical, but then the question is whether to fit two vee berths or one double. For most owners, my choice is the vee berths as they are readily converted to a double when needed and form two separate berths when you have two guests of the same sex aboard, or two argumentative children.

If the boat is to be used almost exclusively by a couple with only occasional guests (who can be stuck in the saloon settees), then the double berth makes sense. It will allow more storage space in a vanity on one side. Such a setup can make a cozy cabin with reasonable privacy. Obviously, the choice of vee berths or double berth forward depends on your preference and where you intend to sleep yourself.

Speaking of double berths, a usable double is four feet wide at the shoulders. Too often you see 40-inch-wide berths advertised as doubles, but they are only for loving couples and too close for comfort in warm weather. Athwartship double berths are fine for yachts that will spend their nights in harbor but are not the most convenient setup at sea. In any case, a double berth that is to be used at sea should have the mattress split down the center so that a lee board or cloth can be set up to keep the sleepers apart; otherwise, a good night's sleep is impossible when the yacht is beating to windward.

To sum up, there are several types of berths, all of which will give a comfortable night's sleep to a tired sailor after a long day on the water. But do not be swayed by the salesman's pitch that the new boat you are looking at will sleep X number of people. The number of sleeping spaces has little to do with the number of people that a boat will accommodate in comfort; too often it is exactly the reverse—the more berths, the less accommodation.

THE HEAD

Unless you are a fan of L. Francis Herreshoff's cedar bucket, your boat will have a W.C. tucked away somewhere. Except on the very smallest boats, under 22 feet or so, there should be space for a private compartment if one of the unnecessary berths is eliminated.

The width needed for a usable head is 24 inches, although 23 inches is just

1. Vetus flexible waste tank
2. water inlet for toilet
3. Two tank connections 1½" for 38 mm I.D. hose (these are supplied with the tank)
4. Valve with skin fitting and hose adapter 1½" for 38 mm I.D. hose
5. Hose 38 mm I.D.

6. Tank fitting 9/16" for 14 mm I.D. hose (supplied with the tank)
7. Air breather nipple 9/16" (14 mm I.D.).
8. Hose 14 mm I.D.
9. Pump
10. T-piece to prevent syphoning
11. Through deck waste fitting 1½" for 38 mm I.D. hose

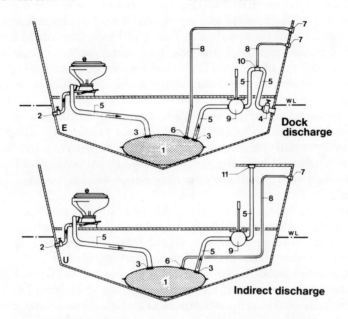

Two systems for holding tanks. A Y-valve at the W.C. will allow direct overboard discharge offshore. Courtesy W.H. Den Ouden (USA), Inc.

adequate. When the space gets to 22 inches or less, you are going to have problems with your elbows. The W.C. is best if it is located fore and aft as it is then equally miserable on either tack. If it is fitted so that it faces athwartship, you can have a problem at extreme heel angles, when your knees are raised higher than your shoulders. Unfortunately, it is not always possible to fit the thing fore and aft without giving up something else, perhaps a private door to the forward cabin, so it can be a compromise situation.

One reason I believe that Herreshoff loathed marine toilets is that too many of the ones made in North America simply have too small a seat for the average person. Measuring the W.C. in my home, I find that the seat is 16 inches from front to back. The standard inexpensive marine toilet used in all too many production boats measures 13 inches. The British seem to do this better. The Simpson Lawrence #401 in my boat is at least 16 inches, and even their smaller #400 model is over 15 inches front to back on the seat. In any case, if you are buying an expensive yacht (and even the smallest are expensive these days), you should get a workable toilet with it and not some child-sized potty. Measure the seat front to back. If it is less than 15 inches, tell the man "no sale" until the situation is rectified.

The problem with marine toilets, of course, is our rather confusing set of laws about what is legal where. My own solution is to fit a Y valve so that the waste can be directed to either a holding tank or overboard discharge to handle in-harbor and offshore usage. If your boat has adequate electrical power, a proper waste-treatment unit (again with Y valve for direct discharge offshore) would be a good choice.

Although it has been said so many times that it hardly bears repeating, a toilet in a sailboat is often below the waterline and must be fitted with a vented loop well above waterline to prevent siphoning and possibly sinking the yacht if the seacock is left open. Even if the top of the bowl is above the waterline when the boat is upright, it may well be below when she is heeled under sail, so the loop is necessary.

As to portable toilets, I think they belong in trailers, but if you can stand the smell and inconvenience, make sure the unit is a good one, if such exists.

A wash basin is desirable in the head if space permits. A folding basin can be installed in very small quarters, even to fold down over the W.C., but these basins are limited to a single cold water faucet as a rule. If you want hot and cold running water, a fixed basin is a must. It is then nice to have a good-sized mirror over it for complete grooming.

Another good feature is a shower, if the water supply aboard is large enough to handle it. The usual shower is in the middle of the toilet room with a curtain arranged somehow to keep the spray off the toilet and basin. A better setup is a separate stall shower, if space permits, but it rarely does on craft under 35 or 36 feet. A decent stall shower should be at least 27 inches wide. Bigger is better, so a shower does take up a lot of room that might be used for other things on a small boat. The shower water should not drain into the general bilge area as it will become sickening in short order. It must drain into a separate compartment or tank and then be pumped directly overboard. The movable telephone-type shower head is probably the best choice for a yacht as it conserves water and has less tendency to spray all over the place.

Good ventilation is essential throughout the boat but particularly so in the head due to the odor and dampness that can pervade the area. An electric exhaust fan is almost a must if a shower is fitted.

THE CHART TABLE

Chart tables have become *de rigeur* on even the smallest cruisers, yet I wonder how often they are really used. I know I do most of my navigating in the cockpit, and I suspect that most other coastal sailors do the same. A chart table is desirable on a blue water cruiser, but on small coastal yachts it generally takes up more good space than it is worth. I think I would rather have a cabin heater there for those cool evenings, or maybe a larger ice box for hot days.

There are yachts where a chart table is a must, of course, and then it should be of good size, 24" x 30" minimum. The sit-down type is the most popular today but wastes a lot of useful stowage space beneath it. I would prefer a stand-up chart table so the space below it could be used for added chart storage. A folding or swing-out seat can then be fitted if you must work there for any long period of time.

If a chart table is fitted, then the yacht will need lockers and shelves for books, navigation instruments, radios, and all the other paraphenalia that goes with them,

A complete navigation station with radar, Loran, satnav, and a full range of sailing instruments (Whitby 55).

and thought should be given to fitting in the Loran, SatNav, speedometer/log, and similar units. On a custom yacht, the owner can specify the equipment that he will require and the designer can lay out the space to suit. On a production yacht, what you see is what you get, so it is up to the owner to select equipment that will fit the available space.

STOWAGE

Storage space should be given more consideration than it usually receives on small craft. Think of the gear that must be stored on even a small boat, and you will begin to see why ample storage space is essential. Separate shelves, bins, or lockers should be provided for each of the following: navigation instruments, books, charts, food, dishes, cutlery, pots and pans, cleaning materials, spare stove fuel, towels and linens, sheets and blankets (or sleeping bags), tools, fishing tackle, spare parts, spare line, extra sails, blocks, fenders and mooring lines, spare anchor and line, foul-weather gear, clothing, dirty laundry, garbage, and so on endlessly. Racks should also be fitted for any items that need to be instantly available—flashlights, binoculars, hand bearing compass, flares, etc.

In the head, it is nice to have a separate small drawer for each crew member for toiletries. And in the sleeping cabins, a separate large drawer is desirable for each crew member's clothing if space permits.

I know my little 23-footer gets terribly crowded when we load it for a short cruise, and I can just imagine the mess if it had four berths instead of two. Perhaps that is why I rant so much about unnecessary berths and chart tables. I've never seen a boat with unnecessary storage space!

AIR, HEAT, AND LIGHT

The standard answer to ventilation on a yacht is still the vents designed by Olin Stephens and first used on his yacht *Dorade* in the late 1920s. The cowl ventilator on a Dorade box is watertight in all but green seas breaking over the deck and passes a reasonable amount of air. It can be improved with a slide inside the cabin to close it off when cool air is not wanted but does not need screens. The Dorade vent is relatively bug free and screens simply reduce air flow.

Flying saucer vents, such as the Simpson-Lawrence Aeolius® and many similar copies, have the advantage that they are flat and do not catch lines. These vents are easily fitted with fans (the Nicro Fico® unit has a built-in solar powered fan) and are ideal in the galley and head where forced air is useful to get rid of heat and odors.

The best ventilation in good weather is an open hatch. The galley and shower areas can have a 10" x 10" vent hatch fitted over them, and the sleeping cabins and saloon will benefit by a larger hatch in the 20" x 20" size range. Fine aluminum hatches are offered by Bomar, Atkins & Hoyle, Lewmar, Goiot, and others. Hatches must be fitted with screens, of course.

Opening ports are not as useful for ventilation as hatches due to their small area. Besides, the wind flow over an anchored boat rarely gets into ports along the cabin or hull side. Screens are a necessity in most locales. Large opening windows, as in pilot houses or dog houses, are useful for ventilation, particularly if they are in the forward end of the house. However, the window, whether hinged, sliding type, or drop sash, must be a proper marine window and not some piece of light aluminum made for RVs. Cornell-Carr Co. Inc. is a supplier of windows to the shipping industry and offers a good selection of types and styles.

Heat can be provided by several different sources. My little U'I *Papela* is heated simply by lighting the cook stove. This warms up the small cabin in short order. Indeed, the first ritual in the morning is to light the stove under the coffee pot without getting out of my sleeping bag. By the time the water is boiling, the cabin is warm enough to crawl out of the sack and start breakfast.

On medium-sized yachts where space permits, a separate cabin heater can be fitted. Solid fuel (coal and briquet) heaters are made by Paul Luke in East Boothbay, Me., and the Luke tiled fireplace adds a touch of class to any cabin. Kerosene and

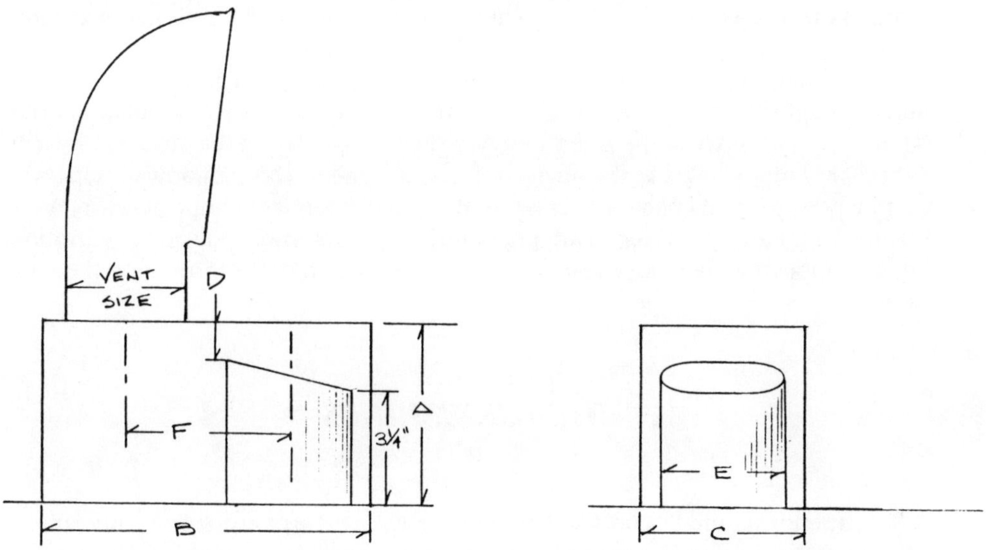

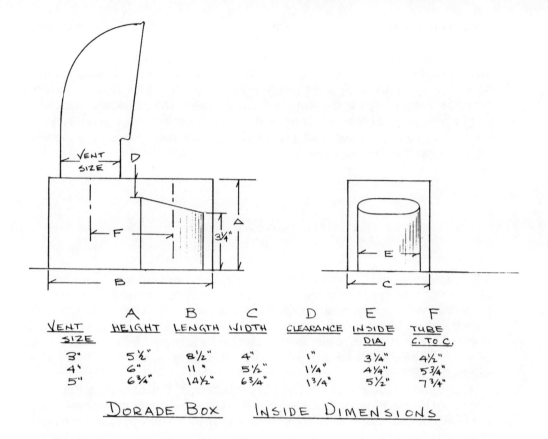

VENT SIZE	A HEIGHT	B LENGTH	C WIDTH	D CLEARANCE	E INSIDE DIA.	F TUBE C. TO C.
3"	5½"	8½"	4"	1"	3¼"	4½"
4"	6"	11"	5½"	1¼"	4¼"	5¾"
5"	6¾"	14½"	6¾"	1¾"	5½"	7¾"

DORADE BOX INSIDE DIMENSIONS

diesel oil bulkhead heaters (Dickerson, Taylor, etc.) are favorites in the cooler northern waters as well. Obviously, these heaters all need smoke stacks for proper draft, but the stack should be removable and have a tight cap to keep water out in storm conditions.

Diesel oil heaters using a gun-type burner (Espar®) will provide forced air heat through ducts to each cabin and are a good answer for the live-aboard yacht and the larger vessel. These units have forced draft so the stack is quite small, about one inch in diameter, and can be led to an area of the deck where it will not be in the way.

Air conditioning is becoming more common on yachts of 40 feet or larger, particularly in southern waters. Unless the unit is to be used only at dockside, and that is when you need it most, of course, a fairly large 110-VAC generator will be a necessity. The engineering and installation of a good air conditioning system should be left to experts.

Lighting deserves more consideration than it usually receives on the average yacht. Natural lighting comes through ports and hatches, but deck prisms can be fitted to brighten up passageways, heads, dark corners of the galley, and other problem areas. Bear in mind, however, that at night the light from below coming through the prisms and hatches can blind the helmsman. Duct tape is handy to close off a prism, and canvas hatch covers can be a blessing at times.

Electric lights should include a reading light at each berth and overhead or bulkhead lights for each cabin. Small lights that can be aimed so they will not bother sleepers are necessary in the galley and navigation area aboard the blue water yacht. As well, red safety lights at the navigation station, galley, companionway steps, and narrow passages will enable the crew to move about safely without upsetting their night vision. Flourescent lights are popular due to their lower power consumption, but remember that they can affect the accuracy of the Loran if both are on at the same time.

THE FURNISHINGS

A boat interior should be constructed of materials that are easily cleaned, not subject to staining by water or dampness, rugged, and, of course, handsome. On modern production yachts, the standard interior is teak or formica with teak trim, and these materials fill the requirements. However, excessive use of teak can result in a dark and gloomy interior. It would be nice to see a yacht done in the old-fashioned way, with white or off-white bulkheads and panels and varnished mahogany trim. To me, that still spells class.

Cabin soles can be teak with holly or maple between the planks. Often, this effect is obtained by teak plywood, but it is not as durable as the real thing. With solid teak and holly, the holly strips can be raised ⅛ to ³⁄₁₆ of an inch to give truly secure footing in any weather. The soles should be removable in sections for access to the bilges, tanks, plumbing, etc., and a teak grating dust bin in the galley is a handy feature. As a less costly alternative to teak, a nice, painted pine, planked sole has much to recommend it.

Carpeting comforts bare feet on a cool morning but tends to absorb water and smell musty in time. If fitted, the carpets should be easily removable for cleaning and airing. Modern indoor-outdoor carpet materials are a good choice for yachts.

Locker and table tops may be of wood or formica. Galley tops are formica as a rule, but well-scrubbed bare ash can be handsome and utilitarian. In any case, all locker and table tops must have high, solid hardwood fiddles (sea rails) around them to keep things in place when it gets rough out there. The fiddles should be a minimum of 1½ inches high and fastened strongly enough that they can be used as emergency hand rails in heavy weather. They will be! Cutesy fiddles made of turned posts and light rails are for motorboats. Where a table top has to do double duty as a berth bottom, as in a dinette, the fiddles should be made removable with brass pegs or the sleepers will truly feel as if they are on rails.

Locker doors should have provision for ventilation by louvres, caning, metal vents, or similar devices in order to eliminate those musty odors that can accumulate in a little used locker. Magnetic catches are useless at sea as they will rust and will also pop open and spill the locker contents on the cabin sole when the boat heels. The commonly used nylon clip-type catch is little better in this regard. The elbow catch through a finger hole is acceptable, but I prefer the Simpson-Lawrence #195200 push-button catch, available in the U.S. from Jay Stuart Haft Co., as there is less chance of tearing your finger off in a rough sea.

Drawers may be fitted with the Simpson-Lawrence catches or may be of the type that lift a quarter inch to open. Drawers should be fitted with center guides also, or they will twist and jam when you try to open them. The new nylon guides can work well, and one of the neatest and cleanest drawers I've seen was the plastic unit used by Morgan, onto which they fitted a solid wood face. If the drawer is of wood, the corners should be dovetailed for strength, the bottom rabbeted into a groove in the sides, and the entire unit glued and solidly fastened. It is amazing the beating that a drawer can get when it is loaded with heavy tools and equipment.

All hardware (hinges, door pulls, metal louvres, etc.) must be of solid brass, bronze, or stainless steel. Plated steel, pot metal, zamac, and other such substances will not stand up to a saltwater atmosphere. Aluminum hardware stands up quite well, but I am just not fond of its appearance. Aluminum hinges and similar items have to be quite bulky if they are to be sufficiently strong.

Sailcloth is still one of the best materials for berth and settee cushion covers. The cover should be fitted with a full length zipper so it can be easily removed for cleaning. Some builders are putting fancy velours and other costly and attractive fabrics into their yachts, but while these may look super at a boat show, they look terrible at sea when they are soaked with salt water and spilled coffee. Naugahyde® and similar fabrics stand up well and are easy to clean. They are quite suitable for seating but tend to feel sticky and uncomfortable when slept on and so are not ideal for settee berths, particularly in warm climates.

The cushions themselves should be of a unicellular plastic foam that will not soak up water. Three inches is ample for a berth if the cushion is of fairly firm density; I can sleep like a log on two inches of firm foam and wake up feeling chipper. If you must have a soft mattress, you may feel more comfortable with a four-inch thickness.

A few examples of furnishings that make a yacht more livable but are too often forgotten by designers (including me) and builders: a good trash bucket, or place to stow one, handy to the galley; a folding shelf to extend the chef's counter space, could be removable to double as a serving tray; a paper towel rack in the galley; a proper rack to hold a set of canisters; condiment bins on the dining table; a hole to contain a wine bottle to keep it from spilling; small shelves at the head of each bunk to hold your wallet, glasses, keys, flashlight, etc., on those stormy nights when you turn in half dressed, expecting to be called on deck at any time; a shelf outboard at the top of each hanging locker to stow caps and other small items that always seem to get lost; a folding table at the end of the settee to serve as a drink and snack tray; overhead racks to stow the seat back cushions when the settee is being used as a berth; a curtain to close off a pilot or quarter berth so the occupant can sleep despite the watch on deck storming below to use the galley or W.C.; if the boat has standing headroom, overhead hand rails in the saloon and passages for safety when moving about at greater angles of heel; a small drawer for each crew member in the head to hold personal toiletries; a grab rail at waist level near the W.C. to assist the occupant in raising or steadying himself when the boat is being tossed around by the seas.

There are many other items similar to the above that can make life aboard more comfortable for everyone, and I'm sure the reader has his own favorites.

141 □

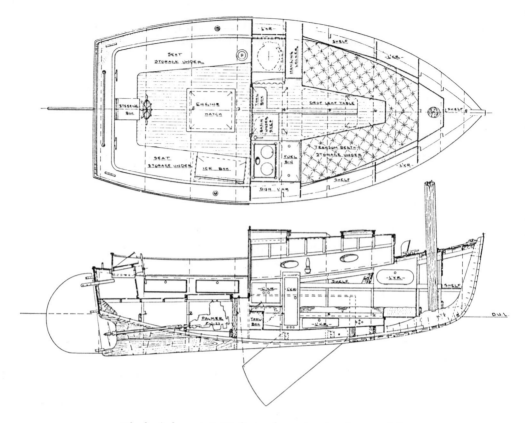

The basic layout. A 21-foot catboat contains the essentials.

BASIC ARRANGEMENT PLANS

Having discussed the details of the interior layout, it is time to address the variety of ways in which the components of head, galley, navigation area, berths, and settees can be arranged.

AFT COCKPIT

The standard aft cockpit layout for many years has had the sleeping cabin forward, the head and hanging locker abaft that across from each other, the saloon next, perhaps with some bureaus, and finally the galley and navigation area aft. The arrangement makes good use of the space since it places the galley and chart table handy to the cockpit, the saloon in the area of easiest motion, and the forward berths in the pointy part of the boat that isn't of much use for anything else.

In recent years, designers have used their ingenuity to change and in some cases improve on this basic layout. Placing the head aft, across from the galley, is one

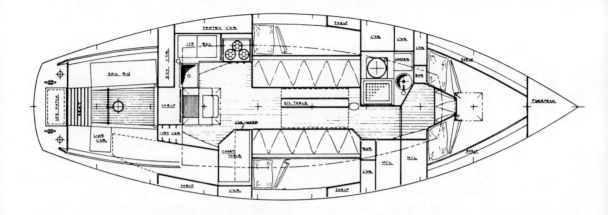

Basic aft cockpit layout in the Murray 33, a steel sloop.

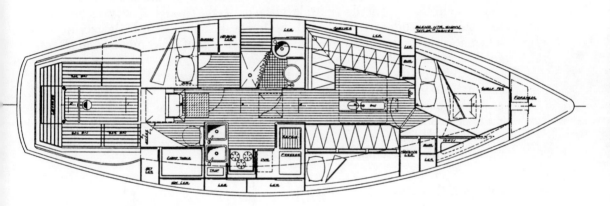

At 38 feet, a private owner's cabin aft becomes practical, as on the Kaiulani 38. Note midship head.

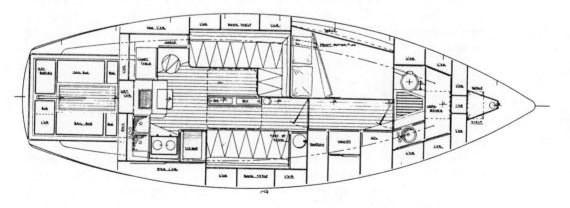

Forward head location on this 33 allows a good owner's cabin but is awkward for guests.

143 □

variation seen on smaller boats, and it does allow the preferred fore-and-aft W.C. location. On boats over 35 feet or so, the trend, pioneered by Bob Perry on the Valiant 40, is to fit a private owner's cabin aft with double berths. These cabins range in size from small dog kennels to fairly sumptuous staterooms, and I would advise the buyer to try such a cabin on for size before he plunks down his money. You must bear in mind that the privacy you obtain by means of small, separate sleeping cabins can only be at the expense of a truly spacious and comfortable main saloon.

Another arrangement places the galley amidships on the starboard side in place of the settee and then fits a large dinette to port with quarter berth(s) and navigation area aft. The useful saloon area is halved, and the dinette is not a particularly good seat when heeled under sail in any case. This is not one of my favorite arrangements.

A layout that does have some advantages for boats in the 30-to-35-foot range is to eliminate the forward cabin altogether, perhaps in favor of a small bosun's storage area, move the rest of the layout forward, and fit two quarter berths. I know I have spoken against quarter berths, but if the layout is moved forward as above, then the quarter berth does not need to intrude too far under the cockpit. Thus, valuable deck stowage is not completely lost, and the forepeak storage helps to make up the difference. This arrangement puts the berths in an area of easier motion and makes good sense for an offshore cruiser.

By and large, the tried and proven basic layout works as well as any for most aft cockpit boats in the 28-to-40-foot range. At 40 feet and above, there is room for the private cabin aft without crowding the saloon out of existence. Below 28 feet even, the basic layout starts to become cramped so there is some excuse for experimenting with other solutions to the problem of getting four berths, a galley, a head, and a few other amenities into a pint pot.

CENTER COCKPIT

The center cockpit arrangement became popular in the early 1970s with the introduction of such boats as the Morgan Out Island 41 and the Whitby 42. It provides good privacy in two or three sleeping cabins along with all the usual features for extended cruising or charter use. The cockpit space is usually short in order to gain extra accommodation room below decks, but it is also wider than the average aft cockpit.

There are two basic center cockpit setups. The most common is to have the owner's cabin aft, the engine room under the cockpit, the galley and saloon amidships just forward of the cockpit, and the typical head and sleeping cabin forward. The other layout, usually seen on boats of the character type, is to have a great cabin aft, often with the galley there as well, and to have the area forward of the cockpit given over to sleeping cabins.

One advantage of the center cockpit arrangement is that the engine room is usually much more spacious and accessible than that of an aft cockpit boat of the same size. Usually, but not always, as some designers use the space on both sides of the engine for passage and accommodations, and this can result in a tiny, but still accessible, engine compartment.

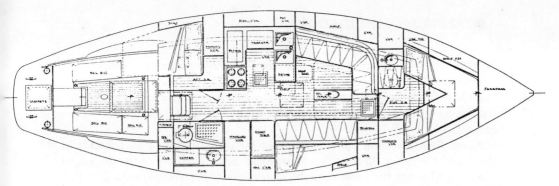

More variations on the aft cockpit layout. **Above,** Traveller IV, *a 42-foot sloop.* **Below,** *the Lazyjack 32 schooner.*

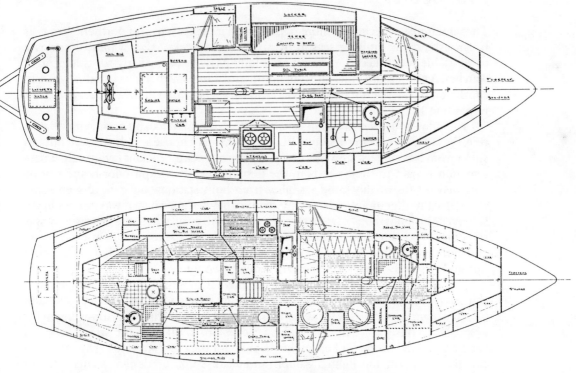

The basic center cockpit layout in an Olympic 47.

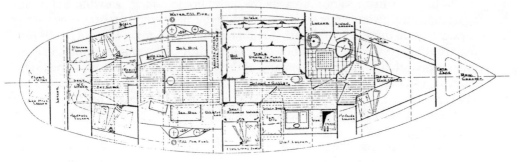

Center cockpit arrangement in a 37-footer. Galley to starboard.

145 □

But when both sides of the engine are used for accommodations, the deck storage suffers, since there is no space for a sail bin in the cockpit. Unless the designer has the foresight to fit a large lazarette, the deck stowage may be inadequate. The adequacy of good locker space accessible from the deck is a point to consider when looking at center cockpit boats.

Again, there are some center cockpit layouts with a dinette on one side of the saloon and the galley on the other. This reduces the livability of the saloon, in my opinion, and is not the most desirable arrangement for average use.

PILOT HOUSE

The pilot house is becoming more popular, and it makes sense for northern waters as it can extend the cruising season by six to eight weeks. Also, a pilot house is a comfortable watch-keeping station on a long passage, particularly for colder night watches. As a measure of its growing popularity, I can say that in my first 20 years in the design business I did only two pilot-house yachts while in the past seven years I have done 18.

The pilot-house vessel can be an aft cockpit or center cockpit arrangement. As a rule, the latter gives better visibility from both the pilot house and the cockpit but can suffer from lack of deck stowage, just as the normal center cockpit layout can, unless attention is paid to these needs in the design. The aft cockpit pilot house can be designed for reasonably good visibility from both stations, but I have seen some boats, usually alterations of a standard trunk cabin design, where it was impossible to see over the pilot house from the outside helm even when the helmsman was standing. This is a feature to check out if you are in the market for a pilot-house boat, and don't accept the salesman's comment that you can see along the sides of the pilot house. Not ruddy likely, as our British friends would say.

Another choice in the pilot-house vessel is what goes into the pilot house itself. It can be a small pilot house with room for the helm, navigation area, and one settee and with the main saloon below forward. This, in my opinion, is the ideal arrangement for an offshore cruiser since the pilot house can be closed off from the saloon area and can be darkened inside for best night visibility for the crew on watch. The off watch can then relax in the lighted saloon and read, cook, or design yachts without bothering the helmsman.

Putting the main saloon area in the pilot house, along with the helm and navigation area, gives a larger and more comfortable pilot house so that the rest of the crew can be up there in friendly association with the helmsman. This is a nice layout for a coastal cruiser that does not do a great deal of overnight sailing. It is an arrangement that is preferred by many as the pilot house *cum* saloon is bright and cheerful, while the visibility from it is much better than from a below-decks saloon. However, it must be remembered when selecting this layout that for night sailing you must either darken ship or kick the helmsman out into the cockpit until everyone else hits the sack.

Regardless of type, the pilot house will probably be seen more and more on our waters in years to come. The well-designed pilot-house yacht can offer good sailing performance plus the inside steering comfort of a motor yacht in cold or drizzly weather. Many yachtsmen and women are beginning to appreciate this advantage.

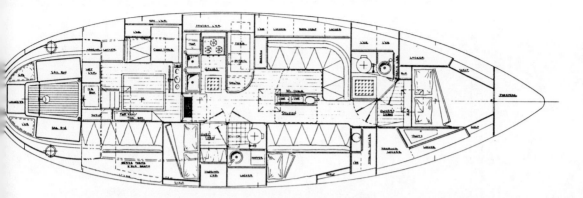

A pilot-house layout on a 43-footer with saloon separate from the helmsman's station.

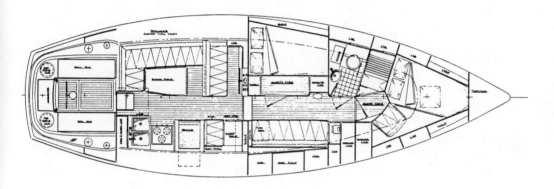

A 40-foot pilot-house yacht with saloon and galley in the pilot house.

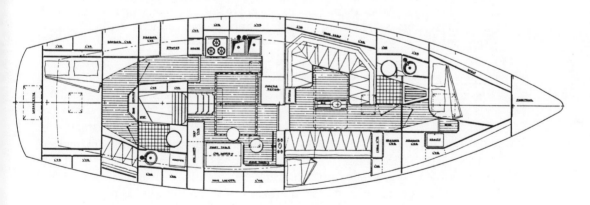

A pilot-house auxiliary with raised center cockpit. The MT 42 by Mao Ta.

8

□
□
□
□
□
□
□
□
□
□

THE MOTORSAILER

"Motorsailer" is a term that could encompass any sailboat with an auxiliary engine and might be stretched to include some motor yachts with steadying sails. However, most of us think of a motorsailer as a yacht with somewhat more power and less sail for its size than the normal auxiliary cruiser.

Motorsailers vary widely in type depending upon the relative emphasis placed on sail and power in the design. For example, the widely used classification system will call a yacht a 30/70 if the design leans 30 percent to sail and 70 percent to power. A 50/50, of course, puts equal weight on each form of propulsion while a 70/30 has the accent on sail.

THE 30/70

This yacht is primarily a displacement powerboat in hull form with sufficient sail area, lateral plane, and rudder area to place it a good notch above the powerboat with only a steadying sail rig. The *Arielle* illustrates the type and is a boat that can reach and run effectively under sail, while its prime mover when the wind is forward of the beam is the engine. The sails steady the motion in beam seas, increase the cruising range, and provide those blissful moments of silence when the wind is right.

□ *148*

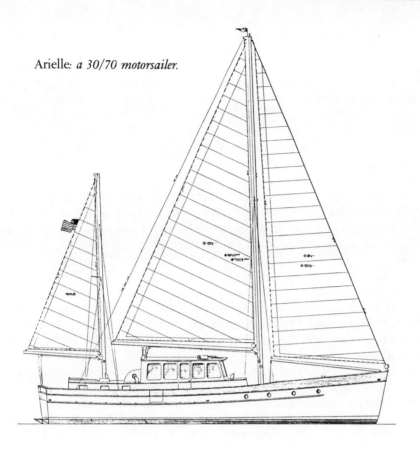

Arielle: *a 30/70 motorsailer.*

The 30/70 is, in effect, a powerboat with auxiliary sail rather than a sailboat with auxiliary power and requires a powerboat hull form for efficiency at V/√L ratios of 1.4 to 1.5. This means a prismatic coefficient of .6 or slightly over, a moderately wide stern to prevent squatting, and a flat run to the buttocks. The wide stern also adds to form stability and enables the lightly ballasted hull to stand up to its modest sail area in a breeze.

The lateral plane is shoal and spread well fore and aft as deep draft is not essential for reasonable performance in beam winds. The leeway made while sailing can be quickly offset by a short period under power. A centerboard would reduce leeway and is of benefit to the 30/70 but is rarely fitted as the owners of such craft are obviously not all that concerned with sailing performance. The added cost and maintenance of the board is, in my view, not worth its minor advantage.

The 30/70 will have a very low ballast ratio, sometimes none at all, and rarely over 20 percent. This means she is not self-righting in an extreme knockdown, but the low rig keeps the heeling moment reasonable and is advantageous in that a low aspect ratio sail is more efficient downwind than a tall rig. For the 30/70, primarily concerned with performance off the wind, the low aspect ratio rig makes sense, and, with her limited stability, a sail area/displacement ratio of 10 to 12 seems to fit.

149 □

THE MOTORSAILER

The 30/70 is more capable of long offshore passages than a powerboat of similar size, more comfortable at sea due to the steadying effect of the sails, and more economical to operate. She makes a good alternative for the motor yacht owner who wants some of the benefits of sail while retaining the advantages of the pure displacement powerboat.

THE 50/50

A 50/50 is not a vessel that can travel just as fast under sail as under power, but rather one that will use both its sail and its engine about the same amount of time. A good 50/50 may be able to cruise under power at a $V/\sqrt{L}$ of 1.3 to 1.4 but will rarely exceed speeds of 1.1 under sail due to the limitations of her modest sail area and stability.

She will have a lower Cp than the 30/70, perhaps in the .57 to .59 range. Her hull form will closely resemble that of the pure sailing yacht but will be slightly more full and usually of heavier displacement to enable her to carry the weights of a large engine and fuel tankage. The lateral plane will be deeper for sailing on the wind and to resist leeway more effectively, and a centerboard will, or should, be fitted if she is of shoal draft.

The rig will be taller and spread more generous area, perhaps a sail area/displacement ratio of 13 to 15, and to enable her to stand up to this, the ballast ratio will be higher, in 25-to-30-percent range. The sailplan should still be fairly low and well spread fore and aft to keep the heeling moment reasonable as the moderate draft is most effective in resisting leeway at lower heel angles.

The 50/50 is quite capable of ocean passages since she will be self-righting as a rule, and her rig and hull form permit her to handle any weather conditions under sail alone. The *Cape Race* design is an example of the 50/50, and the first of these yachts, the *Zig Zag*, has lived up to her name by cruising the canals of Europe, sailing the Mediterranean to Turkey, crossing the Atlantic, cruising the East Coast to Maine and the Mississippi to the Great Lakes, and crossing through the Panama Canal to wind up in San Francisco.

The good 50/50 is a nice compromise for the yachtsman who wants more comfort than the pure auxiliary can provide yet does not want to give up the fun of sailing. It is an extremely versatile craft well suited for the type of cruising that so many of us do.

THE 70/30

The dividing line between this class of motorsailer and the "husky" auxiliary yacht is a fine one today. The 70/30 will have a larger engine and fuel capacity and probably more comfortable accommodations than the auxiliary, but otherwise the differences between them are slight. The 70/30 can be of shoal draft with centerboard, of deep draft, or even fin keel. Her displacement can range from moderate to heavy, but her

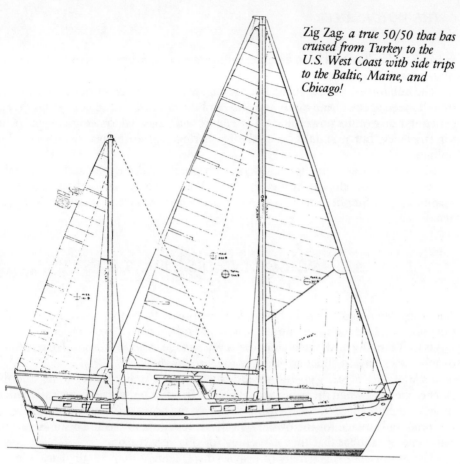

Zig Zag: *a true 50/50 that has cruised from Turkey to the U.S. West Coast with side trips to the Baltic, Maine, and Chicago!*

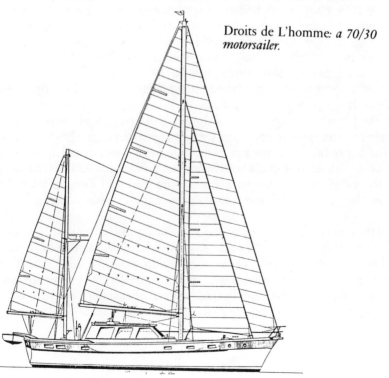

Droits de L'homme: *a 70/30 motorsailer.*

sail area and ballast will be in keeping so that she can perform to standards that will please the sailing man.

The hull form is pure sailboat, but the engine power will be sufficient to drive her to hull speed against headwinds and seas, and the tankage will be large enough for a generous range under power alone. The engine will be geared to swing a big propeller for efficiency, but it should be of the feathering type to reduce resistance when sailing.

Many modern production cruisers, with good-sized engines and comfortable accommodations, closely approach the 70/30 concept, or perhaps 80/20, as Sparkman and Stephens named one of their center cockpit auxiliaries a few years ago.

ADVANTAGES AND DISADVANTAGES

A motorsailer can combine the best of both worlds or the worst. There are some that sail poorly and are inefficient under power, and others that do well under power and sail as well as many husky auxiliaries of a few years ago. A good motorsailer, regardless of type, does have distinct advantages for some owners.

Its large fuel capacity gives it a wide cruising range under power alone, and this can be extended when the winds are favorable. In addition, the power is sufficient to drive it at hull speed dead to windward even in heavy seas, and this can be an important advantage for the owner who has a schedule to meet. To some, it is the only type of sailboat that they can enjoy for this very reason.

The motorsailer is generally of heavier displacement than an auxiliary of equal size and will usually have more freeboard and higher deckhouses. The extra displacement gives an easier motion in a seaway, and combined with the higher topsides, it adds up to more space below and roomier accommodations. Also, the heavier displacement provides the ability to carry greater weights of fuel, batteries, generator set, air conditioning, and other comforts.

On the debit side, the extra displacement adds to cost, as does the extra equipment, while the larger engine increases both the initial price and the operating expense. Then the heavier displacement and usually greater beam add to resistance, as does the larger propeller and aperture and the windage of the higher freeboard and deckhouses. The net result is that the best motorsailer still does not sail as well as a pure auxiliary of the same size. Even when the hull and rig are capable of top sailing performance, the weight of the heavier engine and added fuel detracts from the ballast that can be carried and reduces stability so that sailing performance suffers.

However, if the owner operates the yacht as a true motorsailer, using both sail and engine power at the same time, the results are impressive. The combination gives better speed, better windward performance, and less leeway than sail alone. To a sailboat moving to windward at five knots, an extra knot given by the engine running at a fast idle means 20 percent less time that the hull will be making leeway for every mile covered. The actual gain is not quite that high since the extra speed brings the apparent wind ahead, forcing the boat to point higher. Actual gains are probably in the 15-percent range but still that means that a well-handled 50/50 can almost match tacks with a hot club racer. The combination of sail and power is certainly one of the most relaxing and pleasurable ways of driving a boat to weather. It is particularly advantageous to the true 50/50 as the sails steady the boat compared to a pure motor yacht, while the moderate sail area does not create the large heel angle of the pure sailboat.

Motorsailers are not for everyone, and there are still the few rugged individualists who would not have an engine in their boat regardless. Still the motorsailer makes good sense for those yachtsmen who want to cruise extensively, whether coastwise or blue water, yet must still meet a schedule, and also for those who find their cruiser-racer becoming more burdensome to handle with each passing year. Indeed, if cruising yachtsmen kept a log of their hours under sail, under power alone, and with both sail and power, they might find that they were actually using their auxiliary cruiser as a motorsailer, and that perhaps a true motorsailer would better fit their needs.

THE DECK LAYOUT

The deck layout of the cruising yacht is obviously governed by the basic interior arrangement, although "center"cockpit boats rarely have their cockpit amidships, despite the name. (For example, the Whitby 42's cockpit begins 62 percent of the LOA abaft the bow and runs to 77 percent aft; hardly "center"by anyone's definition.) On the other hand, the deck layout of an out-and-out racing machine will be the governing factor and the interior will be a secondary consideration. Perhaps the major point to consider in deck layouts is whether the deck is flush or whether a trunk cabin is fitted. Both have their advantages, and disadvantages.

The flush deck yacht has the benefits of greater volume below decks and, of course, wide open and relatively uncluttered decks to ease sailhandling for the crew. She will also have greater reserve stability and will have to be knocked down to a much deeper angle of heel before her decks are awash and her righting arm curve begins to decrease. On wooden yachts, the flush deck adds strength by eliminating four corners and reduces the chance of leaks. This advantage does not carry over to fiberglass or metal craft. Indeed, the trunk cabin on a fiberglass yacht may add some longitudinal stiffness to the structure.

The trunk cabin yacht, on the other hand, has the advantage that the weight of the deck is lower, thus lowering the yacht's center of gravity and giving her greater stability at more normal heel angles. Also, there is less windage and weight, particularly forward, so she should go to weather a bit better and will have less tendency to sail around her anchor at the mooring. Then, since it is normal to use the windward side of the ship when going forward to handle sails, having the trunk cabin to leeward gives better footing and added security in heavy seas.

In effect, the choice is a tossup, depending upon your own preferences. The club racer may well favor the trunk cabin yacht for its slight performance advantages; the cruising man may prefer the extra space of the flush decked vessel. And where headroom is not a necessity, the out-and-out performance sailor may select a flush decked yacht with minimum sitting headroom. In any case, the deck layout has certain requirements.

For a sea-going yacht, a self-bailing cockpit is a requisite, with a least two 1½-inch-to-2½-inch-diameter scuppers, depending upon the size of the cockpit and the boat. Four scuppers are better if the arrangement permits. Still, the bigger the scuppers the better. The cockpit volume should not be excessive, especially on an aft cockpit yacht, so that if the boat does get pooped and fill with water she will not trim down by the stern so far that the seas roll aboard faster than the scuppers can drain the water out.

A bridge deck is desirable but not mandatory, in my opinion, as long as the lower hatch slides can be fastened in place. The purpose of the bridge deck is to keep a heavy sea that fills the cockpit from going below decks. In fact, if the sea remains in the cockpit, it will trim the boat by the stern and may lead to further problems if the scuppers do not get rid of it fast enough. If the water spills into the cabin, it will quickly drain into the bilge so the boat will not be trimmed so badly by the stern and may actually be safer in the long run.

I have only been pooped in heavy seas once so my experience is limited (and I hope it remains that way). Still many small boats with open cockpits and low freeboard have made long offshore voyages in less than ideal weather so I have to believe that the seaworthiness of the boat and the skill of the crew are more important than whether the cockpit has a bridge deck, or even whether it is self-bailing. Regardless, I would not go offshore in a boat with an open cockpit and recommend the same to my readers.

The cockpit needs some good storage hatches as was stressed earlier. These should be watertight or fitted with angled troughs that will drain at a substantial angle of heel, and they must be capable of being locked in heavy weather. Seat backs should be about 12 inches high for support and angled for comfort. Bear in mind that what is comfortable when the boat is upright may dig into your back when she is heeled under sail, but well-rounded corners will take some of the pain out of it. Scuppers in the cockpit seat corners to drain that annoying puddle of water are a nice touch. Channels leading to the locker drain troughs can do a good job in this regard also.

The cockpit coamings should be either narrow enough to step over easily or wide enough to step onto (about 8 inches plus). If they are wide, then for obvious reasons it is imperative that the top be nonskid. If the yacht is steered with a tiller, the helmsman will get a better view of things if he sits up and outboard, and this necessitates a wide coaming for comfort or, in the case of a racing yacht, perhaps no coaming at all.

The winches will be mounted on the coamings if they are sufficiently wide, or on a winch pad outboard of the coaming, and should be angled outboard to meet the lead

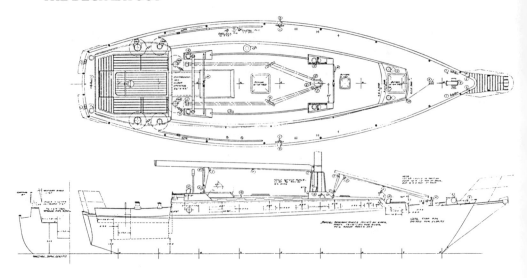

The Kaiulani 38 deck plan shows wide side decks and good working space.

from the sheet or turning block. A winch height about 26 to 30 inches above the cockpit sole works well and fits in nicely with a 16-to-18-inch seat height and a 10-to-12-inch coaming above that. The racing yacht will often dispense with cockpit seats as this allows the crews to stand up to the winches and work more efficiently. Wide coamings permit the fitting of bins, with or without lids, and these are perfect spots for the stowage of winch handles, binoculars, sunglasses, sail gaskets, tag lines, half-full beer cans, and other small, indispensable items.

Large windows are common in modern yachts and an essential of the pilot-house type. These should have husky shutters of plywood or, better yet, Lexan® that can be fastened securely in severe storm conditions. Both Lloyds and the American Bureau of Shipping require solid shutters for all portlights as well, and it is a good idea to have these on any sea-going yacht. Cowl vents and smoke stacks should be removable and have caps that can be fitted over the openings to keep green seas from pouring into the accommodation space.

Wide side decks are desirable for obvious reasons, but on a small boat they reduce the cabin space. I would say that 10-to-12-inch width is a workable minimum on a small yacht, but 16 to 18 inches is better when the size of the yacht permits. In either case, this minimum is at the aft end of the cabin, and the decks should get wider as they run forward. The decks must be nonskid, of course. The choices are: a good nonskid pattern cast into the decks of a fiberglass yacht (and this should be an irregular rather than a diamond pattern as it is easier to match up a repair job); a patterned overlay such as Treadmaster® glued in place; nonskid paint; or a teak deck overlaid on the FRP, metal, or wood subdeck. The teak should be left bare (and scrubbed occasionally) as a wet, oiled deck is about as slippery as a skating rink.

On wood yachts, decks may be canvas covered, but this tends to become slippery after several annual paintings unless sand or other nonskid material is mixed into the paint. Stick-on nonskid strips are useful at the mast and will be appreciated by the crew in heavy weather. Raised wood strips down the centerline of wide cockpits, cabin roofs, and foredecks will also help keep people in place.

Toe rails are required on even the smallest cruiser and club racer, whether the boat has lifelines or not. (Real go-for-the-gold racing yachts might dispense with toe rails to save a few ounces, as long as the owner has a huge liability insurance policy.) The toe rail helps the crew to move around and to brace themselves to their work when the boat is heeled and the spray is flying. Toe rails should be a minimum of 1½ inches high and may be wood, fiberglass, or aluminum slotted genoa-rail type. Solid continuous rails of wood or fiberglass require scuppers at both the low point and the wide point of the sheer to drain water overboard. The scuppers may be through the rail, but this leads to water stains on the topsides. High-quality yachts will have scuppers in the deck, draining through tubes to seacocks in the boot top or perhaps connecting to the cockpit scuppers.

Bulwarks are fitted to many yachts of the character type as well as to blue water cruisers. These are higher than toe rails, perhaps 6 inches high on a small cruiser up to 18 inches or more on a large vessel. They can hold tons of water and so require good-sized scuppers and, if over 6 inches high, freeing ports. Deep bulwarks do provide security on deck and peace of mind when it is blowing a gale. All too rarely fitted are toe rails down the centerline of wide foredecks and in wide cockpits. These can be a low triangular shape but will still do much to keep the crew in position. Similar toe rails at the mast are useful on smaller yachts, but mast safety rails of husky stainless steel tubing are becoming popular on cruisers of medium size and upwards and give good security when you are reefing or changing headsails. These safety rails should be at least 30 inches high and located about 36 inches outboard of the mast to allow room to swing a winch handle.

If the yacht is of trunk cabin type then handrails must be fitted to the cabin roof. These may be wood or metal but must be through-bolted for strength and large enough to give a firm grip to a terrified hand. Unvarnished teak rails give the best grip and stainless steel rails the poorest. Varnished wood rails are somewhere in between, so it is a case of function over beauty—or perhaps the truly functional, unvarnished teak rail is the most beautiful of all by any sensible standard.

Pulpits and lifelines with husky stanchions are required on ocean racers and *de rigeur* on offshore yachts but are often too low (24 to 26 inches) on smaller craft and may actually trip a crewman and help flip him overboard. A height of 28 to 30 inches is better, but there should also be an intermediate lifeline to ensure the safety of children or crewmen who may be washed to the rail while lying down or unconscious. The stanchion bases must be strongly fastened to resist the momentum of a husky crewman falling across the yacht when she is deeply heeled, and all parts of the system (wires, turnbuckles, padeyes, etc.) should be inspected annually for wear. I came close to getting very damp in a race off Newport once when a lifeline broke under my weight simply due to corrosion.

I am not so sure that lifelines are a good thing on very small yachts. Generally, they are scaled down to the 24-inch height and can give a false sense of security. "One hand for the ship" has served me for hundreds of miles of small boat cruising, but a good safety belt system would not be amiss, and I would not sail singlehanded or at night without one.

If a stern pulpit is fitted, a gate at the center with a folding stern ladder is a nice touch that simplifies boarding from a dinghy or after a swim. Bow pulpits are fairly standard these days, but many could benefit by some design work. A gate would aid in getting ashore by the bow, and double pulpits, with a slot for the genoa jib between them, are an asset when driving to windward as they keep the foot of the sail from being curled up with resultant loss in efficiency.

A critical part of the deck layout is the anchor storage, and recently, both anchor wells and/or bow rollers have become standard on many production boats. Both items are definite assets, in my opinion, but the anchor well needs some thought given to drainage and possibly a hose connection so that mud can be washed off the anchor chain and line. The anchor well is a good place to store the anchor itself on a cruiser-racer and the normal anchor line on a cruiser. The anchor on a cruiser should be set in the bow roller chocks, of course, as this simplifies anchor handling tremendously. However, this arrangement puts the weight farther forward than the racing owner should accept; thus, the racing yacht will store its anchors and line low and amidships.

The anchor rollers can be of nylon, but aluminum or stainless steel is better. The metal rollers will stand up to the wear of an all-chain rode that would destroy plastic rollers in short order.

Unfortunately, we often put in an anchor well and then forget about the owner who wants an all-chain rode or wants space to store a line for a second anchor. The well-thought-out cruising yacht should have a bow roller to store the working anchor, an anchor locker to store the working anchor line, and a chain or rope deck pipe leading to stowage in the forepeak for a chain rode or second anchor line. If the yacht is much over 35 feet, she will also need an anchor windlass, possibly electric, and a pipe to get the anchor line below into its storage space. On larger yachts, over 40 feet or so, it is nice to have the chain locker divided into two compartments: the starboard side for an all-chain anchor rode and the port side for a normal line with four or five fathoms of chain and the balance of nylon.

On top of this, the pointy end of the boat needs one or two large and solidly fastened cleats and chocks for mooring lines. The need for chocks for mooring lines may sound obvious, yet I've chartered 25-footers that had bow cleats but no chocks. Some builders will do anything to save an ounce, or a nickel, but eliminating bow chocks on a cruising yacht or a club racer is simply dumb.

The storm anchor on a larger yacht must be a hefty piece of gear if it is to do any good. In the past, it was common to fit chocks for the storm anchor on the cabin top abaft the mast, perhaps under the dinghy. The weight was aft, but high. A better solution is to use a husky yachtsman's kedge that can be taken apart (such as the Paul Luke storm anchor) and stored under the cabin sole where the weight is aft and low. Another possibility on metal or fiberglass yachts is to build, or mold, a space for the storm anchor into the deck. An overboard drain is necessary to keep the space from filling with water, of course.

Besides the bow cleats and chocks, the cruising boat needs cleats and chocks at the stern and amidships. The racing man can save a bit of weight by having his jibsheet cleats double as stern cleats, but the cruising yachtsman needs a full set of all these goodies. The midships cleats are necessary for spring lines and for getting the boat away from a dock under power when wind and tide are against you. The serious cruising man might also consider storage for a stern anchor and line, stern roller chocks, and even a stern capstan on larger yachts as these all make boat handling safer and easier.

The deck layout should also provide space for whisker pole, spinnaker pole(s), and reaching strut some place where they will not trip the unwary crew member. The racing man will want these items on deck to reduce weight aloft and windage, but the cruising owner might think about stowing a spinnaker pole or whisker pole permanently on the mast. It is out of the way yet immediately available when needed. On fiberglass yachts, the deck can have a recess molded into it to take the poles. This is also feasible on metal construction but will add considerable labor cost to the boat.

STEERING SYSTEMS

The type of steering fitted will affect the cockpit arrangement, of course. The simplest system, and the one that gives the best feel of the yacht for the least cost, is the tiller. It is quite suitable for average yachts up to 35-foot LOA and for well-balanced yachts to 40 feet or larger.

When I started in this business in the late 1950s, George Cuthbertson got me a berth on the *Vision* so that I could gain some sailing experience. She was a classic 8-meter yacht, 48-foot LOA, and tiller steered, as were all the 8s, and so sweetly balanced that the tiller was no effort whatsoever. After racing on her for three years, I had trouble adjusting to wheel steering when I started sailing aboard the Luders 40-foot *Storm*. There is no question but that a tiller has its place.

The biggest advantage of the tiller is its sensitivity, but there are other advantages that, too often, are not considered. First, the helmsman, with or without a tiller extension, can slide to windward to get better visibility and put his weight where it is most advantageous. Plus, in harbor, the tiller can be pivoted up out of the way to give you a clear cockpit for lounging and/or entertaining. And then, for obvious reasons, you don't need those weird keyhole-shaped cockpits with their too short seats designed to let the helmsman get around the wheel.

Wheel steering has grabbed the imagination of buyers, though, and is seen today on boats so small that it would have been laughed at as pretentious two decades ago. Basically, there are four types of wheel steering: cable, geared, rod, or hydraulic; and there are many variations on these.

Cable: two types; open wire or sheathed (pull-pull)

The cables are led to a quadrant or to a radial sheave fixed to the rudderpost. Sheaves should be 15 to 16 times the wire diameter for minimum wear, and there must be a way to take up slack in the wires so they cannot jump the sheaves. An emergency tiller is a necessity, as with all wheel systems, in case things go wrong—as they are bound to do. I never moved so fast in my life as I did on one trip to Bermuda when the wheel went dead in my hands while we were running downwind in heavy seas with everything flying. Before I finished yelling "All hands on deck!," I had the emergency tiller out and connected. Thanks to Alan MacDonald, the well-known rigger, the steering cables were respliced and we were using the wheel again in a few hours.

Perhaps that is the major advantage of the cable system—its ease of repair. It also has the best sensitivity of any of the wheel systems and is the number-one choice of most ocean racing and ocean-going yachts. The pull-pull system is recommended on smaller yachts, where the added friction of the sheathed cables is not a problem and where the leads can be kept fairly straight with any turns being of large radius.

Unfortunately, the larger the wheel, the greater its power and sensitivity. In addition, a large-diameter wheel allows the helmsman to get well off to the side for better visibility and control of the yacht. Thus, the modern trend is to huge wheels that force the use of keyhole-shaped cockpit seats and really muck up cockpit seating. Racing men will laugh at such a complaint since it is common today to have no seats at all in the racing yacht cockpit. Still probably 20 percent of our yachts are used for racing and 80 percent for family cruising and fun, so it makes sense that sailing yachts be designed for reasonable comfort first and absolute efficiency second. The full-length cockpit seat, though not as handy for the helmsman, is still my choice for a family cruiser.

Geared

The Edson Corp. is one of the leaders in this type of steering (as well as in the more common cable systems), and its catalog is a bible of geared wheels. Geared systems are leftovers from the turn-of-the-century fishing schooners and large yachts, but they still have their place on character boats of all sizes from 20-foot Cape Cod catboats to large, commercial sailboats. There are two basic types of geared systems: the rack-and-pinion steerer, and the worm steerer, such as the Simplex®. The worm-geared type has less sensitivity than the rack-and-pinion or the cable systems, but they do have the advantage that you can give the wheel a quarter- or half-turn to compensate for weather helm and it will stay there. In both geared systems, the wheel is mounted in a box at the aft end of the cockpit in the older fashion, and the helmsman can straddle the box or sit to one side. No whacky, keyhole-shaped cockpit is required, and there is no pedestal to jam the middle of the cockpit.

Although they are pure "cruising boat" steerers, both of the geared systems deserve more popularity than they presently enjoy. They are fine, rugged steerers with definite advantages of their own.

Rod Systems

The rod steering system connects the steering wheel to a short tiller on the rudder stock by means of torque tubes and gear boxes, not unlike the steering in many autos. The system is popular in the United Kingdom and on North American motor yachts, but is not common on sailing yachts this side of the Atlantic. Mathieson gear is

Edson Steering Systems

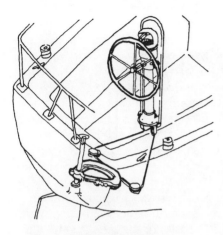

Basic quadrant system

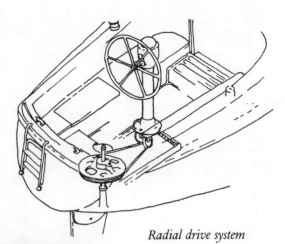

Radial drive system

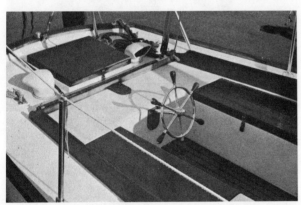

Inboard rack and pinion

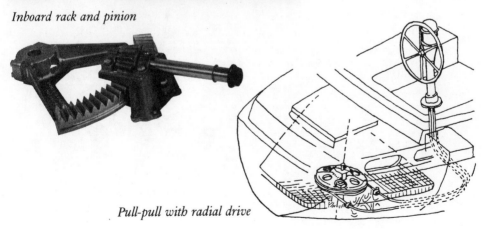

Pull-pull with radial drive

Illustrations courtesy the Edson Corp.

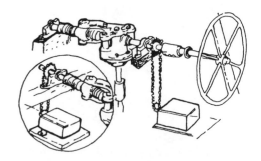

With autopilot

Three typical worm steerer installations

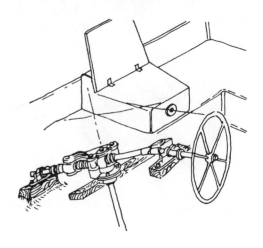

popular overseas, and if you are contemplating a boat equipped with Mathieson steering, you should have no problems. The gear is sturdy and requires minimal maintenance.

Hydraulic Steering

I used my first hydraulic steering gear on a 56-foot ketch in 1968 and sailed on that yacht twice to Hawaii (2nd in Class B in 1969). It was insensitive, and it took some time to get accustomed to it; almost half the crew never did get the feel, but for those of us who did, it was a breeze—one-finger control of a 56-footer spreading 2,400 square feet of spinnaker in winds approaching 40 knots! The newer hydraulic steerers do provide better feel of the yacht by allowing feedback through the system, but the result is still not as sensitive as a cable system.

Essentially, the hydraulic steerer has the wheel turning a hydraulic pump that is connected by hoses to a hydraulic cylinder attached to a tiller on the rudderpost. The hoses are quite flexible and can be led along tortuous routes where it would be difficult to set up a cable properly. For this reason, the hydraulic steerer was popular in center cockpit yachts before the development of the pull-pull cable setup and is still used in many larger center cockpit vessels because of its power and the problem of friction in a long run of pull-pull cable. It is also a good choice for the inside helm of a pilot-house yacht.

WINCHES

Winches ease the work of handling the heavy loads of the modern sailing yacht. With mechanical advantages of from 6-to-1 to better than 65 to 1, today's winches enable a 97-pound weakling to handle sheet loads that would have fazed the mate on a clipper ship.

For maximum efficiency, the sheet winch should be located with its top about 26 to 30 inches above the deck or cockpit sole and its center about 15 to 18 inches from the crewman. Racing yachts will have the cockpit arranged so that the crew stand to the winch as this is more effective than kneeling on a cockpit seat. The cruiser can make up for any drop in efficiency by going to the next larger size; or he can simply accept the fact that it will take a bit longer to get the sheet in!

In recent years, there has been a trend to take the halyard winches off the mast and lead the halyards aft to the cockpit. This makes sense for the main halyard as the reefing lines can be led aft too, and the mainsail can then be reefed quickly without having to go on deck. I still like to see the jib halyard winches at the mast as, when single- or shorthanded, it is difficult to ease the halyard and gather in the jib as it comes down if the halyard is led aft. You have to be forward to gather in the jib in any case, so it seems best to keep the winch up where it is handy to the man on the foredeck. A case can be made for leading a staysail halyard aft *if* the staysail is club footed and fitted with lazyjacks. Otherwise, it still seems better to have it at the mast.

163 ☐

The development of reliable line stoppers in recent years has enabled the modern yacht to get by with fewer winches. The stoppers allow one winch to handle a number of lines, one at a time, of course. I doubt if we will ever get down to the meager two winches recommended by H. A. Calahan in his 1935 book *Learning to Cruise* (one forward to handle the ground tackle and swig on an occasional halyard, and one aft to trim the mainsheet), but intelligent use of line stoppers is a step in the right direction.

The actual number and size of winches will depend on the size of the yacht and, to a considerable extent, its type and purpose. You will see small 27-to-28-footers bristling with winches, and I know of a 45-foot gaff rigged schooner that manages nicely with one. For the average cruiser, two primary winches for the jibsheets, one mainsheet winch, one jib halyard winch, and a main halyard winch would be a basic outfit and can be expanded as fancily as the owner's wallet allows.

The self-tailing winch has proven to be a real boon for the cruising sailor as it eliminates the need for two men to operate one winch. The operation is not as fast as when there are separate winchmen and tailers, but this is critical only to the racing yacht, and even then only on certain operations such as the genoa sheets. The shorthanded cruiser will undoubtedly find the self-tailing winch faster as there is no need to uncleat and recleat the line every time, or struggle with one hand tailing and the other cranking. The benefits of the self-tailing winch to the cruiser are so great that I feel every winch on the boat should be self-tailing.

Another type of winch that bears mention is the bottom action winch as produced by Murray in New Zealand and a few other die-hards. The advantages of the bottom action winch are that you can put the lines on and off it without removing the handle; the handle remains in place—doesn't fall overboard. The Murray winches come with a top cleat that allows small tightening adjustments without having to uncleat and recleat (as does a self-tailer, of course). Bottom action winches are useful as halyard winches, but they are very slow for sheets as you cannot make a full turn with the handle. These winches are not for everyone, but many yachtsmen swear by them.

And then, for the larger yacht, there is the electric winch. Couple this with self-tailing, and you have the epitome of convenience and ease, provided your yacht has adequate electrical power. And with a winch that draws up to 57 amps at full load on 12 VDC, we are talking about ample battery capacity and a heavy-duty alternator or, better yet, an auxiliary generator. I will say that my clients who have fitted electric winches to their yachts would never sail without them again. The retired couple planning to cruise seriously a yacht of much over 40-foot LOA might well take a serious look at the electric winch.

THAT DARNED DINGHY

One of the biggest problems on the under-35-foot auxiliary today is where to put the dinghy. Between 35 and 40 foot LOA, the cabin top is usually long enough so that the dinghy can be stowed there, unless the space is mucked up with midboom sheeting or a center cockpit. Over 40 feet or so, the yacht is large enough to hang the dink on stern davits, provided she is not one of those reverse transom rocketships that would need 10-foot-long davit arms to clear the stern. In that case, there may be sufficient length on the deck or cabin top somewhere to fit the dinghy.

The under-35-footer poses the difficulties. On modern sloops and cutters, the mast is usually so far aft that there is not enough length between the mast and the companionway to handle a decent-sized dinghy. The yacht is too small for stern davits, obviously, and this leaves few alternatives.

One of them is the pram-type dinghy with a removable transom to allow it to be stowed to the aft end of the companionway hatch. A second choice is the folding or two-part dinghy, where the bow part nests in the stern section; I believe that Robert Harris has plans for one of these. The third choice is the inflatable, which, if too long for the cabin roof, can have its bow section deflated and folded aft, or which can be completely folded up and stowed in a locker somewhere. Indeed, on my little 23-foot yawl I have a "raft locker" in the cockpit sole that will just take a 7-foot Achilles if I fold it carefully and leave the floorboards at home.

I will not go into the controversy of solid versus inflatable dinghies, except to say that if your yacht is at all large you should probably have one of each. If she is not big enough to carry two boats, then it is owner's choice, but get it as large as possible and ensure that it has a good set of oars that can move it in head seas and winds and ample flotation. Then pray you never need it except to row ashore for groceries and beer.

H. A. Calahan once wrote that the way to design the perfect yacht was first to design the perfect dinghy, then draw a deck under it, and finally design a yacht to fit that deck. That advice still has considerable merit.

GALLOWS FRAMES

The gallows frame is making a comeback on cruising yachts as more sailors come to realize its merits. A gallows frame is simply an athwartship support for the lowered boom, running the width of the cabinhouse as a general rule, and with several notches in it so the boom can be dropped and held in various positions. It can be fixed or folding, but it is better than a boom crutch in any conditions and safer than a topping lift (which does not stop the boom from swinging wildly in rough seas) when you are trying to tie in the reef points while the yacht does a hula dance beneath your feet.

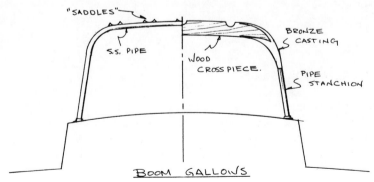

Gallows frames are usually made with pipe stanchions and a husky wood or tubular metal (bronze, stainless steel, or aluminum) cross bar. Handsome cast bronze fittings to take the pipe stanchion and the wood cross bar used to be made by Merriman but are now only available from some importers of Taiwanese yacht hardware. They are worth searching for if you want a strong and good looking gallows. The notches in the cross bar should be leather lined to prevent scarring the boom.

The gallows frame is not an essential piece of gear for the coastal cruiser, but I recommend it highly for any blue water yacht that will be venturing to far-off places.

10

□
□
□
□
□
□
□
□
□
□

CONSTRUCTION, SCANTLING AND RACING RULES

This is not a detailed dissertation on all forms of construction (scantlings, etc.) but is an attempt to discuss the good and bad points of the many ways that a boat can be assembled from various materials. References will be given for those interested in going into more detail in any of the materials. To cover any one form of construction completely would require a book in itself and would be of little interest to the average reader.

WOOD

Wood yachts can be built by many different methods and, with reasonable care, can have a long life. There are quite a few wood yachts and workboats still sailing that are on the plus side of 100 years of age. One of the big advantages of conventional wood construction is that the boat is built of many bits and pieces fastened together with nails and screws. This creates its own problems but does allow any one piece to be replaced easily if it starts to deteriorate. Most of the older wood boats have little original material left in them, having had major surgery, bit by bit, over the years.

I was aboard one Friendship sloop in Maine that had been completely rebuilt by Bald Mountain Boat Works. Every timber in her had been replaced one at a time by

The steam bent frames for a wood 60-footer are being formed over the ribbands.

new wood. In effect, she was a brand new boat but legally, she was the original 1900 Friendship sloop since she had never been broken up and had never lost her original shape. This was a striking example of reconstruction, but many fine wooden yachts have been restored to good-as-new condition without such drastic measures. Wood will always be an excellent boatbuilding material.

One of the oldest wood construction methods is clench-built (also called clinker, clencher, lapstrake) planking on closely spaced athwartship frames. The Viking ships were built in this fashion, as well as fairly recent wood yachts such as the popular Folkboat of the 1950s and literally thousands of small sailing and rowing dinghies. Lapstrake planking can be thinner since the plank thickness and strength is doubled at each lap. Thus, the boat can be lighter or the ballast heavier. The Folkboat had a 50-percent ballast ratio, not at all bad for a 40-year-old wood cruising boat. The drawbacks are that the planks depend on a close fit instead of caulking for watertightness so the seams will open and leak if the fastenings, often copper rivets, stretch or loosen with age. Refastening or setting up on the rivets is not an uncommon chore every 10 years or so. The lapstrake boat cannot be caulked, of course, since the caulking will open the seams farther and simply increase the problem. There is added wetted surface and turbulence to a clench-built hull so the method was never popular for high-quality racing yachts, although it was quite common in workboats, particularly in Europe.

Carvel (some individuals call it "smooth skin") planking has the planks butted edge to edge and caulked. A slightly different form of carvel is the glued seam, used in many light racing yachts (5.5 meters, etc.) where a particularly smooth finish was required. The glued seam hull depends on a tight fit of the planks and top-quality workmanship for watertightness. True carvel planking will require recaulking from time to time, and that is a job for experts. A bad caulking job can almost destroy the hull. Both carvel and glued seam planking may require refastening after 20 years or so, and the glued seam may need to have its seams cleaned out with a router and a new strip glued in place, particularly if it is raced hard.

Strip planking uses relatively square strips, edge nailed and glued. It is strong and tight, but repairs are more difficult than to regular carvel planking. It is an ideal system for the amateur builder as the strips are easily handled, easily bent into place (regular carvel may require steam bending of some planks), and do not require the fine fitting of carvel or glued seam construction. The end result is a monolithic structure, and if the strips are made thicker than normal, the frames may be more widely spaced than with carvel or entirely eliminated if bulkheads are used for framing. Strips may be hollow and round to eliminate gaps between them at the hard turn of the bilge, or they may be tapered to shape. Some builders do neither, but fill the gap with an epoxy/microballoon mix, and this seems to work well.

Double-planked carvel hulls were the sign of quality not too many years ago. The inner layer of planking has its seams fitted tight and glued and the outer layer is set on glue against the inner layer, also with glued seams. When the glue used was epoxy, as on the 12-meter *American Eagle*, built by Luders, the seams remain tight despite hard racing. Older double-planked boats may have canvas set in white lead or glue between the layers and these boats did develop problems as the canvas deteriorated. Some double-planked boats had the inner layer run diagonally, adding athwartship strength.

The rage today is the laminated hull as developed by Bill Luders in the 1950s. These are formed of multilayers of veneer, all glued together to form a strong, one-piece hull. Luders used resorcinol glue between the layers and then placed the hull in a large pressure vessel where it was cured under heat and vacuum bags. Many of these hulls are still sailing after well over 30 years of intense racing.

Since few modern builders have access to a huge autoclave, the modern laminated hull is cold molded using epoxy glue but usually with fewer layers than the Luders boats. Where the Luders 27 had 10 layers of one-eighth-inch mahogany veneer in its hull, the modern cold-molded boat may have three to five heavier layers to create the same thickness. In either case, the inner layers are laid diagonally and alternate in direction while the final layer is usually run fore and aft.

The Gougeon brothers have popularized cold molded hulls in recent years using their WEST (wood epoxy saturation) system. The hulls are glued up with epoxy resin and then coated with epoxy inside and out. Of course, the resin does not actually saturate the wood; it is merely a coating, but it does prevent the entry of air and moisture, and without those two necessities of life, the dry rot fungus cannot grow.

Obviously, epoxy coating will benefit any wood boat. Indeed, Luders was coating the laminated 40-footer *Storm* with epoxy when I first sailed on her almost 25 years ago, and the *American Eagle* was similarly treated in 1964. Epoxy glue is particularly useful for gluing the veneers of a cold molded wood hull, though, as it is thick enough to fill slight gaps between the layers. The superior resorcinol glue is not a good gap filler and needs the pressure of the autoclave to perform up to specification.

169 ☐

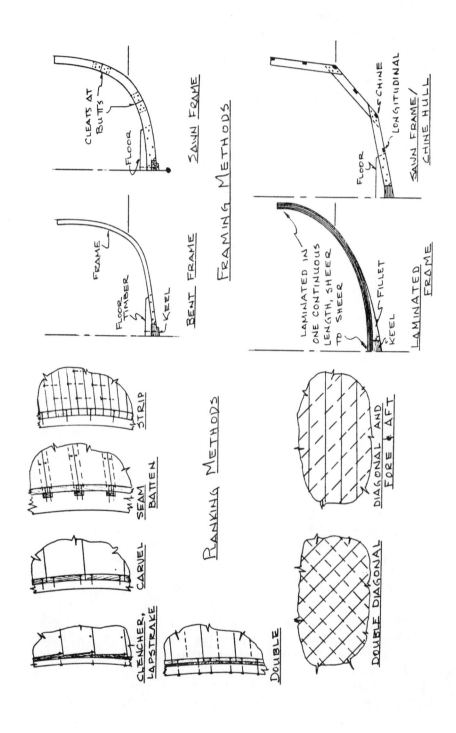

CLEATS AT BUTS

FLOOR

SAWN FRAME

CHINE

LONGITUDINAL

FLOOR

SAWN FRAME /
CHINE HULL

FRAMING METHODS

FRAME

FLOOR TIMBER

KEEL

BENT FRAME

LAMINATED IN ONE CONTINUOUS LENGTH, SHEER TO SHEER

FILLET

KEEL

LAMINATED FRAME

STRIP

SEAM BATTEN

CARVEL

PLANKING METHODS

CLENCHER, LAPSTRAKE

DOUBLE

DIAGONAL AND FORE & AFT

DOUBLE DIAGONAL

A laminated hull is receiving a layer of veneers laid diagonally.

The framing systems used in wood hulls over the years are just as varied as the planking methods. The lapstrake and carvel planked hulls require fairly closely spaced athwartship frames to hold everything together. The frames may be steam bent, sawn of solid timber, or laminated to shape. Sawn frames are generally associated with larger, heavier vessels, usually of workboat type, as well as with plywood planked hulls or carvel planked, hard chine hulls. As a rule, the round bilged yacht will have steam bent frames or a combination of steam bent and laminated frames, i.e., two steam bent frames between each pair of laminated frames. If the boat was all bent framed, it was common to double up several frames or fit sister frames at highly loaded areas such as the mast.

Composite construction, using athwartship metal angle frames with carvel wood planking bolted to them, was popular in the past but is rarely seen today. The frames were usually of steel, galvanized after being bent to shape, or of bronze. I have surveyed 30-year-old steel composite yachts that were structurally as good as new, and I have to believe that a bronze composite yacht would be just about the epitome of fine carvel construction—but hellishly expensive today. One or two metal angle frames are often used at the mast area instead of sister frames in many boats that otherwise are entirely of steam bent or laminated framing.

The strip planked hull will often have only bulkhead framing, not unlike a modern fiberglass yacht, but may have additional frames laminated in place at stress areas such as at the mast. Metal frames could also be used, of course.

On the other hand, the modern cold molded hull will probably have most of its framing longitudinal instead of athwartship. The longitudinal stringers are supported by the bulkheads, and again there may be laminated frames or additional web frames at highly stressed areas. The designer has a choice of either using a thin skin with fairly closely spaced longitudinals or going to a thicker planking and spreading the longitudinals farther apart or eliminating them altogether. *Storm* was basically a frameless hull with bulkhead supports only at the mast and engine. The Canadian designer Graham Shannon is using this method today on cold molded cruiser-racers, and it certainly produces a clean interior.

The thin skin hull with closely spaced longitudinals is lighter for a given strength. However, in the smaller sizes under 32 feet or so, you need a reasonable skin thickness to reduce the chance of penetration if the boat hits a deadhead or a pier. I would say that ⅝-inch skin thickness is about minimal for a cruising yacht, and this thickness in a small yacht does not require a great deal of support from framing. The settee berths, shelves, and cabin sole, if fastened to stringers glued to the skin, will be about all the framing that is required between bulkheads.

The strongest, lightest, and tightest deck for a wood hull is marine grade plywood with strip planked decks a close second. The advantage of strip planking is that if a top grade of clear fir or pine is used, the deck can be simply sanded and oiled and will give good footing without the need for fiberglass covering or nonskid paint. Plywood must be painted or fiberglass covered, of course.

Often teak planks are laid over a plywood subdeck, the teak being set in epoxy or a bedding compound such as Thiokol®. This is poor construction, in my opinion, as the teak deck can develop leaks that run between the layers, often show up many feet from where the water is entering, and are difficult to cure. The result is that the plywood rots out after a few years, necessitating extensive and costly repairs.

Laid decks of solid pine, fir, or teak are another story entirely. The planks are screw fastened to the beams and properly caulked, the seams being finished with black seam compound. If the deck does leak, the water drips right on through so the source of the leak is evident and can be repaired with little fuss. An enthusiastic owner can scrub away a fair thickness of deck over the years, though, so older yachts may be getting to the point where the decks are thin enough that the plugs keep popping out. This is a sign of a costly repair job. Teak is the most common laid decking on yachts, but fir or pine will be seen on older vessels and traditional craft and will last for many years if oiled and maintained without excessive scrubbing.

One of the problems with wood yachts is the mixture of metals in the fittings and fastenings. Reactions between different metals can cause electrolysis, which will eat away the less noble metals. Galvanized iron or other ferrous metals must be kept away from bronze or lead. Generally, bronze screws and bolts are the best fastenings for a good yacht, but galvanized iron nails can be used for edge fastening of strip planked hulls as the nails are completely buried in the wood and sealed off from moisture by the epoxy glue used between the strips. Lead ballast keels should be fastened only with bronze bolts. Stainless steel bolts are often used for this but are less noble than the lead and will be eroded in time with disastrous results. Iron ballast keels may be fastened with stainless or galvanized steel bolts with satisfactory results.

Even if the hull is entirely bronze fastened, stray electrical currents from nearby boats or the yacht's own electrical system can cause problems. Sacrificial zinc plates should be fitted to the hull near the major masses of metal (propeller, shaft, rudder bearing, etc.) to protect them.

PLYWOOD

Plywood has long been popular for small craft and chine hulls of all types. Its strength and lightness, ease of construction, and general availability endear it to the amateur builder. My three most popular designs, the Grand Banks 22, Cape Cod 21-foot catboat, and Deer Isle 28, have all been plywood boats, and plans for them have been sold by the hundreds over the years.

Where the hull is of single-chine type, it must be designed to suit the material. Plywood will only bend in one direction, of course, so the hulls must be conically developed if there is a great deal of twist to the sections and the plywood planking is to lay tight to the frames. Hulls with straight sections between the keel and chine and a lot of twist in the sections will not accept plywood planking. If you are not certain that a design may be plywood planked, check with the architect before you purchase the plans.

Single-chine plywood hulls are set up with widely spaced sawn or bulkhead framing as a rule and have longitudinal stringers let into the framing to support the planking between frames. Multichine hulls, particularly if more than two chines, may have the planking narrow enough that the longitudinals are not required for additional support.

Extremely attractive sailing yachts have been built with three or more chines, and though their shape closely resembles a round bilged hull, they are plywood planked. Plywood can also be ripped into planks for lapstrake hulls and has some advantages for this use. The plywood has less tendency to soak up water, swell, and later shrink as it dries again, so there is less strain on the lap fastenings, and the hull stays tight over the years. For this use, only the finest marine grade plywood is suitable, and the edges must be carefully sealed (with epoxy) to keep moisture out of the layers.

Where plywood is used in wide panels, as on single-chine hulls, the butts of the panels are a weak point. Normally, a wide doubler is fitted inside and glued and screw fastened to the planking. This can create a hard spot in the hull, and the edges of the plywood in the seam can absorb water over the years and delaminate. A long scarf joint is a better method of joining the panel. Alternately, several thin layers of plywood can be used and the butts well staggered. Several of my designs use three layers of quarter-inch plywood to form, in effect, a cold molded bottom. This multilayer plywood construction is also suitable for conically developed hulls with a great deal of curvature in the forward sections. It goes on much easier than a solid sheet of the same total thickness, and once the layers are glued up, it forms an extremely strong and tight structure. This was proven by one of my powerboat designs that hit the rocks at a speed in excess of 15 knots yet was not holed; lots of damage, but no hole!

Plywood also lends itself nicely to fiberglass covering. The material is dimensionally stable compared to other forms of wood planking, and thus, the FRP (fiberglass-reinforced plastic construction) covering does not delaminate as easily. Unfortunately, plywood does not do so well with ordinary paints; the grain seems to creep through and the boat always screams "plywood." A treatment with the WEST system epoxy helps to eliminate this problem as it seals out moisture from the surface of the panel, and it is this that causes the grain to lift.

Plywood comes in two grades that are suitable for marine use. Both marine and exterior grades are glued with the same waterproof glue, but the cheaper exterior grade will have voids, or gaps, in the inner layers. These will be noticed when you saw across a sheet and see the small holes in the inner laminates. The marine grade plywood has a solid core with no voids and is the only choice for hulls and decks. Exterior grade can be used for interior furniture, but the voids in the edges should be filled with epoxy or otherwise sealed to avoid future problems. I used to advise amateur builders that they could use exterior grade for hulls that were to be fiberglassed, but on thinking it over, it seems foolish to put all that hard labor into your dream boat and then risk serious problems after a few years just to save a few dollars.

A form of construction that is not widely known is the plywood "sandwich," in which a core is glued between two thin sheets of plywood. Using 3⁄16-inch plywood skins and a 5⁄8-inch foam or edge grain balsa core, you get a panel that is much stiffer than solid 3⁄4-inch plywood and yet is 20 percent lighter. The stiffness of the panel allows further weight savings in the framing as well. The plywood sandwich can be used for chine hulls and decks. It can be fiberglass covered, of course, or the outer skin of plywood can be completely replaced with FRP to form a fiberglass/plywood sandwich. This would be an excellent form of construction for multichine hulls as it would give a warm wood interior with a tough FRP outer skin.

It is unfortunate that there are not more plans available for good multichine plywood yachts. They make an ideal project for the home craftsman and with modern glues and coatings can give a lifetime of pleasure.

STEEL

Steel has long been accepted as a superb material for cruising yachts in Holland and Germany, but its acceptance in America has been slow. It is only in the past eight to 10 years that it has caught on to any extent, and now it is on the upsurge. Both stock and production builders offer steel yachts, and the amateur builder is welding up everything from Cape Cod catboats to 50-foot auxiliaries. Part of the reason for this popularity is that modern hot zinc sprayed and epoxy coatings have reduced maintenance to little more than that of a fiberglass yacht; it is no longer a neverending battle with wire brushes and red lead! Any good skipper should be able to keep his yacht Bristol fashion with a modest amount of labor and reasonable care.

The major advantage of steel is its strength. With a tensile strength of 50,000 to 60,000 pounds per square inch, and the ability to stretch 30 to 40 percent before failure, a steel hull is able to take strandings and collisions that would reduce a fiberglass boat to splinters and a wood yacht to matchsticks. Steel is also hard and so is the best material for withstanding the abrasion of sand and coral if the yacht does go aground.

Another advantage of steel is that the joining of the parts by welding makes it a one-piece structure with no opportunity for water to find its way in through leaky hull or deck joints, improperly bedded chainplates, or any one of the dozens of places that can leak on wood or fiberglass yachts. The welded "fastenings" on a steel hull are as strong as the metal being joined and are not subject to being fatigued or loosened by working in heavy seas. Steel hulls are tight and remain tight throughout their life.

The cabin doors open as easily in heavy weather as they do in harbor; a good sign of a strong hull that is not wracking itself to death in its continual battle with the seas.

Steel is also an inexpensive building material. While production fiberglass yachts may beat it in price, no custom building material can. Steel has the edge over FRP, wood, or aluminum in material costs and, except for aluminum, in labor costs as well. The repair costs will be lower also. In the first place, the damage will be minimal compared to FRP or wood, and the materials for the repair will cost less than for any of the other materials. A point to consider for the blue water voyager is that any little South Seas island has a steel welder and a scrap yard. How many have the facilities to weld aluminum, the resins and cloth to repair fiberglass, the oak and mahogany to repair a wood hull? It is food for thought.

The other advantages of steel include fire resistance (at least the hull might be saved) and the fact that steel does not deteriorate with age. Given proper initial coating and reasonable care, there is no reason a steel boat should not last your lifetime. The second owner can worry about it after that.

There is another side to the picture, of course. Steel is heavy. Very thin steel plates cannot be welded without buckling so the lightest plate that can be used is about .10 inch, and most builders will not tackle anything lighter than .125 inch. Even .125-inch plate is as heavy as .35-inch aluminum, .5-inch FRP, or 1.5-inch-thick mahogany. To give a better picture, .125-inch steel is suitable for the average 30-to-40-foot cruiser, .35-inch aluminum is heavy enough for a 65-to-70-footer, 1.5-inch mahogany is ample for yachts to 60 feet or more, and .5-inch fiberglass will do for a 40-footer with reasonable framing. The weight disadvantage of steel is obvious, but not as bad as it seems. The steel hull can be built to about the same weight as a conventional carvel wood hull in the 40-foot-and-over size since she does not have the solid deadwood, clamps, bilge stringers, knees, and other structural members of a wood boat. Under 40 feet, the steel boat will be heavier as her plate thickness cannot be reduced with size, and of course, she will be heavier than a modern laminated wood, aluminum, or FRP hull in all sizes.

The weight consideration is not vital to the cruising sailor since the heavier displacement of the steel hull means added stability and motion comfort while she can be given extra sail area to compensate for her added weight. Moreover, the cruising man does not need or want a lightweight, skinned-out racing hull. With modern steel construction, the steel boat can be built to displacement/length ratios of about 300, and this is a good compromise for performance, weight carrying ability, and motion comfort.

Where a lighter displacement and a lower center of gravity are desired, the steel hull can have plywood decks bolted to the beams at considerable weight savings, and wood or aluminum deckhouses can be fitted. The aluminum can be fastened to the steel by bolting over a neoprene gasket. Or, a special metal is available, in effect, aluminum bonded to steel under immense pressure. The steel side is welded to the steel framing, of course, and the aluminum side welded to the superstructure. This has been used in fishing vessels for several years with excellent results.

The second disadvantage of steel is shape. European builders have been turning out wineglass sectioned steel hulls since before World War II but few North

A radius chine steel 45-footer being plated. The framing, both longitudinal and athwartship, shows clearly.

American builders have the equipment or the skills to do this type of work. In most yards, the hull is limited to single-chine or multichine types, but since we started the radius chine hulls in the mid 1970s, more builders are turning to it, and a few are able to turn out the more complex wineglass-shaped vessel.

The radius chine hulls are simply that, a vee bottom hull with a large radius at the chine. Some designers and builders use a constant radius from stem to stern, but I find the results are happier if the radius tapers, being greatest at the bow. For example, on a 36-to-40-footer, the chine radius might be 6 feet forward and reduce gradually to 2½ feet aft. Such yachts are not that much more difficult to build than a chine hull, and amateur builders have completed substantial 45-footers as a first project, although that is more boat than I would care to tackle.

Steel is low on the galvanic scale so bronze and copper cannot be used below the waterline or electrolysis will result. Indeed, it is best to eliminate cuprous metals wherever possible. Fortunately, with stainless steel valves, nylon seacocks, stainless shafting and propellers, and many fine aluminum fittings available today, it is not too difficult to attain this goal. Sacrificial zinc anodes are still required, of course, and these can be pocketed flush with the hull. I like to see two aft and two forward for good protection. Because of the problems of electrolysis, lead ballast keels should be poured inside the steel fin and not be a bolted-on casting.

Steel hulls may be framed completely athwartship, and this was the standard method for many years. However, modern yachts generally have widely spaced athwartship frames and closely spaced longitudinals as this permits the use of the lightest possible plating and helps ensure a fair hull. It is quite feasible to build a steel hull similar to a fiberglass yacht, using frames only at the bulkheads and stiffening the plate with longitudinals between the bulkheads. In an interesting experiment, the

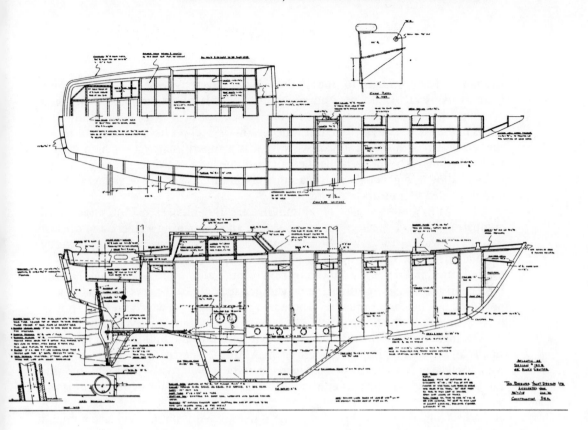

The Atlantic 45. Typical steel construction. (The hull longitudinals are not shown to avoid a confusion of lines.)

builder of a new steel 40-footer made up two 6-foot long panels, one of .125-inch steel with longitudinal frames and another of the .4-inch-thick unframed fiberglass typical of a boat of this size. The panels were suspended at the ends and weight applied in the middle. It took 700 pounds to bend the steel panel two inches and 60 pounds to bend the fiberglass panel an equal amount. The result says much for the strength of a steel hull in comparison to that of the common type of construction used in the majority of production fiberglass yachts. I think we still have much to learn about steel construction, and I believe that we will be seeing lighter steel boats in the future.

Steel decks are the rule, of course, although plywood can save weight up high. I do not like to see teak decks over a steel subdeck as I feel it is an invitation to rust and leaks, similar to teak over plywood. Perhaps with a heavy epoxy coating the steel subdeck will stand up, but we will not know for another 10 years or so if it is truly a long-term solution. If a teak deck is desired on a steel yacht, I much prefer to see it bolted directly to the beams and properly caulked. At least, if it leaks, you can find the leak and fix it. At the moment, a painted steel deck or plastic nonskid material over the steel deck seems the best bet.

ALUMINUM

Aluminum has been used for many years now for every type of craft, from fishing boats to luxury yachts, as it has numerous advantages. It is light, strong, and corrosion resistant—highly desirable qualities for any vessel. Consider that marine aluminum alloys in the 5000 series are one-third the weight of steel yet have almost two-thirds the tensile strength, and you can see why it is a superb material for high-quality yachts. Sailing yachts in particular benefit from the light construction weight of the hull as it allows a higher ballast/displacement ratio with its benefits of greater stability and improved windward performance.

The main disadvantages of aluminum are the higher cost of material in comparison to steel, the need for highly skilled and specialized welders, and the fact that it is lower on the galvanic scale than steel so electrolysis has to be carefully considered. Like steel, no copper-based metals (copper, bronze, brass) can be used in the hull, and protection by anodes of zinc or pure aluminum is essential. Further protection against electrolysis is given by impressed current systems such as Capac®, produced by Englehart Industries. These are active systems in which the ship's power is used to reverse the normal flow of galvanic current and so prevent electrolysis.

The higher cost of the material is not that serious as the hull is only a relatively small part of a well-equipped, modern yacht. A 20-to-25-percent increase in hull costs could well be only a 5-to-10-percent increase in the overall cost of the yacht, and this can be repaid several times over in resale value. One 56-foot aluminum yacht that I designed in 1967 has been resold for twice its initial cost and is probably worth two-and-a-half times its new cost on today's market. Aluminum yachts command premium prices.

Barring electrolysis, aluminum of the 5000 (high magnesium content) series is virtually corrosion free. It does not even need to be painted to protect it against the effects of sea water. Indeed, some commerical fishing vessels do not put antifouling paint on the bottom, figuring it is cheaper to haul every couple of months to scrub the bottom than it is to haul and repaint once or twice a year.

There are two basic types of aluminum alloys. The 5000 series metals are preferred for hulls as they are not heat treated. Thus, when welded, they do not lose as much of their strength as the heat treated 6000 series alloys. The latter alloys are easily extruded and thus widely used for spars. However, they lose about one-third of their strength in the vicinity of a weld as the high temperatures of welding anneal the metal. The alloys commonly used in hulls are 5083 or 5086 and will develop tensile strengths of about 34,000 pounds per square inch.

Like steel, the aluminum hull cannot be less than about .10 inch thick due to the problems of buckling from the heat of welding. Indeed, most builders prefer .15 inch as a minimum. The answer for a really lightweight aluminum hull is to use even thinner plating, support it in an "eggcrate"-type framing, and fasten it with epoxy glue and rivets to avoid the distortion caused by welding. Such construction has been used in racing yachts, but I would not recommend it for a cruising yacht as a thicker, welded hull will be better able to withstand the day-to-day impacts that are a natural part of the cruiser's life.

The 56-foot aluminum ketch Mystic *on her way to second in class in the 1969 Trans-Pac race.*

The framing will be similar to a steel yacht, either all athwartship frames or, more commonly today, widely spaced athwartship frames with closely spaced longitudinal stringers to support the plate. In both steel and aluminum, the frames and longitudinals can be angles, T sections, or flat bar. The latter is slightly stronger for a given weight but takes up much more space inside the hull. For example, with .125-inch skin plating, a 1.5"x1.5"x.1875" angle will give a section modulus of .468. With the same skin plate thickness, a 3"x.1875" flat bar frame gives a section modulus of .532 for the same weight of material but takes a full 3-inch width out of the accommodations due to its greater depth. Flat bar framing has one advantage in the steel hull as it is easier to paint around, but this is of no consequence to the aluminum hull as the inside does not need to be painted. A common combination is to use angle stock for the athwartship frames and flat bar for the longitudinals.

Both steel and aluminum hulls need to be insulated to prevent condensation, maintain temperatures inside the hull, and dampen noise. I have used common house-type fiberglass bat insulation with good success, or foam sheets lightly contact-cemented in place. I am not fond of the spray-in foam insulations as some of them give off toxic gases in a fire, and they are difficult to remove if repairs are required. The builder should ensure that any foam insulation, whether spray-in-place or sheet-type foam, is nontoxic and will not readily burn in case of fire.

Aluminum hulls can have teak decks laid over the aluminum subdeck without any fear of the subdeck corroding through in time. The teak, if it is not of too thin a planking, can be blind-fastened to tabs welded to the aluminum deck, thereby avoiding having to drill a thousand or more holes through the watertight aluminum subdeck. The aluminum deck can also be painted with nonskid paint or covered with a vinyl nonskid material. All deck hardware should be of stainless steel or aluminum; bronze fittings should be avoided wherever possible to eliminate any chance of electrolysis. If bronze hardware must be used, then it has to be carefully insulated from the aluminum and fastened with stainless steel bolts. To avoid dozens of fastening holes through the deck, it is possible to have a thick aluminum base plate welded to the deck, drilled and tapped to accept the fitting bolts.

There are no limitations to hull shape in aluminum, of course, so the larger yachts turned out by the top yards are almost universally of wineglass or round bilge form. Few of the smaller builders have mastered the techniques necessary to accomplish this as yet, so most of the yachts under 35 or 40 feet are of chine or radius chine shape. I consider this unfortunate as aluminum is a superb material for a custom cruising yacht of any size.

FIBERGLASS-REINFORCED PLASTIC (FRP)

FRP construction (also known in Europe as GRP, for glass-reinforced plastic) accounts for the vast majority of the production-built yachts of today and is probably the single major factor in the increase in yachting activity since the early 1960s. In essence, the material is composed of strong strands of glass bonded together by plastic resin, not unlike the rods of reinforcing steel that are laid up in concrete to reinforce our bridges and buildings. The main difference is that the steel is a relatively small part of the reinforced concrete, while the glass content of a good FRP hand layup will be from 33 to 45 percent of the total material. The FRP is layed up in a female mold, speeding up construction so that labor costs are much lower. This has brought down the cost of boats and opened the market to people who could not afford a quality wood yacht. The lower cost, combined with a more affluent economy and more people with more leisure time, creates a larger demand for yachts than ever before in our history.

FRP weighs about 106 pounds per cubic foot, about three times the weight of mahogany. However, the skin of the FRP yacht will be about half the thickness of that of a carvel planked wood yacht, and it will not have the heavy deadwood, the frames, the clamp, carlin, etc., of the wood vessel. Thus, the FRP boat turns out lighter all around, unless it is horribly overbuilt—and far too many are.

The fiberglass material comes in several different types. Mat is a fabric made with chopped strands about two inches long, randomly woven together. The mats used in boatbuilding will weigh from .75 to 2 ounces per square foot and vary in thickness from .022 to .06 inches per layer. Woven roving is a coarse fabric made with bundles of strands interwoven at right angles and comes in weights of 16 to 24 ounces per square yard, giving thicknesses of .023 to .035 inches per layer. FRP is weak in flexural strength compared to other boatbuilding materials so the mat is useful in building up

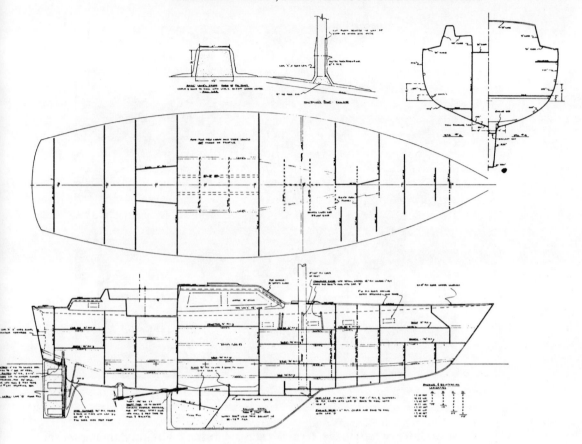

Fiberglass construction using a light skin and longitudinals. The Brewer/MT 42.

the required thickness. The woven roving, having over twice the tensile strength and flexural modulus of mat, is used to increase the strength of the laminate.

Woven roving is very coarse so there may be resin-filled gaps between two layers. This reduces the interlaminar shear strength so most builders will put a light layer of mat between the layers of woven roving to ensure a good bond. A "chopper gun," which spits out a mixture of chopped glass strands and resin to form a mat, can also be used to improve the interlaminar shear strength. Chopper guns have been used to build entire boats, but the result is not as strong as even a hand-laid-up, all-mat hull and should only be used for small dinghies.

Cloth is a tightly woven fabric of fiberglass yarns and is available in a wide range of weights. The 9-to-10-ounce-per-square-yard "boat cloth" is the common weight used. It is stronger than woven rovings but only builds up .016-inch thickness per layer. Building an entire boat out of cloth would be too laborious and costly, but it is often used as the outside layer to prevent print-through of the woven roving pattern and may be used in other areas where a strong reinforcement is desired.

Unidirectional rovings are bundles of filaments all running in the same direction, not woven across each other. The advantage of the unidirectional material (UD) is

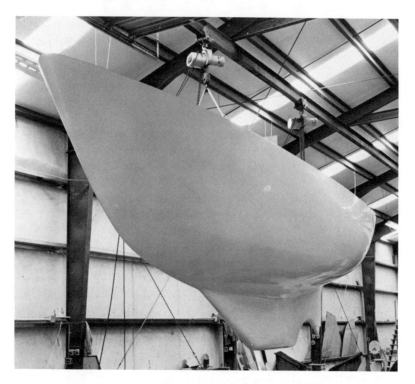

The fiberglass Jason hull is popped from its mold.

that the layers lie closer so smaller resin pockets are formed. The interlaminar shear is stronger, the glass content of the laminate is higher, and the strength is greatly increased over that of woven roving—doubled if the layers are set at 90 degrees to each other, almost tripled if they are all run in the same direction as on a deck beam or a frame. Stronger still is the UD made of S glass, a better quality structural glass fiber. High-tech racing yachts are now using UD made of S glass combined with strands of Kevlar or graphite for even greater strengths, thus permitting thinner skins and lighter hulls, though at higher cost, obviously.

Kevlar is a fiber made by Dupont that is becoming widely used in such diverse creations as IOR racing yachts, lightweight rowing shells, and kayaks. Its stiffness is almost double that of standard fiberglass, and unlike glass, it is not brittle so the result is a much lighter and tougher boat. The material is much more expensive than fiberglass, of course, so it is but rarely used in standard production yachts and then only in expensive high-tech racers.

One way to build a single-skin hull without an expensive female mold is by the use of C-Flex®. This material is a "plank" of FRP rods saturated with resin alternating with bundles of unsaturated rovings, all held together by a light UD cloth on each side. The C-Flex® bends easily in fair curves over a wood framework and can be held to the wood with staples or light brads. Once wetted with resin, the C-Flex® sets up hard and strong, and further layers of mat and woven rovings are applied to build up the necessary thickness. The result is a single-skin hull, but the C-Flex® is, essentially,

Today yachts such as the Nimble 30 canoe yawl are built with cored hulls for strength, lightness, and insulation.

a UD material and provides excellent directional strength. (The wood framework is, of course, removed once the glass sets up and the hull is turned over.)

The average cruising yacht of today is a single-skin hull, hand laid up of mat and woven roving layers, set in polyester resin. Epoxy resin is stronger and more flexible, but its much higher price and toxic qualities limit its use to custom one-offs and racing yachts. Vinylester resin has appeared on the scene recently and is priced between the two. Like epoxy, it is stronger than polyester, more flexible, and has better shear strength but is still not widely used by production builders.

The standard production yacht and many one-offs use little framing other than the bulkheads and perhaps the glassed-in sole, berth tops, and shelves. Since FRP is weak in flexural strength, the skin has to be thicker to make up for this lack of framing. The result is a yacht that is heavier than it needs to be. This disadvantage can be overcome by using two thinner skins of FRP with a lightweight core between. The core acts like the web of an I beam, holding the flanges (the FRP skins) apart and thus stiffening the structure. By using this sandwich construction, the yacht can be made both lighter and stronger than a single-skin sister, plus the core provides advantages of insulation and sound deadening.

The Cabot 36, one of the first production yachs with an Airex core. One of these boats survived the Cabo San Lucas disaster, proving the toughness of this construction.

Edge grain balsa has been used as a core in decks for many years, and a number of builders, notably C&C Yachts, have used it as hull core also. It is one of the strongest cores for its weight, with excellent compression and shear strength. In recent years, foam cores have increased in popularity both in production yachts and in one-offs. There are two basic types of foam, the noncrosslinked PVC foam such as Airex®, and the crosslinked PVC foams such as Termanto® and Divinycell®. The basic difference

☐ 184

is that the noncrosslinked foam is more elastic. It can be bent to almost 180 degrees without breaking and will then slowly return to its original condition when released. The crosslinked foams are more rigid and while they have better shear strength (but still not up to balsa in that regard), they are brittle and will snap in two if bent to any degree.

I will not get into any argument about which is the best core material. They all have their advantages and disadvantages, but I do feel that in the case of a major collision, the Airex® cored hull would have the least damage and delamination and be the easiest to repair. On the other hand, a collision is not something we worry about every day, and the more rigid foams have their advantages in producing a stiffer, and perhaps lighter, hull. I will say that a cored hull of any material, if well built, is far superior to a standard, unframed, solid FRP hull.

The cored hull lends itself to amateur building also as the sandwich hull can be built over a simple wood framework. The best way to do this is to cover the framework with mylar to prevent the resin adhering to the wood. Next, lay up the inner skin laminate, fit the core to it in a mix of resin and filler (preferably with a vacuum bag to get a solid bond), fair the core, and finally lay up the outer FRP skin. Such a hull is quite stiff when it is turned over and the framework removed, thus eliminating the serious problems of distortion that can occur if the inner skin is not applied until after the hull is turned.

The usual core materials are relatively weak in compression and not able to handle the loads of keel bolts or deck hardware bolts. Thus, it is essential that the core in these areas be replaced by solid plywood or solid FRP.

Many production boats have a FRP inner liner, which forms the basis for the furniture and is bonded to the hull at certain places to form a stiffener. The liner is easy to clean, but it can make repairs difficult and reduce access to the hull, wiring, plumbing, etc., for inspection and maintenance. The underside of the cabin roof and deck may have a FRP headliner as well, but a removable soft liner is to be preferred, in my opinion. It greatly simplifies adding deck hardware (and we all do that) as well as making it easier to track down and cure leaks through weepy fastenings.

Structural bulkheads normally are of plywood and are bonded to the inside of the hull using FRP tapes on each side. The American Bureau of Shipping rules require that these FRP bonds be reinforced by mechanical fastenings such as stainless steel bolts. This is rarely done unless the boat is to be classed by the ABS. Another good way to provide a mechanical bond is to drill ½-to-¾-inch-diameter holes along the edge of the bulkhead and ensure that the FRP tape is pressed deeply into each hole as it is applied. Again, this is rarely done, and bulkheads tearing loose from the hull are not uncommon in boats subjected to the strains of rough weather. Some extra care in building would eliminate this danger. Another problem with bulkhead installations is hard spots in the hull caused by the bulkhead pressing against the inside. The bulkhead should be fitted onto a foam pad flared to spread the load. This practice is becoming fairly standard today.

The hull/deck joint has long been a weak spot in FRP boat construction, with a reputation for serious leaks and even pulling apart on occasion under the strains of hard sailing. The best joint is one where the deck laps at least three inches onto the hull flange and is set into a strong sealant, such as 3M® 5200. This is then reinforced with closely spaced stainless steel through-bolts, and in fine-quality yachts, the joint is taped on the inside with FRP tape to reinforce it further. Some builders will use pop rivets to hold this vital connection. However, such rivets are not up to the job unless, as many good builders do, the rivets are only used to hold things in line until a teak rail or aluminum genoa track is fitted over the joint and through-bolted to lock everything in place.

We are now finding that FRP yachts are not quite as maintenance free as was originally believed. Besides the chalking and fading of the colors, the crazing of the gel coat, and the structural cracks that may develop in highly stressed areas of the hull and deck, we now have osmosis. This shows up after 5 to 15 years as blisters in the underwater areas of the hull. Polyester resin is *not* waterproof so water can seep into tiny voids in the gel coat or laminate and create an acidic solution and an eventual blister. If left unattended, the blister may break open due to inside pressure, and the eventual result can be a weakening of the laminate. The best prevention is to epoxy-coat the bottom of the new yacht before the first layer of antifouling paint is applied. If the boat is already blistered, the cure is to open the little devils up, dry them out, and fair up the hull with epoxy, coating the entire bottom for long-term protection while you're at it. Because of the dangers of osmosis, built-in water and holding tanks should be epoxy coated inside. It is a good idea to paint or epoxy-coat the bilges as well since bilge water is likely to cause problems over the years.

Regardless of its problems, the FRP hull is still one of the best methods of construction for the mass market. In future years, we may see more cored hulls and other advances, but they will still be FRP yachts.

FERROCEMENT

Concrete weighs one-third as much as steel, but steel boats can be built of $\frac{1}{10}$" to $\frac{1}{8}$" plate, while a ferro skin is rarely less than $\frac{5}{8}$-inch thick. Thus, the ferro hull will weigh in at somewhere between one-and-a-half to two times as heavy as a steel hull. Since I'm always concerned with the weight of steel hulls and constantly trying to think of ways to build them lighter, I just cannot bring myself to consider ferrocement a viable material for yacht construction, particularly when there are so many better materials available.

SCANTLING RULES

Scantlings are the dimensions of the planking (or plating), frames, keel members, beams, etc., of the vessel; scantling rules are written rules that control the scantlings and thus the strength of the yacht. The rules are written by various groups or societies to ensure that the craft classed by them are built to a reasonable standard of strength, usually based on size. Rules for wood yachts were produced many years ago by Lloyds, Nevins yacht builders and Nathanael Herreshoff, among others, and generally produced a solid vessel. The Herreshoff rule used lighter scantlings, allowing a lighter weight of hull, but required more skilled and careful workmanship. Lloyds's rules produced a slightly heavier yacht, and the Nevins rule the heaviest, though many U.S. yachts were built to this rule. Lloyds also published scantling rules for metal hulls and in the late 1960s and early 1970s came out with rules for FRP and ferrocement yachts. There are other rules, including those for Scottish fishing trawlers, but the basic idea is that the scantling rule ensures that the vessel is built to a minimum (and good) standard.

The scantlings are usually based on a rule length, or L, which may be an average of the LOA and the LWL, or the length measured at half the height of the midships freeboard. The depth of the hull, the beam, and even the displacement might be taken into account, depending upon the rule being used. Applying the rule formulae produces the required dimensions for skin thickness, frames, and other members of the structure. Most of the rules permit a reduction of strength and a lighter scantling in the ends of the hull where the strains are slightly less.

A few years ago the American Bureau of Shipping looked into scantling rules, did a great deal of research, consulted many designers (including Gary Mull who has had a long-time interest in this problem), looked at successful and unsuccessful yachts, and came out with the ABS Rules for Offshore Racing Yachts. These cover wood (carvel and laminated), FRP (single and cored skin), and steel and aluminum construction. In my opinion, these are the most intelligently developed scantling rules yet worked out for sailing yachts. The ABS rule, while specifically for racing yachts, also serves well for cruisers since these are rarely subjected to the strains that a racer will encounter in heavy weather. The rule establishes an L from the average of the LOA and the LWL and takes in the depth of the canoe hull of the yacht plus many other factors.

Essentially, the formulae in the ABS rule establish a head of water for the part of the yacht being examined, take into account the size of the unsupported panel of the skin, and then set forth the required minimum skin thickness of the hull or deck. With further information as to the frame chord, the rule comes up with the section modulus of the frames or beams required to support the skin under the developed heads of water. From tests, the ABS has concluded that the maximum loads are developed in the area from about 5 percent to 40 percent of the LWL abaft the bow, and that both ahead and abaft these areas the structure can be progressively lightened. My experience with the rule has been good, and I feel that it creates a strong but light hull with the strength concentrated in the vital areas. I use the rule exclusively in new design work and have developed a computer program to handle it.

Builders have accepted the rule wholeheartedly, and I have had the construction drawings of several yachts approved by the ABS to date; the Whitby 55, an aluminum custom 51-foot motorsailer, the Brewer/MT50, and the Brewer/MT42. Even when the client does not want to pay for ABS approval (about $1,500), I still use the scantling rule for the boat as I feel it is a sensible and workable rule that ensures a solid but not overweight vessel.

It must be borne in mind that a builder who advertises that the boat is built to ABS or Lloyds rules (the favorite phrase is "in excess of") is putting forth absolute hogwash unless he can show you a set of construction plans with the ABS or Lloyds stamp on them. Even then, having the drawings approved does not necessarily mean that the builder is going by them. I heard of one Hong Kong builder who stationed a small boy where he could watch the harbor and then turned on the air conditioning in the laminating shed only when the lookout reported that the Lloyds surveyor's launch was in sight. Of course, if they have invested the money in plan approval, most builders will stick carefully to the scantling so they can continue to advertise honestly, "built to the ABS (or Lloyds) rule."

Even if the builder has the plans approved, the owner cannot get a 100A* class on the yacht unless the surveyor is physically there during certain periods of construction to check hull thickness, etc., or unless tests are done on the hull after it is built to ensure that it meets the standards. Lloyds will issue a blanket approval on production FRP hulls, but their surveyor will then visit the plant at regular intervals. In order to get a full 100A* class on a yacht, the machinery, wiring, ground tackle, and many other items of the yacht have to be inspected. In any case, no classification society concerns itself with the spars, rigging, chainplates, or sails, leaving that up to the owner/builder/designer completely. The 100A* class is good for a couple of years, and then the boat must pass a rigid survey to remain in class. For the average owner, it may not be worth the hassle, but it is a darned fine reassurance if you are buying a used boat that has remained in class over the years. If a boat still has the 100A* class, it is obvious that the previous owner(s) must have spent money to have it surveyed and repaired as necessary.

There are separate scantling rules set by Lloyds for boats racing in the 5.5-, 6-, 8-, and 12-meter classes. The purpose of these is to ensure that all the competitors are built to a reasonable standard and the same construction weight so that no one can have an edge by building an ultra-light, six-race, disposable boat.

Generally, any older yacht you might consider as a purchase will be well built if she was classed originally by Lloyds, ABS, Norske Veritas, or one of the other societies and will be in good condition if the owner(s) have maintained her in class. A new yacht built to approved plans will be a strong yacht as well, but beware of the yacht built "in excess of the rules." First, the phrase means nothing unless the plans are approved and the builder trustworthy; second, it could mean an overbuilt boat with inadequate ballast. The rules produce a good boat, too heavy for IOR racing but amply strong for cruising yachts. Exceeding the rule is not really in the best interests of the buyer. It may save the builder some money, though, as it is cheaper and simpler to add another layer of FRP and charge it to the buyer than it is to design a good structure and have it approved by the societies.

IOR racing yachts are rarely built to the rules (even to the ABS Offshore Racing Yacht rule) as designers and owners are insistent on building as lightly as possible to ensure maximum performance. There is a move afoot to require that yachts on long offshore courses be ABS approved, and I hope this will come to pass for the good of the sport. Certainly, if all the yachts have to meet the same scantling rule then no one yacht will have an unfair weight advantage, and this will ensure a semblance of sanity and longevity in the construction of IOR racers.

RACING RATINGS

Yacht racing is conducted in three basic forms. One-design classes such as the Lightning, Star, International One-Design, and several small cruiser classes race with boats that are built to the same design. The yachts all start at the same time and the first one across the finish line, barring protests, is the winner. The second type of racing is the international meter classes such as the 5.5-, 6-, 8-, and 12-meter yachts. The designs are all different but done to a rule that allows slight variations in hull shape, displacement, sail area, and other factors but limits minimum beam, maximum mast height, sail area, and other factors. Again the boats start together, and the one that romps home first gets the silver.

To enable yachts of widely different sizes and types to race together, we have an assortment of handicap rules: the IOR rules, the Midget Ocean Racing Club (MORC) rule, the Measurement Handicap Rule (MHR), etc. Under any of these rules, literally dozens of measurements are taken of the hull and rig and put through a formula (usually quite complex) to arrive at the rating for the yacht. Then a handicap is determined based on the rating and the distance of the race. Obviously, the designers and owners will take advantage of any loopholes in the handicap rule in order to win so, over the years, the boats built to any given rule tend to become similar in general type.

At the turn of the century, the British handicap rule then in use developed the plank-on-edge cutter as the rule gave no credit for beam. Similarly, in the 1960s the Cruising Club of America rule turned out beamy, keel-centerboard yawls while the Royal Ocean Racing Club rule produced narrower and deeper cutters. In the 1960s, a group of yachtsmen from both sides of the Atlantic got together to create a handicap rule that would be suitable to both European and American yachtsmen and, with Olin Stephens to head up the work, put together the International Offshore Rule. With periodic changes to plug loopholes, the IOR has been the major handicap rule throughout the world for almost two decades and is used for most top-level racing.

The major fault of the IOR is that it does not properly assess displacement. The CCA rule required that the yachts actually be weighed and while this is essentially foolproof, it is also a costly procedure. The IOR takes measurements at certain points on the hull and uses these figures to estimate displacement. This is a reasonable method if there are enough points, but the few required by the rule allow designers to design to the dots, so to speak. As a result, we see rather strange, flat bottomed hulls produced in an attempt to make the rule think the boat is heavier than it actually is and so give it a lower rating.

Dissatisfaction with the IOR resulted in the Measurement Handicap Rule being developed in the U.S. The complete lines of the yacht are measured with an electronic device so there is no point in designing to the dots and a fairer hull is assured. The MHR also requires more complete interior accommodations and, if it becomes popular, may result in a return to the true cruiser-racer types that were prevalent in the 1960s as opposed to the stripped-out racing machines that are the present vogue for top-flight competition.

The Offshore Racing Council has attempted to develop level racing by creating a group of classes of different IOR ratings as follows.

Mini-ton	16.5 feet
Quarter-ton	18.5 feet
Half-ton	22.0 feet
Three-quarter-ton	24.5 feet

Like the one-design classes, boats in these groups, though of quite varied design, start together, and the winner is the first over the finish line. The idea is good but has not proved popular in America, perhaps due to the wide variety of small, one-design distance racers that are available as well as the expense of measuring to the IOR and building a new boat every year or two to keep up with developments as designers find new loopholes in the rule. It is simpy much easier and less costly to buy a J-24 and race with other J-24s than it is to have a quarter-tonner designed and custom built. Also, there is much more racing available in an active class, such as the J-24, for the real die-hard racing skipper while class limitations on the number and type of sails can help reduce expenses.

The Midget Ocean Racing Club rule is another handicap rule current in America, and it has a substantial following. It originally started off with a 24-foot LOA limit but has expanded to 30 feet. The original rule was similar to the CCA rule but has been modified over the years as designers discovered loopholes. The first MORC boats were almost miniature CCA yachts, like Bill Shaw's sweet little 24-foot keel-centerboard yawl *Trina*. Present competition in the class is a beamier, lighter displacement craft, and the average size has grown to 27 feet or so.

If you are interested in distance racing, find out what classes are seriously racing in your area, whether IOR level rating, a one-design cruiser-racer, MORC, etc. There is no point in buying one type of boat simply because it appeals to you if all the good competition is in a completely different class.

11

PLANS AND DESIGNERS

THE CLIENT AND THE ARCHITECT

No two designers are alike; they will vary in their style of boats; in their interpretation of the problems involved; in their preference as to rig, layout, construction, and machinery; and in their fees. In effect, yacht designers are a reflection of the yachting public. Selecting a designer is not a difficult task, though, whether you are looking for stock plans to build yourself or have built for you or want to commission a custom design.

You cannot pick an architect out of the yellow pages, but you can spend some time looking at the work of various designers to decide which one does the type of yacht that pleases you both aesthetically and practically. Root through the design sections of the various yachting magazines and read all the books you can on actual designs. Some of the good ones to start with are: Henderson's *Choice Yacht Designs*, Beiser's *The Proper Yacht*, Mate's *Best Boats*, and Taylor's *Good Boats, More Good Boats*, and *Fourth Book of Good Boats*.

Once you find a designer whose work agrees with you, then write him with your requirements. Be specific. Don't say "I want plans for a 30-foot boat." Tell him your preferences in material, rig, layout, style, machinery, where you will use it, and all the details that you want in your dream boat. Then you should get a reasoned and thoughtful reply.

Some architects do not have stock plans for sale, others may not sell plans to amateur builders, some specialize in plans for amateur builders and do very little custom work. We are getting to be like doctors, every one with a specialty. Still many designers do both production boats and custom yachts, and many have stock plans available.

As to specialization, some designers do only IOR racers or modern-style cruisers and have never worked with carvel planked hull construction or a traditional design. Others do only traditional boats or character types and may never have worked with cored FRP, aluminum, or laminated wood. A few, and I like to think I am one of them, will tackle anything within reason, although I do draw the line at ferrocement. In my years in this business, I have designed boats in steel, aluminum, solid and cored FRP, carvel wood planked on steam bent frames and on bent bronze frames, chine plywood and round bilge strip and laminated wood, and even Fer-a-lite®. In types they have ranged from Cape Cod cats, pilot schooner types, sharpies, traditional CCA styles, and Down East pinkies to ultra-light racers and modern fin keel production cruisers. Many other designers can make similar claims. Just be sure that the designer you select, if it's a custom design you're after, is willing, able, and experienced to tackle the type of yacht that you want.

Fees may vary widely. Generally, a good stock plan will run about one percent of the value of the completed yacht, a custom design somewhere between five and 15 percent of the value, depending on how much supervision is involved on the part of the architect. Be sure you find out what you will get for your money. The following section describes the drawings that should be part of a set of plans for the average yacht.

Some designers catering to the amateur builder offer full-scale patterns of the lines. These can be useful if they are printed on mylar so that they will not shrink and stretch with changes in the weather. My feeling is that a person who does not have the skill and the space to loft a boat properly certainly does not have the skill or the space to build it. The amateur builder who lofts his own boat will be way ahead of the person working from patterns in the long run. No designer can afford to give patterns of every little part of the yacht, but if you have lofted it full size, you can go to the lofting and take off the part you need. If you have built from patterns, then you have to go by the cut-and-try method. No professional builder would dream of building a boat without lofting it; I'm always impressed that so many amateur builders think they know a better way.

If you order stock plans you will receive them by return mail as a rule. A custom design, depending on size, may take from three months to a year to turn out, so plan ahead. You may find a stock plan that will suit your needs with some modifications. If these are minor, you can make the changes yourself, but if you require major changes in rig, construction, or arrangement (particularly where major weights are involved), then you must consult the architect. If the changes are truly great you might well be better off with a custom design right from the beginning. One of the most common changes that I get asked for is to convert a FRP design to wood construction. Of course, the wood boat needs beams and frames, all of which reduce interior volume and headroom, necessitating a new arrangement plan; and then the keel structure forces relocation of the engine, ballast, and other items. It is usually best to start from scratch in such a case.

Altering rigs can also pose problems as you suddenly find that the mast has been relocated right into the middle of the head. This means a new arrangement plan, and that calls for new joiner sections and possibly a relocation of the tanks; then that means recalculating the ballast and, of course, new chainplate drawings, mast steps, and deck layout. In effect, all you reuse is the lines drawing, and the client wonders why the simple rig change cost so much! Changes can be made to designs and sometimes the work is simple, but all too often it turns out to create more problems than anyone expected. For this reason, many architects will only take modification work on an hourly basis. I'm one of them.

THE PLANS

A complete set of plans consists of a number of drawings and usually a set of written specifications. On yachts up to 30 feet or so, the major drawings may be at a scale of 1 inch to the foot; from 25 to 50 feet LOA, a scale of ¾ inch to the foot is common; and above this ½ inch to the foot. Detail drawings of items such as chainplates, stemhead fittings, rudder bearings, etc., will be done at larger scales, from 1½ inches to the foot to full size. The complete set of plans will consist of the following:

LINES DRAWING

This will show the three views of the hull—plan, profile, and section—and the diagonals on a round bilged yacht. Only half the yacht is shown in the plan and section views as, with any luck, the other half will turn out reasonably similar. A table of offsets will be on the drawing or may be a separate sheet. The offsets are the dimensions of the hull and will be given in feet-inches-eighths. Thus 6.3.4 indicates 6 feet, 3½ inches, 4 eighths being one-half inch, of course. A plus sign may be used to indicate an additional ¹⁄₁₆ inch, that is 6.3.4+ = 6 feet, 3⁹⁄₁₆ inches. Some designers have switched to the metric system, and this is common overseas. I've done two designs to the metric system—my first and last.

Yachts that have fin keels or outside ballast may have larger scale drawings of the fin or ballast. Large-scale lines drawings of spade and skeg-type rudders are also usual, and these will all have their separate offset table.

ACCOMMODATION PLANS

These consist of the arrangement plan view and profile. The port side inboard profile is normally shown, but many designs will also show the starboard profile, or chunks of it where it differs from the port side, on another sheet. The joiner sections are also part of the accommodation plans and are usually on a separate sheet. These are athwartships sections through the hull showing the furniture and often the tanks and similar detail.

CONSTRUCTION DRAWINGS

This may be on one or several sheets and will include the construction profile, showing the hull as if it were sliced lengthwise down the centerline. One or more construction sections will detail the scantlings of the various parts, or laminate schedule. If the boat is wood or metal, there will be a deck framing plan, and if it is a chine hull there may be a bottom framing plan. Some architects will show a separate keel structure plan on wood boats as well. The engine room layout will be included on larger vessels where the machinery is complex, and detail drawings of such items as chainplates, stemhead fitting, mast step, tanks, ballast keel, rudder construction, etc., will be included as necessary.

DECK PLAN

This will show the location, size, manufacturer, etc., of all the hardware and may have offsets for the deck structures, cockpit, and similar items. On a FRP production boat, this may be combined with the deck mold drawing.

SAILPLAN

The sailplan will show the general appearance of the yacht and will have details on the sail measurements, rigging sizes, and possibly a block list. Because of the size of this drawing, it is usually to a smaller scale than the lines, construction, and arrangement plans.

SPAR DRAWING

If the boat has hollow wood spars, there will be a separate drawing showing the mast construction, tangs, masthead fitting, etc. On boats with aluminum spars, the spar drawing is generally placed on the sailplan and does little more than give the minimum moments of inertia and the basic dimensions of the mast—basically enough data that the client can take the drawing to a reputable sparmaker and have it built. Racing yachts will often have custom spars, and this will require a well-detailed sheet of drawings, but it is rare to find custom spars on a cruising yacht. If a bowsprit is fitted, this will appear on a separate sheet along with the bobstay attachment and other hardware.

MISCELLANEOUS DRAWINGS

These will depend on the size and complexity of the vessel. Electrical schematic diagrams, piping plans, centerboard detail drawings, tanks, and special joinerwork may all be covered as required.

SPECIFICATIONS

Written specifications accompany most designs and will contain much data now shown on the plans, i.e., material specifications, hardware description, glue, fastenings, machinery detail, paint schedule, equipment list, etc. A good set of specs will fill in any gaps and ensure that the complete set of plans can form the basis for a contract between the owner and the builder.

Even if there are questions after you receive the plans, the conscientious architect will fill in the gaps with special sketches or verbal advice. Most of us want to see our creations properly built and our clients happy and will put in as many hours as necessary to achieve this end.

THE CUSTOM DESIGN

When the average yachtsman hears the words "custom designed," he immediately visualizes a gold plated floating palace that epitomizes the proverbial hole-in-the-water into which money is poured. Many custom yachts fit into this category, but equally many are simply average craft designed to fit a particular need. Indeed, quite a few custom designs are created with an eye to saving the owner money, as will be discussed later.

One reason for a custom design is to obtain a craft that you cannot buy "off the shelf," such as this 50-footer with only 3-foot-6-inch draft with board up.

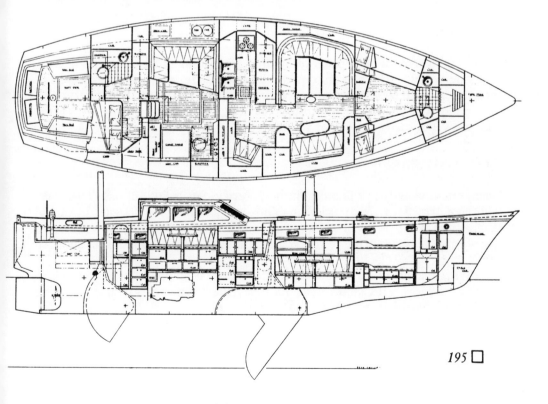

The reasons for having a custom design created vary widely, so let's examine a few of these reasons. You might just find that you fit into one of these categories.

RACING YACHTS

Racing craft are custom designed because the owner wants a winning boat. Such yachts can range from a 14-foot international dinghy to a 100-foot entry in the Observer Singlehanded Transatlantic Race. The reason for the design is usually that the owner or the designer has an idea that he feels will swing the scales in his favor, either by improved performance or a lower handicap rating.

A racing yacht may be created for a particular series, such as the America's Cup, in which case a custom design is essential as no production boats are built for events in this category. Large ocean racing yachts, over 50 feet or so in length, are also custom designed as there are few, if any, stock production models in this size range modern enough for today's stiff competition.

The custom racing yacht, from the earliest era of the sport, has pioneered many ideas that have filtered down to the present modern cruising yacht. Ideas such as the modern Bermudan rig, aluminum masts, inside halyards, winches, fin keels, jiffy reefing, folding propellers, spinnaker poles, genoa jibs, and even outside ballast all began with the idea of better performance for racing. Indeed, if it were not for racing and the custom yacht designed to win, we would probably all be cruising around in deep vee bodied, full keel, gaff rigged yachts today.

Unfortunately, the intensity of competition today means that most top-flight racing yachts are gold platers as far as equipment and sails are concerned. A sign of the times, perhaps.

GOLD PLATERS

A large number of true gold plater yachts are designed simply because no production boats are available that meet the owner's needs as to size, type, or luxury. Such craft can range from large motorsailers and auxiliaries up to such exotic craft as brigantines. Custom design and custom building at the highest quality yards is the only answer to such a yachtsman's needs.

ECONOMY CRAFT

Many sailors would be surprised at the number of yachts sailing our waters that were custom designed with one purpose in mind—economy. A good designer, by careful attention to materials, details, equipment, and building yard, can save his client a fair percentage of the cost of the vessel, certainly enough to offset the design fee and then some.

By suggesting certain hull types that are more economical to build (such as sharpies, deadrise hulls, radius chine hulls, etc.), the designer may be able to give his client more boat than he expected to obtain for his money. Similarly, by knowing from experience those yards that provide acceptable quality at a reasonable price, the

The 34-foot pinky sloop Lucia: *a very traditional yacht with a modern fiberglass hull.*

designer can often achieve economies for his client with no sacrifice of comfort or durability.

Many custom designs are created for amateur builders who cannot find the stock plan that meets their needs. The object of the home builder is economy in most cases. By turning to a custom design, he can obtain the size and type of boat that he requires, and the designer can plan it to suit the builder's skills, available materials, simplified hull shapes, or other particular requirements requested by the builder.

CHARACTER YACHTS

Few traditional boats are available as stock fiberglass production boats either, so the owner who wants a Boston pilot schooner, a sharpie, a skipjack, a pinky, or other particular type must commission a custom design if he cannot find a suitable used boat or a stock plan to build from.

Some of the character boat types might be classed under the economy reason as well. Many traditional shapes can provide a lot of boat for the money and are also simple-to-build craft suitable for amateur construction. The owner looking for a traditional yacht to build himself could have several good reasons for considering a custom design.

The larger and more elaborate character yachts, such as the coasting or pilot schooners, are usually professionally built as the project is too large for the average amateur, no matter how skilled. Still I never cease to be amazed at what a dedicated amateur builder can turn out. I have seen a 38-foot Friendship sloop, a 45-foot steel auxiliary, and a 40-foot schooner all built by the owners for whom they were originally custom designed.

SPECIAL PURPOSE

Special purpose vessels must be custom designed and built in the large majority of cases. In my experience, such designs have ranged from a 19-foot aluminum cat schooner to a Tern schooner rated to carry 125 passengers. Each was a vessel whose owner had special requirements that could not possibly be met by anything other than a custom design.

METAL YACHTS

With a few exceptions, metal yachts are custom built, and many are custom designed. Steel and aluminum yachts, particularly the radius chine hull shapes, are fairly recent arrivals on the boating scene and so there is not, as yet, the wide variety of stock plans available that there is for wood and FRP. As a result, the custom design is quite a normal thing.

AVERAGE CRAFT

Despite the varied reasons for custom designing that have just been discussed, most custom designs are for average vessels whose owners simply were not satisfied with the usual production yacht and could not find anything suitable on the used boat market. Many times such owners are very experienced yachtsmen who have developed, through the years, their own ideas about rig, layout, machinery, or other specific areas of design or construction and must go to a custom design to satisfy their exact requirements.

Most of the production yachts on the market are average craft for the average buyer. While a visit to the Annapolis Boat Show might lead one to believe that every conceivable size and type of craft is available from the manufacturer, when your needs are for something just a little bit special you either compromise your ideas a bit or start to think seriously about a custom design.

MODIFICATION

A number of years ago, I did a 40-foot, gaff rigged, double-chined steel schooner as a custom design for an amateur builder. Since that design was completed, other clients have had me make the following modifications to it: Lengthen the ends to make her 42 feet; change the gaff main to Bermudan; design a cutter rig for her; alter the hull to radius chine shape, etc. If you find a stock design that is fairly close to your needs, then some custom modifications to the design might turn her into your ideal.

□ *198*

The moment of truth—a new yacht is launched.

CLIENT AND DESIGNER

If you are to get the design that suits your exact requirements, you must provide the designer with as much information as possible. Besides the usual data on size, type, draft, general arrangement, equipment, power, cruising radius, and similar details, let the architect know your sailing habits—cruising area, usual number of guests, whether you normally anchor or go into marinas, dinghy preference, etc. It is hardly possible to provide too much information, and it will all help the designer do a better job for you.

Once the designer has this information and a signed contract with deposit, he will begin work on the preliminary sketches. These are his interpretation of your needs and as such are open to critique, comment, and suggestion on the part of the owner. It may take two or three drawings before the client is completely satisfied, but if it drags out much more than this it might well be wise to look for another architect as the two of you may be on different tracks.

When the final preliminary sketch is approved by the client, the designer assumes the client is happy and he will get started on the lines drawing. If further changes are demanded after the prelims are approved and work on the final plans has begun, the designer is justified in charging extra if the changes result in added labor for him.

Depending on the contract arrangements, the designer may provide added services, sending out for and recommending on bids, ordering special equipment for the yacht, making inspection trips during construction, and attending the trials once the boat is launched. The designer may also act as the client's representative in any disputes with the builder, and these do occur! All in all, the architect earns his pittance, and, whether the boat is a 25-foot sloop or a 125-foot gold plated motorsailer, he will be doing his best to ensure that it is a successful example of its type.

GLOSSARY

Aback: With the wind on the wrong side of the sails.

Abaft: Behind an object in relation to the bow, i.e., "abaft the mast" means "behind the mast."

Abeam: At a right angle to the line of the keel, off the beam.

Aft: Toward the stern.

After body: The aft section of a vessel.

Alee: Downwind, to the leeward side.

Aloft: Above deck.

Amidships (also *midships*): The center of the vessel. May refer to either the fore-and-aft or athwartship direction.

Apparent wind: The wind direction that is felt on the deck of a moving vessel. It differs from the true wind as a result of the vessel's speed and course.

Anchor light (also *riding light*): A white light carried high in the vessel, often at the masthead, and visible in a 360-degree circle.

Astern: Abaft the vessel.

Athwartships: At a right angle to the centerline of the vessel.

Auxiliary: A vessel propelled by both sails and engine, separately or together. Also, the engine in an auxiliary.

Back: The wind backs when it changes direction to the left. See *veer*.

Backstay: The part of the standing rigging that supports the mast from the aft part of the vessel. May be "permanent" or "running," depending upon whether the backstay is fixed or adjustable.

Balanced rudder: One that carries a small part (10 percent or so) of its area forward of its pivot point.

Baldheaded schooner: A schooner that carries no topmasts.

Ballast: Weight, usually iron, lead, or other heavy substance, carried low in the vessel to increase stability.

Ballooner, balloon jib: A large, full jib carried when off the wind in light airs.

Bare poles: With no sail set, as in a storm.

Barney post: A wood or metal post in the cockpit to which the lower end of the mainsheet is fitted.

Battens: Light wood or plastic strips fitted to support the roach of a sail.

Batten pockets: Pockets sewn into the aft end of a sail to hold the battens.

Beam: A timber fitted athwartship to support the deck. Also, the maximum breadth of a vessel.

Beamy: A relatively wide vessel.

Beat: Sailing to windward on alternate tacks.

Bed: The support for an engine or other heavy piece of equipment, e.g., engine beds, tank beds.

Bermudan rig: A triangular sail with the luff secured to the mast. Also called *marconi rig*. Original name, now rarely used, was *leg-o-mutton* rig.

Berth: A narrow, hard, wet place in which one sleeps aboard a yacht.

Bilge: The turn of the hull between the topside and the bottom. Also, the dark, smelly place above the keel where all the oily water collects.

Binnacle: The container (box or modern metal hood) that contains the compass.

Bitts: Wooden or metal vertical posts at bow and/or stern for mooring or towing line attachment.

Bluff bowed: Full or round bowed vessel.

Bobstay: Chain or wire rigging running from the forward end of the bowsprit to the hull just above the load waterline.

Body plan: The lines of a yacht as seen from the bow. Also called *sections*.

Boom: The spar to which the foot of a fore-and-aft sail is fastened, e.g., *mainboom*, *stays'l boom*.

Boomkin (also *bumpkin*): A spar extending abaft the stern of the vessel, designed to provide added length for sheeting home a sail, such as a mizzen or the mainsail of a schooner, or for fitting a permanent backstay.

Bow: The forward end of the vessel. Also called the *pointy end*.

Bowsprit: A spar extending forward of the bow from which the headsails (jibs) are set. *Bowsprit shrouds* or *whisker shrouds* support the bowsprit athwartship.

Brightwork: Varnished wood surface.

Bulb keel: A keel shape with a streamlined bulb of iron or lead at its bottom end, designed to add to stability. Usually slows the boat.

Bulkhead: A vertical partition, either athwartship or fore-and-aft, that forms the "walls" of the various compartments. In modern yachts, most bulkheads add structural strength as well.

Bullseye: Round wood or plastic fairlead with edges grooved to accept a line. Used for lazyjacks, etc.

Bulwark: The extension of the vessel's frames and planking above the weather deck.

Bury: The part of a mast below the deck or cabin roof.

Buttock: The part of the vessel's stern abaft amidships.

Buttock lines: Those lines on the lines drawing of the vessel that represent vertical saw cuts through the vessel for the length of the craft, at various distances from the centerline.

By-the-head: Used to describe a vessel that is trimmed down forward below her designed waterline.

By-the-lee: Sailing downwind with the wind and the mainboom on the same side of the vessel. Can be dangerous.

By-the-stern: Used to describe a vessel that is trimmed down aft below her designed waterline.

Camber: The athwartships curve of the decks of a vessel. The maximum camber height above the sheerline is called *crown*.

Carvel construction: Smooth-sided wooden construction with planks edge butted and caulked.

Catboat: Single-masted sailboat, carrying mainsail only, no headsails.

Cat schooner: Two-masted vessel with fore-and-aft sails, carrying almost equal-sized sails on both masts, no headsails. Also see *periauger*.

Cat yawl: Two-masted vessel with fore-and-aft sails, carrying a main and small mizzen, no headsails.

CB (Center of Buoyancy): The center of the vessel's displacement.

CE (Center of Effort): The center of the vessel's sail area.

CF (Center of Flotation): The center of the vessel's waterline area.

CLP (Center of Lateral Pressure, also CLR, the Center of Lateral Resistance): The center of the underwater area of the vessel viewed in profile.

CG: The Center of Gravity. Also, *VCG*, the vertical center of gravity. Note that the fore-and-aft CG must be at the same location as the CB.

Centerboard: A device that can be lowered through the hull to increase the lateral area in order to reduce leeway under sail.

Chainplates: The fittings on a yacht that accept the lower ends of the shrouds in order to support the mast.

Cheek block: A block with one side fastened to a spar or to the deck.

Chine: The angle between the topside and bottom of a flat or vee bottom boat.

Clamp: Longitudinal structural member in a wood vessel, running inside the hull along the sheer, that supports beam ends.

Clew: The lower aft corner of a fore-and-aft sail; the two lower corners of a square sail.

Clencher *or* clinker planking: A method of wood boatbuilding in which the upper plank overlaps the lower.

Clipper bow: A bow shape reminiscent of that of the clipper ships, with a graceful, reverse S curve.

Close-hauled: Sailing to windward with sails trimmed as close to midships as possible.

Close-winded: A boat that will sail well to windward. *Weatherly* is another term used to denote this desirable feature.

Club: The boom on a jib or staysail, i.e., *club jib*.

Coaming: The raised sides of the cockpit. Also, the side of the trunk cabin.

Coffeegrinder: A large sheet winch with the drum operated by two handles on a raised pedestal.

Collision bulkhead: A watertight bulkhead just abaft the bow, intended to keep the vessel afloat in case of a bow-on collision.

Come about: To change tacks by bringing the bow through the eye of the wind.

Companionway: The access to the interior of the yacht, generally from the cockpit (*companionway hatch, companionway ladder*).

Composite construction: A yacht with wood planking on metal frames, usually steel or bronze.

Counter: The stern of the yacht abaft the aft end of the waterline.

Covering board: The deck plank that covers the top of the hull frames, the outermost deck plank.

Cranse iron: The band at the outer end of a bowsprit, fitted with eyes to accept the headstay, bobstay, and bowsprit shrouds.

Crosstrees: Light timbers placed athwartship on the trestles at the masthead to support the topmast and spread the topmast shrouds.

Crown: The height of the arc of the deck athwartship; the amount of camber.

Cruiser stern: A rounded stern with moderate overhang.

Cutter: A single-masted yacht with two or more headsails, the mast being located farther aft than the mast in a sloop.

Cutwater: The leading edge of the stern.

Daggerboard: A centerboard that is hoisted vertically in its trunk instead of pivoting.

Dead light: Fixed glass ports. Also, the metal plate that closes off an opening portlight in an emergency.

Deadeye: Round wood block with three holes for passing a lanyard to set up tension. Fitted to the lower end of the shroud with a matching deadeye on the hull chainplate.

Deadrise: The measure, athwartship, that the bottom of a vessel makes with the horizon.

Deadwood: Heavy timbers at the stern of a wood vessel connecting the keel to the ballast or to the sternpost.

Deck: The planked "floor" of a vessel. Note that in yachts the interior deck is called the *cabin sole*; the decks are exterior.

Diagonal planking: A wood construction method where the planks are laid diagonally and covered by a second layer, also laid diagonally but in the opposite direction. Additional layers may be fitted diagonally or fore-and-aft.

Dipping lug rig: A fore-and-aft rig where the tack of the mainsail is at the stemhead. The vessel is tacked by letting go the tack, passing the sail abaft the mast, and resetting the tack. The halyard must be eased to permit tacking. The rig is weatherly but requires a large, skilled crew (similar to a modern ocean racer).

Displacement: The weight of water displaced by the vessel; the weight of the vessel.

Dolphin striker: A spar beneath the bowsprit that acts as a spreader to provide a better angle to the bobstay. Only seen on traditional and character (and "cartoon") boats.

Dorade ventilator: A self-draining ventilator. See text.

Dory: A flat bottomed boat, originally designed for rowing and fishing. See text.

Double-ender: A sharp sterned hull.

Downhaul: A line or tackle used to pull down a sail or spar *(spinnaker pole downhaul, jib downhaul)*.

Draft: The depth of water required to float a vessel. Also refers to the shape of a sail.

Drag: Used to denote resistance. Also, a fin or keel that increases its draft toward the aft end is said to have drag to its shape.

Drop keel: Old term for *centerboard*.

Earing: A rope used to hold a sail cringle to a yard or boom.

Eddy: Water or air currents moving in confused, circular patterns.

Entrance: The vessel's bow at and just above the waterline. The half-angle of entrance is a measure of the fineness of the waterline at the bow.

Factor of safety: The relationship of the ultimate strength of a material or item (e.g., a turnbuckle) to the working loads it will face.

Fair: Used to describe a hull without distortions, humps, bumps, or hollows.

Fairlead: An eye of plastic or wood used to lead lines in the desired direction.

Feathering propeller: A propeller in which the blades turn to line up with the flow of the water when the vessel is under sail.

Fiberglass: Actually should be called *fiberglass reinforced plastic* (FRP). See text.

Fiddle block: A block with two sheaves in line.

Fiddle: A rail used to keep items in place in heavy seas. Also mistakenly called a *sea rail.*

Fife rail: A semicircular pinrail fitted around a mast.

Fin keel: A deep, narrow fin, separate from the rudder, to provide lateral resistance. It is not actually a keel.

Fisherman staysail: A quadrilateral light weather sail set high between the masts of schooners. Its head runs from the main to the foremast.

Flush deck: The deck line from the stem to somewhat abaft the mast if not broken by a cabin.

Flying: Used to describe the setting of a sail that is held only at the corners and not hanked on to a stay or mast.

Foot: The lower edge of a sail. Also, to perform; i.e., to *outfoot* means to sail faster than a rival.

Fore-and-aft: Along the line of the keel; i.e., in a fore-and-aft rig, the sails are set in the direction of the keel rather than athwartships.

Foremast: The forward mast of a schooner.

Forepeak: The stowage compartment in the bow of a vessel.

Foresail: The sail set on the foremast of a schooner.

Forefoot: Where the keel meets the stem.

Frame: An athwartship structural member of a vessel, supporting the planking or plating.

Freeing port: An opening in the bulwarks to drain water on the decks.

Freeboard: The distance from the water to the deck at side, or sheerline.

Frostbite dinghy: A dinghy used for racing in the winter by a bunch of nuts loosely called frostbiters. Good, cool fun.

Full-and-by: Sailing as close to the wind as possible with all sails drawing.

Gaff rig: A rig in which the mainsail is quadrilateral and its upper side, or head, is fastened to a gaff spar attached to the mast.

Gaff jaws: The end of the gaff fitting around the mast to hold the gaff in place.

Gaff topsail: A light weather sail set above the gaff of a gaff rigged vessel.

Gale: A storm with wind speed of 34 to 40 knots.

Galley: The cooking compartment. Also, a type of rowing craft.

Gallows frame: A frame rising above the deck or cabin, used to support the boom when lowered.

Gammoning: The lashing securing the bowsprit to the stemhead. *Gammoning iron*—a metal fitting serving the same purpose.

Garboard strake: The plank of a wooden vessel that fastens to the keel, the lowest plank.

Garvey: A scow-type vessel developed in Barnegat Bay and adjacent waters.

Gasket: Ropes or dacron ties used to secure the sail to the boom when sail is lowered.

Genoa: A large jib that overlaps the mast and is sheeted well aft. Also called *jenny*.

Gimbals: A device forming a pivot, used to keep compasses, stoves, and tables level when the vessel heels.

Go about: To change tack by bringing the bow through the eye of the wind. See *come about*.

Gollywobbler: A large sail set between the masts of schooners, cut full and with much overlap.

Gooseneck: The metal fitting that secures the boom to the mast.

Goosewing jibe: A bad jibe resulting in the boom and gaff ending up on opposite sides of the mast.

Ground tackle: The anchor, chain, rode, etc.

Gudgeon: Eyes set in the stern or rudderpost to accept the rudder pintles and permit the rudder to swing. See *pintles*.

Gunkholing: Cruising in shallow water and overnighting in small, quiet coves.

Gunter rig: A jibheaded rig in which the upper part of the mainsail is supported by a gaff sliding vertically.

Gunwale: The rail of a boat. Also spelled *gunnel*.

Gybe: Changing tack by passing the wind over the stern rather than the bow. *Jibe* is the more common spelling.

Gypsy: The drum of a winch. Used only with capstans and windlasses as a rule.

Halyards (also *halliards*): Lines used to hoist sails.

Jibe: See *gybe*.

Jibheaded rig: See *Bermudan rig, marconi rig*.

Jibstay: The stay from the head of the mast to the stemhead (or bowsprit end, if fitted). Also called *headstay*.

Jib topsail: A light weather jib set high on the headstay of a cutter or other yacht with two or more stays forward.

Jiffy reef: A form of slab reefing with reef tackles arranged so that reefing can be done quickly and simply.

Jigger: A term for a small mizzen on a yawl or ketch.

Jiggermast: Another term for *mizzenmast*, the after mast on a yawl or ketch.

Jumbo jib: The large, overlapping forestaysail used on commercial sailboats.

Jumpers: Stays set up to support the masthead of a ¾ or ⅞ rig. *Jumper struts* are the spreaders fitted to hold these stays in position and apply their force to the mast.

Jury rig: An emergency rig set up when dismasted. Any gear rigged to carry out the job of a broken part.

Keel: The backbone of a vessel to which the floors and frames are fastened. The term *fin keel* is really a poor one; it should be simply *fin* as the structure does not truly serve the purpose of a keel.

Ketch: See text. A two-masted vessel in which the mizzen is forward of the rudderpost and/or over 15 percent of the total sail area.

King plank: On a wood planked deck, the plank down the centerline of the vessel into which the ends of the other deck planks are set.

Kites: Light sails.

Knees: Structural members fitted to strengthen the hull. See *hanging knees. Lodging knees* are fitted horizontally alongside beams to stiffen the deck.

Knot: One nautical mile per hour. A *nautical mile* equals 1.151 land miles, or 6,076 feet.

Lapstrake: See *clinker.*

Lateen: A triangular sail set from a yard along the luff of the sail.

Lazarette: A storage compartment in the stern of the vessel.

Lazyjacks: Light lines running from the mast to the boom to form a simple netting to hold the sail temporarily when it is lowered. The handiest thing since the invention of the marine toilet. See text.

Lay-to: See *heave-to.*

Leach (also *leech*)**:** The after side of a fore-and-aft sail; the edges of a square sail.

Lead: The distance that the center of sail area is ahead of the center of lateral resistance. See text.

Lee: Downwind, away from the wind.

Lee board: A board fitted on the lee side of the vessel to reduce leeway. Similar to a centerboard in purpose. Also, a board fitted to a berth to keep the sleeper in place when the vessel is heeled.

Lee helm: Having to hold the helm to the lee side in order to maintain a course. Undesirable. See text, *helm balance.*

Lee side: The side away from the wind.

Leeward: Downwind. One vessel is said to be to leeward of another.

Leeway: The movement of a vessel to leeward due to the force of the wind on the sails.

Hand rail: Wood or metal rail running along the cabintop.

Hanging knees: Structural knees fitted vertically between the hull and deck, or the cabin side and roof, to strengthen the vessel.

Hanks: Fittings sewn onto the headsails for fastenings the sails to the stays.

Hard-a-lee: The command to put the helm over to come about.

Hard over: To put the helm over as far as possible in either direction.

Hauling part: That part of a tackle that is pulled upon, the other end being the *standing part.*

Head: The marine toilet, also the toilet compartment. Also, the upper part of a gaff sail or the upper corner of a jibheaded sail.

Headboard: A wood or metal fitting sewn into the head of a Bermudan sail.

Headsails: Those staysails and jibs set forward of the fore or mainmast.

Headstay: The stay running from the masthead to the stemhead or the bowsprit end, if fitted.

Heave-to: To bring the boat's head to wind so that she will stay there. This is done by putting the vessel on the wind with helm down and sails trimmed flat so that she will alternately come up and then fall off a bit. The purpose is to hold the general position when riding out a gale.

Heel: The lower part of the mast or rudder. Also, the athwartship inclination of a vessel.

Heeling arm: The vertical distance between the center of effort and the center of lateral resistance.

Heeling moment: The moment resulting from the product of the heeling arm and wind pressure on the sails.

Helm: The tiller or steering wheel.

Helm's-alee: A warning sounded by the helmsman when tacking to brace the crew to their duties.

Hiking: To get the crew weight to windward outside the rail for added stability.

Hogged: A condition of an older wooden vessel where the ends have dropped, usually due to the upward loads on the chainplates.

Hood ends: On a wooden vessel, the ends of the planks that are set into the rabbet in the stem and sternpost.

Hoops: Rings of wood (nowadays plastic) that hold the gaff sail to the mast.

Horn timber: In wood vessels, that timber extending from the sternpost to the transom.

Horse: A rod of metal, usually steel or bronze, on which the traveler for a sheet block can slide athwartship when tacking.

Horsepower: A unit of power equivalent to lifting a weight of 550 pounds one foot in one second.

Inboard: Towards the centerline of the vessel.

Initial stability: The stability of the vessel at small angles of heel.

Irish pennant: A loose line dangling in the rig.

Jaws: On a gaff rig, the fitting, usually wooden, attaching the boom and gaff to the mast.

Jaw rope: The line, often wire and usually fitted with parrel beads, holding the jaws to the mast. More commonly called *parrel*.

Jib: A triangular sail set forward of the fore or mainmast.

Jibheaded: An older term for the *Bermudan, marconi,* or *leg-o'-mutton* mainsail.

Jib netting: A network of rope under the bowsprit and between the whisker shrouds to keep the jib, and crew, from dropping into the sea.

Left hand propeller: A wheel that, when viewed from aft, has its upper blade turning to port.

Leg-o'-mutton: An old term for the *jibheaded mainsail.*

Liverpool head: A type of smoke stack for a cabin heater or solid fuel stove.

Load waterline: The waterline at which the designer prays the boat will float.

Longitudinal bulkhead: A bulkhead that runs fore and aft.

Longitudinals (also *stringers*): Framing that runs fore and aft.

Loose footed: A fore-and-aft sail not attached to a boom or club.

Luff: The leading edge of a fore-and-aft sail. Also, to luff a sail is to allow the vessel to come head-to-wind, or to ease the sheets, so that the wind pressure on the leading edge of the sail is relieved.

Lug foresail: A boomless schooner foresail.

Lugsail: A type of quadrilateral fore-and-aft sail. See *dipping lug rig*. There is also the *standing lug rig*, in which the sail is not dipped.

Lugger: A vessel setting a lugsail on the main and mizzenmast. A usual combination was a dipping lug main and standing lug mizzen. The vessels were fast and weatherly for their time.

Mainmast: The forward mast in yawls and ketches; the aft mast in a schooner.

Mainsail: The sail set abaft the mast on sloops and cutters and from the mainmast of ketches, yawls, and schooners.

Marconi rig: See *Bermudan rig.*

Margin plank: The plank, often teak, around the cabin trunk and hatches, into which the deck planks are nibbed.

Mast coat: The canvas (now often neoprene) around the mast at the deck to prevent water from getting below.

Mast hoops: See *hoops.*

Mast partners: In a wooden yacht, the structural members around the mast where it goes through the deck or cabin roof.

Mast step: The structural member that supports the heel of the mast.

Mast tabernacle: A structure extending above the deck that supports the mast and allows it to be hinged for lowering.

Mast wedges: Wood or hard rubber wedges driven between the mast and the partners to support the spar.

Metacenter: The point at which a vertical line from the heeled center of buoyancy of the vessel passes through the centerline. The distance from this point to the center of gravity is the *metacentric height*, or *GM.*

Midships: The fore-and-aft center of the vessel.

Mizzenmast: The after mast of a yawl or ketch. See *jigger.*

Mizzensail (usually just *mizzen*): The sail set abaft the mizzenmast.

Mizzen staysail: A triangular sail set flying from the mizzenmast head, tacked to the deck forward to windward, and sheeted to the mizzenboom. Used when reaching and running. It is badly named as it is not set on a stay and so is not truly a staysail.

Mule: A triangular sail set from the main backstay of a ketch or yawl and sheeted to the mizzenmast head.

Near gale: Storm with wind speeds of 28 to 33 knots.

Nettles: Reef points.

No higher: An order meaning to sail no closer to the wind.

North river jibe: Jibing quickly without first hauling in the mainsheet. Can be dangerous.

Oakum: Tarred rope fibers, used for caulking.

Off-the-wind: To sail downwind.

Offing: Well out to sea but with land in sight.

Offsets: Dimensions of the hull, taken from the lines drawing, used by the loftsman to redraw the lines full size.

On the beam: At a right angle to the line of the keel.

On the bow: 45 degrees or less from the bow.

On the quarter: 45 degrees or less from the stern.

On the wind: Close-hauled.

Outpoint: To sail closer to the wind than a rival yacht.

Out of trim: To be down by the bow or stern, or with an athwartship list.

Outboard: Outside of the hull of the vessel. Also, a portable motor.

Outfoot: To sail faster than a rival yacht.

Outhaul: A fitting or line used to haul out the clew of a sail.

Outsail: To make better speed and/or point higher than a rival yacht.

Overall: The length on the range of deck. See text.

Over-rigged: Rigging heavier than necessary.

Oversparred: Carrying more sail than stability warrants; i.e., mast(s) too lofty and boom(s) too long.

Overboard: Over the side; in the water.

Overhang: The projection of the bow and/or stern beyond the ends of the waterline.

Painter: The towing line made fast to the bow of a dinghy.

Parrel: Same as *jaw rope*. Parrel is the more common term.

Part: One section of a rope or tackle. Also, to break.

Partners: See *mast partners*.

Patent log: Another term for *taffrail log*, a distance measuring device.

Pawls: The device in a winch or windlass that prevents it from turning backward.

Pay: To fill the seams in a deck with pitch (3M Deck Seam Compound is now used instead of pitch).

Pay off: To turn the bow away from the wind.

Peak: The upper aft corner of a gaff sail. Also, the end of the gaff. Also, a compartment in the ends of the vessel; see *forepeak.*

Peak halyard: The line that hoists the peak of the gaff.

Pelican hook: A form of slip hook, commonly used on lifeline gates and mizzenmast running backstays.

Periauger (also *periaugua*): An early American two-masted rig without headsail; i.e., cat schooner.

Pinrail: A rail with holes to receive belaying pins for fastening the running rigging.

Pinch: To point slightly too high to windward, slowing the vessel and causing the sails to luff.

Pink stern: An extension of the aft deck outboard of the hull of a double-ended vessel. *Pinky*—a vessel with this form of stern, typically a fishing vessel from the Canadian Maritimes or the New England states.

Pintle: The pin that fits into the gudgeon to form a support and hinge for the rudder.

Pitch: The falling and rising of a vessel in a fore-and-aft direction. Also, the distance the propeller would move forward in one revolution if it were threading into a solid material. Also, a material used to pay the seams of a vessel.

Pitch pole: A disaster in which a breaking sea causes a vessel to cartwheel her stern over her bow.

Plain sail: The working sails.

Plow: Another name for the patented *CQR* (secure) anchor.

Poop: The raised after deck at the stern of a vessel.

Pooped: Having a sea break over the stern.

Port: The left side of the vessel when looking forward. Old term for port was *larboard.* Also, an opening in the side of a vessel, i.e., *gun port, portlight* (window).

Port tack: Sailing with the wind coming over the port side.

Preventer: A line running from the boom forward to prevent an accidental jibe.

Pulpit: The railing at the bow or stern.

Quadrant: The fitting on the rudder stock to which the steering cables attach. It is a segment, usually a quarter, of a circle.

Quarter: The side of the vessel abaft the beam and forward of the stern, the aft "corner," in effect.

Rabbet: The groove cut in the stem, keel, and sternpost of a wood vessel to accept the planking.

Rack: A less commonly used term for *fiddle.*

Rail: The top of the bulwarks. *Top rail*—a raised edge at the sheer where no bulwark is fitted.

Rake: The angle of the masts or deck structures.

Ratlines: Rope rungs seized to the shrouds to form a ladder.

Rattling down: The job of fitting ratlines.

Reach: To sail on a course between close-hauled and running free. *Close reach*—wind forward of the beam. *Beam reach*—wind abeam. *Broad reach*—wind on the quarter.

Ready about: The order given to prepare to tack the vessel.

Reduction gear: The gearbox that steps down high engine RPMs to workably low propeller RPMs.

Reef: To reduce sail area. *Close-reefed*—the sail is reduced to its last set of reef points.

Reef cringle: A grommet or eye in the leach and tack of the sail at the ends of the reef.

Reef earing: The line attaching the reef cringle to the boom (*luff earing, leach earing*).

Reef points: Short pieces of rope set in the sail at intervals to secure the foot of the sail when reefed.

Reef tackle: The line that pulls the reef down to the boom until the earings can be tied off. In modern reefing the tackles may be permanent and separate earings not used.

Ribband: A fore-and-aft strip of wood used to support and fair the frames in new boat construction.

Riding light: Anchor light.

Rig: A vessel's arrangement of masts and sails. Also, to set up the masts and rigging in a vessel.

Rigging: The wires and ropes that support the masts (*standing rigging*) and hoist and trim the spars and sails (*running rigging*).

Rigging screw: British term for *turnbuckle*.

Right: To return to upright, as to right a capsized dinghy.

Right handed propeller: A wheel on which the upper blade, when viewed from aft, turns to starboard.

Righting lever (also *righting arm*): The horizontal distance from the center of gravity to a line drawn vertically through the heeled center of buoyancy. Abbreviated *GZ*. See text, *stability*.

Righting moment: The moment resulting when the displacement of the vessel is multiplied by the length of the righting arm.

Roach: The curve in the leach of a sail. In the foot of a genoa it is called *foot roach*.

Rode: The anchor line. Often *anchor rode*.

Roll: Side-to-side oscillation of a vessel.

Roller furling gear: The sail rolls up on a wire luff or aluminum foil. Commonly used for headsails, becoming more frequent on mainsails either inside or just abaft the mast. Roller furled sails cannot have roach or battens.

Roller reefing gear: A method of reefing by rolling the sail around the boom. Now obsolete, largely replaced by slab or jiffy reefing.

Rose box: The strainer at the bottom of the hose leading to the bilge pump. Also called *strum box.*

Rudder: The plate at the stern used to steer a vessel.

Rudder irons: The pintles and gudgeons.

Rudderpost: The structural member that is forward of and supports the rudder on a wood or metal vessel.

Rudder port: The tube through which the rudder stock enters the vessel.

Rudder stock: The metal tube or rod to which the rudder is attached. May be wood on older and/or commercial vessels.

Run: The hull of the vessel underwater toward the stern. Also, to sail downwind, as in "running free."

Running backstays (also *runners*): Temporary backstays that are set up to tension the jib or staysail luff. The weather backstay is set up when changing tack, and the leeward backstay is let go.

Running lights: Lights carried when underway at night.

Samson post: A single bitt. See *bitts.*

Scandalize: To reduce sail on a gaff rigged vessel by letting go the peak halyard.

Scantlings: The dimensions of the structure of a vessel.

Scarph: To join two timbers by beveling and overlapping the ends.

Scend: The lifting of a vessel to a swell or passing sea.

Schooner: A fore-and-aft rigged vessel with two to seven masts. The usual two-masted schooner has a foremast and a taller mainmast abaft the foremast.

Scow: A shoal-draft, square ended vessel. The *scow sloop* is a popular open racing class in the Midwest.

Screw: Another term for *propeller.*

Scud: To run before a gale with storm sails or no sails. Also, driving mist or broken clouds moving fast under nimbus clouds.

Scuppers: Drains on deck or in the cockpit to carry water overboard.

Sea chest: The intake between the hull and the seacock.

Seacock: A type of valve connecting a vessel's piping to the seawater.

Seakindly: A vessel with an easy motion in heavy seas.

Sea room: Being a safe distance from the shore or from shoals.

Seawater: Weighs 64 pounds per cubic foot. Thirty-five cubic feet weigh one ton, or 2,240 pounds.

Seam: The joint between two planks of the hull or deck.

Seaworthy: A vessel that is well designed, built, equipped, and in satisfactory condition to meet conditions at sea.

Seize: Binding ropes together with light line or marline.

Set: The direction of the current; the direction in which a vessel is moved by the tide and/or wind.

Shackle: A horseshoe-shaped metal fitting with a bolt or pin across the open end.

Shaft: The rod that connects the engine to the propeller.

Shaft tube: The tube in which the shaft passes through the hull.

Shake: A crack in a spar or heavy timber.

Sharpie: A flat bottom, shoal-draft hull developed in the Long Island Sound area. See text.

Sheer: The curve of the deck line.

Sheet: The line attached to the clew of a sail, or to the boom of a boomed sail, in order to trim the sail.

Shipshape: Everything in its place.

Shiver: The luff of the sail shaking from pointing too high into the wind.

Shoot: To luff and move to windward by the vessel's momentum.

Short board: A short tack.

Short ended: A vessel with short overhangs.

Shorten sail: To reduce sail area by reefing or taking down a sail.

Shrouds: The wires that support the mast athwartships. See *stays.*

Shutter: The last plank in a wood, carvel built vessel.

Side lights: The red (port) and green (starboard) running lights.

Siding: The thickness of a timber. *Molding* is the dimension to which the timber is cut.

Simpson's rule: The rule for an approximate form of integration that is commonly used by naval architects to calculate the displacement of a vessel from its lines drawing.

Skeg: The extension of the hull forward of and supporting the rudder.

Slab reefing: Reefing by lowering the sail to a line of reef points sewn in parallel to the foot.

Sliding Gunter rig: See *Gunter rig.*

Sloop: A single-masted vessel with one or more headsails. The mast is farther forward than in a cutter, though the distinction is a narrow one today.

Slot effect: The theory that the improvement in speed from carrying a large overlapping jib is due to the effect of accelerated air flow to the lee side of the mainsail, rather than simply to the larger sail area of the jib.

Snatch block: A block that can open to allow the line to be placed in it, rather than having to pull the whole length through the block.

Snotter: The line holding the heel of the sprit in a spritsail rig.

Sole: The cabin floor.

Spade rudder: A rudder that is supported only by the strength of its rudder stock and is not attached to the hull or to a skeg.

Spars: A general term for the mast, boom, gaff, spinnaker pole, etc.

Spinnaker: A large, light triangular headsail used off the wind and when reaching. Sets with its tack held outboard by a spinnaker pole. A very unseamanlike sail, in my view.

Spinnaker net: A net spread between the mast and headstay to prevent the spinnaker from wrapping around the headstay.

Spitfire jib: A small jib for use in stronger winds.

Spreaders: The wood or metal (aluminum) struts used to spread the shrouds to a better staying angle.

Spring stay: A stay between the mastheads of a schooner.

Spritsail rig: A quadrilateral sail with the peak extended by a spar (the sprit) running from the peak down to the mast.

Squatting: The sinking of the stern due to excess speed.

Stability: The moment or force that tends to return a vessel to upright. See text.

Stanchions: Upright support posts. The term is usually used to mean the lifeline stanchions.

Standing backstay: One that is permanently set up and not shifted with the tack. Also called *permanent backstay.*

Standing lug: A lugsail that is not changed over when the vessel tacks. See *dipping lug, lugger.*

Standing part: The part of a rope or tackle that is made fast to an eye or block.

Standing rigging: The rigging that supports the mast, consisting of stays and shrouds.

Starboard: The right side of the vessel when looking forward.

Starboard tack: Sailing with the wind coming over the starboard side.

Start: To ease off on a line.

Stay: The wire rigging that supports the mast from forward. The backstay supports it from aft.

Staysail: The triangular sail set on the forestay.

Staysail schooner: A schooner in which the foresail is replaced by a staysail set from the mainmast.

Steeve: The angle of the bowsprit with the waterline.

Stem: The timber or steel bar that supports the planking between the keel and the deck. On a fiberglass boat, that part of the hull at the bow between the waterline and the deck.

Step: see *mast step.* To step a mast is to set it in the vessel.

Stern: The after part of a vessel.

Sternpost: The structural member between the keel and the horn timber.

Stern sheets: The space abaft the thwarts of a small boat.

Stern tube: Same as *shaft tube*.

Stopwater: In wooden construction, a wood dowel driven at a joint to prevent water seepage.

Storm: Officially, wind speeds of 48 to 55 knots.

Storm sails: Sails of small size and heavy material, usually hand roped on the edges for extra strength, intended for gale winds. Commonly, a storm jib and storm trysail are carried.

Stow: To place. *Stowage*—an area where items are stowed.

Strake: A line of planking or plating running the length of a vessel.

Strapped down: Sailing as close to windward as possible, with sheets in tight.

Stringer: A fore-and-aft structural member, e.g., *bilge stringer*.

Strong gale: A storm with wind speeds of 41 to 47 knots.

Strum box: See *rose box*.

Strut: The appendage that supports the propeller shaft.

Stuffing box: A device to prevent entry of water around a propeller shaft or rudder stock.

Swaging: A terminal fused to the end of wire rigging; the act of fitting such a terminal.

Swamped: A boat awash with water.

Tabernacle: See *mast tabernacle*.

Tachometer: An instrument that measures the rpm of an engine or shaft.

Tack: A course sailed with the wind on one side of the yacht. To *tack* or to *change tack* is to change course (*come about*) by bringing the wind across the bow to the other tack. Also, the forward lower corner of a sail.

Tackle (pronounced *taykle*): A purchase composed of rope and blocks to increase power. The power is equal to the total number of running parts, less a small amount for friction.

Taffrail log: See *patent log*.

Tangs: Metal fittings that attach the rigging to the mast.

Telltale: A light yarn or ribbon suspended in the rigging to indicate wind direction.

Telltale compass: A compass suspended over the captain's berth so he can check the course without going on deck.

Tensile strength: The measure of a material to withstand a pulling strain, measured in tons or thousands of pounds per square inch.

Thimble: A ring with grooved edges to accept a rope or wire.

Thole pins: Wood pins set in the rail of a rowing boat to retain the oars.

Throat: That part of the gaff nearest the mast. The forward upper corner of a gaff sail or spritsail.

Thwartships: See *athwartships*.

Tiller: A wood or metal bar connected to the rudderpost to steer a vessel.

Tiller head: The part of the tiller farthest from the rudder.

Tiller ropes: Lines leading from the tiller or quadrant to the steering wheel.

Tip clearance: The distance by which a propeller blade clears the hull.

Toe rail: A low rail around the deck edge.

Ton: 2,240 pounds, or 35 cubic feet.

Tongue: The vertical piece of wood between the jaws of a gaff that rides on the aft side of the mast to ease hoisting and lowering of the sail.

Top hamper: The spars and gear above the deck.

Topmast: The mast next above the lower mast.

Topping lift: A line running from the mast to the boom to support the boom when the sail is lowered. A *spinnaker-pole topping lift* supports the spinnaker pole.

Topsail: The sail above the mainsail on a gaff rigged vessel. Also called *gaff topsail*. Also, a square sail above the mainsail.

Topsail schooner: A schooner having a square topsail on the foremast.

Topsides: The area of the hull between the boot top and the deck.

Trailboards: Carved boards at the bow of a clipper bowed vessel that support the extension of the cutwater.

Transom: The stern of a square sterned vessel.

Traveler: The track with car or slide, or the athwartship rod, to which a boom is sheeted. A *bridle* is a wire traveler.

Treenail: A wood pin used in wood boat construction in place of metal fastenings. Now obsolete.

Trestle trees: Timbers supporting the crosstrees and the heel of a topmast.

Triatic stay: The stay that leads from the mainmast head to the mizzenmast head of a yawl or ketch, or from the foremast head to the main crosstrees of a schooner.

Trice: Haul up.

Trick: Time spent at the wheel.

Trim: The fore-and-aft flotation of a vessel. "Trimmed by the head" means trimmed down by the bow.

Truck: The top of a mast, particularly the wooden cap on a wood mast.

Trunk cabin: A cabin raised above the main deck.

Trunnel: A treenail.

Trysail: See *storm sails*. The storm trysail is set when the mainsail is lowered.

Tuck: The part of the hull where the bottom meets the keel or fin.

Tumblehome: The inward curve of the sides of a vessel above the waterline.

Turn of the bilge: The part of the hull where the topsides turn to form the bottom.

Turnbuckle: A metal fitting composed of two bolts threaded into a central cylinder. The bolts have eyes or jaws at the ends to fit onto the rigging and chainplates. The turnbuckle can be adjusted to tension the rigging as required.

Two-blocked: A tackle taken up so completely that the blocks meet and no further takeup is possible.

Una boat: English term for *catboat*.

Underfoot: The anchor is on the bottom, and the anchor line is straight up and down.

Underway: A vessel that is cast off from the pier and has her anchor up (whether she is moving or not).

Up and down: Used to describe the anchor line just before the anchor leaves the bottom.

Vee bottom: A hard chine hull with deadrise to the bottom.

Vangs: Lines leading from the peak of the gaff to the deck to trim the gaff amidship. *Boom vang*—a tackle to haul down on the boom to flatten the mainsail.

Veer: To pay out anchor line. Also, for the wind to change direction to the right.

Vessel: A general term for any floating structure.

W.C.: Water closet.

Wake: The disturbed water behind a moving vessel.

Wale: A heavy strake running fore and aft below the sheer.

Wall sided: A vessel with flat, vertical topsides.

Waterline: The line at which a vessel floats. Lines used by a naval architect in fairing up the drawing of a hull.

Waterplane: The shape of the hull at the load waterline.

Wear: To change from one tack to another by bringing the wind across the stern. Square riggers could rarely come about into the wind so they changed tacks by "wearing ship."

Weather: Toward the wind. The side of the vessel toward the wind is the weather side, also the *windward side*.

Weather boards: Planks above the deck edge to keep water out.

Weather cloths: Canvas panels laced around the aft lifelines to give protection against wind and spray in the cockpit.

Weather helm: The tendency of a vessel to come head-to-wind, requiring that the helm be to weather to maintain the desired course.

Weatherly: A vessel that performs well to windward.

Web frame: An extra deep frame, fitted at the mast for added strength.

Weeping: A slow, steady leak.

Weigh: Raise the anchor.

Wheel: The steering wheel. Also, a term for *propeller*.

Whisker pole: A pole used to hold out the clew of a headsail when running.

Wide berth: A safe and comfortable distance from another vessel, a shoal, or the land.

Winch: A mechanical device for increasing power for hauling on running rigging.

Wind sail (also *windscoop*): A cloth air scoop to ventilate a vessel.

Windlass: A mechanical device for hoisting an anchor.

Windward: The direction from which the wind is blowing. See *weather*.

Wing-and-wing: To sail downwind with sails on opposite sides of the vessel. Also called *wung out*.

Withe *or* **wythe:** A metal ring on the end of a spar through which another spar can be run out.

Working sails: Those sails that are regularly used, excluding light sails and storm sails.

Working to windward *or* **Work up:** To tack to windward.

Yacht: A vessel used for pleasure. A hole in the water into which the owner pours money.

Yard: A spar from which a square sail is set. Lugsails are also set from a yard. The *yardarm* is the outer quarter of a yard.

Yaw: To steer badly, veer continually off course, particularly when running.

Yawl: A two-masted vessel in which the mizzenmast is set abaft the sternpost or the mizzensail is less than 15 percent of the total sail area.

Yoke: A wood or metal fitting across the rudderhead of a small boat, enabling the vessel to be steered by lines.

Zincs: Zinc plates fitted to the hull to prevent electrolysis.

Zulu: A Scottish lug rigged fishing boat of double-ended hull form.

BIBLIOGRAPHY

Design-General

Baader, Juan. *The Sailing Yacht 2nd*. New York, New York: W.W. Norton & Company, 1979.

Chappelle, Howard I. *Yacht Design and Planning*. New York, New York: W.W. Norton & Company, 1971.

Herreshoff, L. Francis. *The Common Sense of Yacht Design*. 1946. (Reprint: Jamaica, New York: Caravan-Maritime Books, 1974.)

Kinney, Francis S. *Skene's Elements of Yacht Design*. New York, New York: Dodd-Mead Publishing Company, 1981

Miller, Richards T. & Henry, Robert G. *Sailing Yacht Design*. Ann Arbor, Michigan: Books on Demand.

Phillips-Birt, Douglas. *Naval Architecture of Small Craft*. New York, New York: Philosophical Library, Inc., 1957.

Design-Technical

Gutelle, Pierre. *The Design of Sailing Yachts*. Camden, Maine: International Marine Publishing Co., 1984.

Hammit, Andrew G. *Technical Yacht Design*. New York, New York: Van Nostrand Reinhold Publishing Co., 1975.

Kay, A.F. *The Science of Yachts, Wind, and Water*. Tuckahoe, New York: John de Graff Inc., 1971.

Marchaj, C.C. *Aero-Hydrodynamics of Sailing*. New York, New York: Dodd-Mead & Company, 1979.

Marchaj, C.C. *Seaworthiness: The Forgotten Factor*. Camden, Maine: International Marine Publishing Co., 1987.

Historical

Chappelle, Howard I. *American Small Sailing Craft*. New York, New York: W.W. Norton & Company, 1951.

Chappelle, Howard I. *American Sailing Craft*. New York, New York: Bonanza Books, 1976.

Phillips-Birt, Douglas. *The Fore and Aft Rig*. London, United Kingdom: Seeley Service & Co. Ltd., 1962.

Leather, John. *Gaff Rig*. Camden, Maine: International Marine Publishing Co., 1970.

Construction

American Bureau of Shipping. *Guide for Building and Classing Offshore Racing Yachts*.

Chappelle, Howard I. *Boatbuilding*. New York, New York: W.W. Norton & Company, 1969.

Colvin, Thomas E. *Steel Boatbuilding*, Volumes 1 and 2. Camden, Maine: International Marine Publishing Co., 1985 and 1986.

Guzzwell, John. *Modern Wooden Yacht Construction*. Camden, Maine: International Marine Publishing Co., 1979.

Hankinson, Ken. *Fiberglass Boat Building for Amateurs*. Bellflower, California: Gen-L Marine Designs, 1982.

Johannsen, Thomas J. *One-Off Airex Fiberglass Sandwich Construction*. Buffalo, New York: Chemacyrl, Inc., 1973.

Klingel, Gilbert C. *Boat Building with Steel*. Camden, Maine: International Marine Publishing Co., 1973.

McIntosh, David C. "Bud." *How to Build a Wooden Boat*. Brooklin, Maine: Wooden-Boat Books, 1987.

Nicolson, Ian. *Cold-Molded and Strip Planked Wood Boatbuilding*. London, United Kingdom: Stanford Maritime Press. (Distributed by Sheridan House, Dobbs Ferry, New York.) 1983.

Nicolson, Ian. *Small Steel Craft*. Camden, Maine: International Marine Publishing Co., 1983.

Steward, Robert. *Boatbuilding Manual*, 3rd Edition. Camden, Maine: International Marine Publishing Co., 1987.

Vaitses, Alan. *Lofting*. Camden, Maine: International Marine Publishing Co., 1980.

Plans and Designs

Beiser, Arthur. *The Proper Yacht, Second Edition*. Camden, Maine: International Marine Publishing Co., 1978.

Cole, Guy (editor). *The Best of Uffa*. Camden, Maine: International Marine Publishing Co., 1978.

Gerr, Dave. *Pocket Cruisers for the Backyard Builder: 30 Small Sailboats You Can Build for Less Than $12,000*. Camden, Maine: International Marine Publishing Co., 1987.

Henderson, Richard. *Choice Yacht Designs*. Camden, Maine: International Marine Publishing Co., 1979.

Henderson, Richard. *53 Boats You Can Build*. Camden, Maine: International Marine Publishing Co., 1984.

Henderson, Richard. *Philip Rhodes and His Yacht Designs*. Camden, Maine: International Marine Publishing Co., 1981.

Herreshoff, L. Francis. *Sensible Cruising Designs*. Camden, Maine: International Marine Publishing Co., 1973.

Taylor, Roger. *Good Boats*. Camden, Maine: International Marine Publishing Co., 1977.

Taylor, Roger. *More Good Boats*. Camden, Maine: International Marine Publishing Co., 1979.

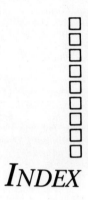

INDEX